AF540296

Tribal Studies and Social Development in India

Tribal Studies and Social Development in India

Dr. V. Shriram Naik

Tribal Studies and Social Development in India

First Published : 2017

ISBN 978-81-8342-412-7

Published by:

CRESCENT PUBLISHING CORPORATION

4806/24, Mathur Lane,
Ansari Road, Darya Ganj,
New Delhi - 110002
Mob.: 9711991838, 9999021668
Fax : 011-23257835
e-mail : crescentbook@gmail.com
Website : www.crescentpublishingcorp.weebly.com

Printed at :

Roshan Offset Printers

Delhi

Contents

Preface

India has given shelter to a large number of tribal people with diverse cultural and biological identity in diverse environmental and geographical conditions. The tribals with diverse ethnic and cultural identity have been living in different corners for centuries. They adjusted themselves with peculiar ecological conditions of the area and started the way of life suitable in their respected ecosystem.

Tribal studies have been traditionally pioneered by anthropologists over the last hundred years. However, the purpose of the studies were different in those times than what they are conceived now. The tribes for understanding the evolution of human institutions which were imagined to have originated in the primitive cultures of the tribes. Some of the Westerners were interested in spreading the gospel of their religion. From the methodological point of view, it has been easier to study simpler tribal cultures as compared to the urban complex cultures. The British and Indian civil - servants - turned - anthropologists studied castes and tribes were not meant to be scientific ethnographic studies of tribes but were meant to provide the basic information of Indian cultural groups to facilitate administration by indirect rule.

Social development is an integral part of any society for the development and prosperity of the people living in the nation. It is multidimensional in nature. It includes variegated aspects and areas such as eradication of poverty hunger gender equality education health reducing child mortality, maternal health economic development educational development, rural tribal and urban development, social welfare creation of a new social order, industrialization agricultural development and a host of other things.

The concept of tribe or tribal social formation was referred by most social anthropologist as a stage destined to move toward a better or more developed stage towards the 'Mainstream' society by means of history within their own political space, promising to change whatever existed for long. There is no doubt that there has been a significant change in the lives of the tribals especially in the North east region in the past 60 years of independence. But the question is, has the majority of the tribals in India benefitted from this model of development? Tribals continues to occupy the lowest economic strata, its areas of habitation is the least developed in infrastructure and all aspects of development.

The Tribal Development Blocks were introduced for the developments of tribal areas. These Tribal Development Blocks were expected to have their role in matters of economic developments, education, health and communication. By the end of Third Five Year Plan there were more than 500 such Tribal Development Blocks serving around 40 per cent of the total tribal population, in the country. But no further expansion of the TDBs to other areas of tribal concentration took place after the Third Five Year Plan.

The book will prove an informative and most useful asset for students, scholars and teachers in this field.

– Author

Chapter 1

Introduction

TRIBAL DEVELOPMENT IN INDIA

The chief measures regarding tribal development are as follows:

1. Constitutional Provisions and Safeguards: The Constitution of India provides for the special provisions relating to Scheduled Tribes. Article 342 lays down that the President may by public notification, specify the tribes or tribal communities or part of or groups within tribes or tribal communities or parts which shall for the purpose of this Constitution deemed to be Scheduled Tribes….".According to this provision, President of India has specified these communities through Constitution (Scheduled Tribes) order, 1950 S.R.0.570.
2. Article 164 provides for a Ministry of Tribal Welfare in each of the State of Bihar, Madhya Pradesh and Orissa which have large concentration of Scheduled Tribes population. These Ministries are required to look after the welfare of the Scheduled Tribes in their respective States.
3. Article 244 provides for the inclusion of a Fifth Schedule in the Constitution for incorporating provisions for the administration of Scheduled Areas and Tribes of the States which have sizeable tribal population (other than those of Assam)
4. Article 275 provides for the grant of special funds by the Union Government to State Government for promoting the welfare of Scheduled Tribes and providing them with a better administration.,

5. *Representation in Legislatures and Panchayats*: The Constitution of India prescribes protection and safeguards for Scheduled Tribes with the object of promoting their educational and economic interests. Under Article 330 and 332 of the Indian Constitution, seats have been reserved for Scheduled Tribes in Lok Sabha and state Vidhan Sabhas.
6. Following the introduction of Panchayati Raj, Suitable safeguards have been provided for proper representation" of the members of the Scheduled Tribes by reserving seats for them in the Gram Panchayats, Block Panchayats, District Panchayats etc.
7. *Reservation in the Service*: Government has made provisions for their adequate representation in the services. To facilitate their adequate representation certain concessions have been provided, such as:
   - Exemption in age limits,
   - Relaxation in the standard of suitability.
   - Inclusion at least in the lower category for purpose of promotion is otherwise than through qualifying examinations.
8. *Administration of Scheduled and Tribal Areas*: 'Scheduled Areas' have been declared in the States of Andhra Pradesh, Bihar, Gujarat, Madhya Pradesh, Maharashtra, Orissa, Himachal Pradesh and Rajasthan. The scheme of administration of' Scheduled Areas under the Fifth Schedule visualises a division of responsibility between the State and Union Governments. The State Governments have been given the responsibility of screening the legislations which are unsuitable for extension to the tribal areas. They are also responsible for framing rules for the prevention of exploitation of the tribals by the money-lenders. They implement schemes for the welfare of the tribals living within its boundary.
9. The Union Government provides guidelines in regard to the administration of Scheduled Areas. It also provides necessary funds that are required to raise the standard of administration and for the improvement in the quality of life of the tribal communities. The Union Government also

has the power to give directions to the State Governments about matters relating to the welfare of the Scheduled Tribes.

10. *Tribes' Advisory council*: The Fifth Schedule of the Constitution provides for the setting up a Tribes' Advisory Council in each of the States having Scheduled Areas. According to this provision, Tribes' Advisory Councils have been set up so far in the states of Andhra Pradesh, Bihar, Madhya Pradesh, Orissa, Punjab, Rajasthan and West Bengal. The duty of these Councils is to advise the Government on such matters concerning the welfare of Scheduled Tribes and development of Scheduled Areas. Advisory Boards for the Scheduled Tribes have been set up in Assam, Kerala and Mysore to advise the State Governments. Tribes' Advisory Committees have also been formed in the Union Territories of Andaman and Nicobar Island, Himachal Pradesh, Manipur and Tripura.
11. *Commissioner for the Scheduled Castes and Tribes*: Under Article 338 of Indian Constitution a Commissioner has been appointed by the President of India. The main duty of the Commissioner is (i) to investigate all matters relating to the safeguards for Scheduled Castes and Scheduled Tribes under the Constitution and (ii) to report the President on working of these safeguards.
12. *Welfare Department in the States*: Under Article 164 (i) of the Constitution there is a provision of Welfare Department in the States of Indian Union. In Bihar, Madhya Pradesh and Orissa, Welfare Departments in the charge of a Minister have been set up. Welfare Departments have been set up in these States as well us in Andhra Pradesh, Assam, Kerala; Tamil Nadu, Karnataka, Punjab, Rajasthan, Uttar Pradesh, West Bengal, Himachal Pradesh, Manipur and Tripura.
13. *Educational Facilities*: Measures to provide educational facilities have been taken by the Government.Emphasis is being laid on vocational and technical training. According to these measures, concessions, stipends, scholarships, books, stationery and other equipments are provided. Residential schools have been set up for them.
14. *Scholarships*: The Central Government awards scholarships

to deserving students for higher studies in foreign countries. Seventeen and half per cent of the merit scholarships are granted by the Centre, to deserving students of lower income groups.

15. *Economic Opportunities*: A large number of tribal people practice shifting cultivation. This problem is in acute form in the States of Andhra Pradesh, Assam, Bihar, Madhya Pradesh, Orissa, Manipur and Tripura. A scheme to control shifting cultivation has been started.
16. Besides this, Andhra Pradesh, Bihar, Tamil Nadu, Orissa, Uttar Pradesh have launched schemes to improve irrigation facilities to reclaim waste land and to distribute it among members of the Scheduled Castes and Tribes. In addition, facilities for the purchase of livestock, fertilizer, agricultural equipment, better seeds are also provided to them. Cattle breeding and poultry farming are also being encouraged among these people.
17. The Governments of different States are encouraging the development of cottage industries by providing loans and subsidies through various schemes. Multipurpose co-operative societies which provide credit in cash and kind to the Scheduled Castes and Scheduled Tribes have been established in various States such as Andhra Pradesh, Bihar, Tamil Nadu and Orissa etc.
18. *Tribal Research Institute*: Tribal and Harijan Research Institutes, which undertake intensive studies of tribal arts, culture and customs have been set up in Bihar, Madhya Pradesh, Orissa, Rajasthan and West Bengal.

The Indian Constitution has made important provisions for the welfare of Scheduled Tribes. The Central Government and State Governments have made incessant effort in the direction of tribal welfare. Special programmes for their welfare and development have been undertaken in the successive Five Year Plans.

The primary objective of Community Development Programme was to achieve rural development. This was envisaged by making available the required services at the doors of people. But there were remote inaccessible areas and there was almost total absence of additional infrastructural facilities. Therefore, special efforts and greater financial investment were required to extend the services available under the Community Development Programmes to tribal areas. Initially 43 such blocks were selected for the purpose soon it was realised that it would not be possible to sustain such an intensive development approach for a long.

The Tribal Development Blocks were introduced for the developments of tribal areas. These Tribal Development Blocks were expected to have their role in matters of economic developments, education, health and communication. By the end of Third Five Year Plan there were more than 500 such Tribal Development Blocks serving around 40 per cent of the total tribal population, in the country. But no further expansion of the TDBs to other areas of tribal concentration took place after the Third Five Year Plan.

In the Fourth Five Year Plans, a series of programme such as Small Farmers Development Agencies (SFDA), Marginal Farmers and Agricultural Development Agencies were conceived and implemented.

The above mentioned programmes were introduced on an experimental basis in tribal areas. The Tribal Development Agencies were identified on the same pattern as that of the Small Farmers' Development Agencies. Each Tribal Development Agency covered a group of Tribal Development Blocks.

During Fourth Plan, six Tribal Agencies were started and anthers two were added during the Fifth Plan. These Agencies were expected to incorporate elements of economic development, social services and other progressive measures. In actual practice the TDAs could not do anything other than agricultural development and construction of roads. But the experience gained from the TDAs provided valuable means for evolving better policies and programmes for the development of Scheduled Tribes.

The approach and strategy for tribal development was, revised comprehensively on the eve of Fifth Five Year Plan. It was thought as recommended by the Shilo Ao Committee that Tribal Development Blocks as an instrument of tribal development were unsuitable to tackle complex tribal problems. Besides, the situation in tribal areas in terihs of resources, target groups, local priorities were different from non-tribal areas. Even within the tribal areas, problems faced by all the tribal people are not uniform in nature.

To tackle the complex and diverse tribal problems effectively, a comprehensive programme of development known as Tribal Sub-Plan was prepared under the Fifth Five Year Plan. Accordingly, all areas with more than 50 per: cent tribal population were treated as Sub-Plan areas. A development block was taken as the smallest unit of development under this new strategy. This unit is known as the Integrated Tribal Development Project (ITDP).

VARIOUS APPROACHES TO TRIBAL DEVELOPMENT IN INDIA

Approaches to tribal development in India are based on three models, to conserve, assimilate and integrate.

First, there was a school of thought which favoured isolation. Hutton, who was a Commissioner for Census of 1931, gave a solution to the tribal problems of uncontrolled acculturation. He suggested the creation of self-governing tribal areas with free power of self-determination.

Earlier Verrier Elwin suggested the creation of "National Parks" where the tribal people could live safely without being victims of what Elwin calls an" "over-hasty and unregulated process of belief and civilization". But later on Elwin discarded the idea of a national park. Both Hutton and Elwin were severely criticised for recommending this policy of isolation which was looked upon as a proposal to create a museum or zoo, instead of helping the tribal people to utilise the resources of modern knowledge and improve their condition of life.

Second, there is another school which favoured assimilation. According to G.S. Ghurye, the tribals are backward Hindus and they should be completely assimilated into Hindu culture. D.N. Majumdar has put forward a philosophy and programme of tribal welfare. He says that it is not possible to ignore the entire.tribal population and leave them to their own lot. It is not also possible to completely assimilate them in the Hindu culture.

Therefore, a gradual transformation of the tribal population is the best policy. We should try to help them in assimilating in their own way of life the elements of alien culture which they readily accept. This view was also supported by social reformers and voluntary organisations. The Christian missionaries and some social reformers like Thakkar Bapa have recommended and have worked for the assimilation of these tribal groups either into Christianity or into Hinduism.

The third view, which is followed in the recent years, is that of integration. The policy of integration, as against isolation and assimilation, was laid down in five principles by Nehru in 1957 in forwarding to Verrier Elwin's the philosophy for NEFA.

The tribal 'Panchasheel' as enunciated by him are as follows:

(1) People should develop along the lines of their own genius and we should avoid imposing anything on them. We should try to encourage in every way their traditional art and culture.
(2) Tribal rights in land and forests should be respected.
(3) We should try to train and build up a team of their own people for the work of administration and development. Some technical personnel from outside will, no doubt be needed especially in the beginning. But we should avoid introducing too many outsiders into tribal territory.
(4) We should not over-administer these areas or overwhelm them with a multiplicity of schemes. We should rather work through and not in rivalry to their own social and cultural institutions.
(5) We should judge results not by statistics or the amount of money spent but by the quality of human character that is evolved.

To conclude, the policy of isolation was neither possible nor desirable. Assimilation as advocated by some was not accepted because it would mean imposition. Only therefore, the policy accepted which would make available to the tribes the benefits of modern society and yet retain their separate identity is integration. However, the process of assimilation is bound to continue as some of the tribal groups are adopting Hindu customs because of their association with the village people. Others have been converted to Christianity.

PLANNED DEVELOPMENT OF TRIBAL AREAS

The British Legislature in India passed the Scheduled District Act XIV of 1874 by which local governments were empowered to identify and declare certain areas as Scheduled Areas. The British had at different times created the semi-autonomous territory of Kandh Mahal and promulgated Tenancy Protection Legislation in Orissa. The Indian Education Commission of 1882 made suggestions for the preferential treatment of tribal children in the form of non-payment of school fees and additional grants to schools located in tribal areas. Later the Government of India Act of 1919 and 1935 created a number of partial and fully excluded areas. A review of such privileges provided by the British suggests that they were compelled to grant such status perhaps not to improve tribal communities, but in response to the revolts and protests of the minorities, and with the purpose of containing them. In the post-Independence era, in consideration of tribal people's socioeconomic backwardness, constitutional experts drew up 20 articles, clauses and sub-clauses and two special schedules in the Constitution of India, which elaborately explained the protective privileges for tribal people, and which came into force on 26 January 1950.

TRIBAL WELFARE PROGRAMMES IN ORISSA

The First Plan made it clear that all tribal development programmes must reflect the expressed wishes of the communities concerned, while the Second Plan stated that programmes should be formulated by consulting tribal representatives and their councils. The Nehruvian Panchsheel also influenced tribal development policies in the state. To examine the backwardness of the tribal people and tribal regions of Orissa, the Partial Excluded Areas Enquiry Committee, under the chairmanship of A. V. Thakkar, visited Orissa in 1938 and submitted its report, which was reviewed during 1946 by the Backward Classes Welfare Section. Finally, the GoO formed a separate department in 1948, known as the Backward Class Welfare Department. Not finding the name of the department appropriate, the GoO thought of changing it to the Rural Welfare Department or the Welfare Department; presently it is known as the ST and SC Development Department.

In spite of the constitutional provision for a separate minister in charge of the welfare of SCs, STs and Backward Classes (although the states of Bihar and Madhya Pradesh have already made separate provision for the development of STs), the state of Orissa is yet to have such provision. The Tribes Advisory Council (TAC) formed in

Orissa on 24 June 1950 has been advising the GoO from time to time on matters of the welfare of tribal communities in the state. The Scheduled Areas Order of 1950 first issued in Orissa by the Government of India and revised during 1977 added two full administrative districts as fully scheduled areas, with a few districts as partial scheduled areas. The recent reformulation of these districts in Orissa includes six districts as fully Scheduled Areas and five as partially Scheduled Areas.

In the initial days of Community Development programmes, special projects known as Multipurpose Tribal Blocks were started in 1956 on an experimental basis. The major objectives of these experiments were to develop tribal people in line with their culture and to safeguard their interests in land, the forest and forest-based resources.

Being pilot projects by nature such experiments in financial, administrative and functional autonomy aimed to produce a development model for tribal people. However, these experiments were not methodologically and contextually sound for this purpose. In consideration of the recommendations of the Elwin Committee (1960) regarding implementation of the structure of Tribal Development Blocks (where more than 50 percent of the population was represented by tribals) the state of Orissa initially opened up 62 such blocks, which were later increased to 74.

Since the beginning of the concept of the Community Development Programme in April 1951 and later the Community Development Blocks during the Second Five Year Plan period, planners have given special thought to the advancement of the tribal communities. Despite the constraints of proper policy formulation and impediments in the structural arrangements for tribal development, during the First and Second Five Year Plans, planners earmarked ₹ 390 million and ₹ 470 million to them, respectively. Perhaps the failure of the special Multi-Purpose Tribal Development Projects to find a model organisational and administrative structure for tribal development forced the government to establish both the Dhebar Committee and the Elwin Committee, which had recommended the structure of Tribal Development (TD) Blocks for implementing tribal development programmes. The basic objectives of the TD Blocks were to cover a contiguous area of 150 to 200 square miles and a population of 25,000. With 500 Tribal Development Blocks the expenditure for this purpose during the Third Five Year Plan was ₹ 534 million, an increase of 21.2 percent over the Second Five Year Plan. Compared to the Second Five Year Pan Period (Rs 3.90 per person), the per capita expenditure for tribal development was lower (Rs 3.58) during the Third Five Year Plan period.

This was mainly the result of the increase in coverage of the tribal population and the decrease in budget expenditure for tribal development from 0.81 percent in the Second Five Year Plan to 0.61 percent during of the Third Five Year Plan period. Since there were insignificant qualitative changes in tribal people's life-way processes, an evaluation of this programme was carried out by the Special Multi-purpose Tribal Block Committee under V. Elwin in 1959.

The Committee (1960) observed that alienation of land, the role of moneylenders, and the fraudulent sale of agricultural produce had all resulted in the backwardness of tribal people. The Tribal Development Programme also faced a major halt during India's involvement in war during 1962 to 1965. This forced the state to prepare Annual Plans during 1966 without any change in the thrust and priorities of the TD programme. During the Fourth Five Year Plan (1969-74) the programme started with a Commission headed by P. Shilu Ao (1961) and an assumption that most of the benefits of planned expenditures had not reached the tribals as desired, primarily because of their socio-cultural set up. The Maoist Naxalite movements and the slogans of 'Garibi Hatao'or Poverty Eradication have largely influenced the change of emphasis in tribal development programmes. In order to devote more attention particularly to the weaker sections of society, the Fourth Five Year Plan initiated certain special programmes, like the Small Farmers Development Agency (SFDA), Marginal Farmers and Agricultural Labourers Development Agency (MFALDA) and the Drought Prone Area Programme (DPAP). There was a major shift from a target-oriented development strategy to a family-oriented development strategy. One can say that the approaches adopted, programme content, programme type, their (lack of) integration, and an irregular flow of funds all caused the concept of TD Blocks to suffer. Such inherent deficiencies in policies, programmes, and also in implementation, subsequently provoked planners, executives, scholars and many others to rethink the concept and strategies of tribal development.

A Tribal Sub-Plan (TSP), as an integrated part of the state plan, was conceived during the Fifth Five Year Plan (1974-79) to cover both tribal-concentrated areas (having more than 50 percent tribal populations) and tribal-dispersed areas including those home to PTGs).

The TSP approach had multifarious objectives: to bridge the gap between the levels of development of both tribals and non-tribals; to improve the quality of life of tribal people by wiping out the net of exploitation around them due to land alienation, bonded labour, high rates of interest during lending, low payment for forest products, etc. Allocation of funds for tribal development was streamlined and demarcated from State Plan Outlays, the sectoral outlays of Central Ministries, Special Central Assistance and institutional funds. Policy measures were enacted to protect tribal interests from liquor vendors, land alienation, moneylending and collection of forest produce. The Tribal Sub-Plan approach was introduced in Orissa in 1979, where Integrated Tribal Development Projects (ITDP) were launched. Thus, presently Orissa has 118 TD Blocks distributed over 21 ITDPs and Tribal Development Agencies, for planning and execution of tribal development programmes.

These cover 1,549 Gram Panchayats (GPs) and 17,597 villages. Further, special micro-projects for the development of PTGs were implemented from time to time. Presently, Orissa has 17 micro-projects to bring the 13 PTGs into the mainstream. The first was started in 1976-77, five were started during 1978-79, one each during 1984-85 and 1985-86, three each during 1986-87, 1988-89 and 1997-98 and the last two were started during 1993-94. The basic objective of all these arrangements is to bring tribal people out of poverty and to free them from of exploitation by non-tribals.

SPECIAL TRIBAL DEVELOPMENT PROJECTS IN ORISSA

The Government of India, with the assistance of the International Fund for Agriculture Development (IFAD), set up a special tribal project on 14 May 1988 for a period of 14 years, in two phases and with a budget approval of ₹ 317 million. The project aimed at the all-round development of tribal people in the Kashipur block of Rayagada district (447 villages covering a population of 51,385).

However it was not continued after the first phase of seven years. Similarly, an integrated Livestock Development Project, assisted by the Danish International Development Agency (DANIDA) in Koraput district, which was planned to go into an extension phase, closed down at the end of the pilot phase in 2000.

The Long Term Action Plan (LTAP) in Koraput-Bolangir and Kalahandi (KBK) districts has yet to yield many of the results planned at the initial phase. These projects have by and large failed to achieve their desired objectives. Only recently (2003-04) has the Government of Orissa, with assistance from IFAD, the UK Department for International Development (DFID) and the World Food Programme (WFP), started implementing a special 10-year development project. Called the 'Orissa Tribal Empowerment and Livelihood Programme', it is being implemented in ten blocks of four districts, *i.e.* Gajapati, Kalahandi, Koraput and Kandhamal, and is still in its initial stage.

SPECIAL MICRO-PROJECTS FOR THE DEVELOPMENT OF PRIMITIVE TRIBAL GROUPS

Given the perceived backwardness of the primitive tribal communities, planners realised that these communities required special care and holistic attention under the Tribal Sub-Plan approach. The gamut of development activities planned under the Tribal Sub-Plan covers sectors such as agriculture, horticulture, soil conservation, health, education, animal husbandry, communications and provision of drinking water. In Orissa 17 such special micro-projects have been established at different times.

These projects cover 13 vulnerable tribal communities made up of 61,240 households in 537 villages distributed over 20 CD Blocks in 12 districts. These special microprojects have been formulated for these communities with a 100 percent subsidy under SCA. A review of the flow of funds to these micro-projects suggests that, although there is a standing instruction that 75 percent of the grant is to be spent on income generation programmes, in practice, since the state government is suffering a financial crunch and is unable to provide the necessary expenditure, there is often a slippage of funds from the programme head to the establishment head. Inconsistencies in the flow of funds are observed in respect of the period of release and quantity of funds allotted. This affects the physical achievements of the project and their impact on the development of vulnerable communities. As a result, the timely supply of various inputs, of institutional credit, and of training in improved dry-land farming and dissemination of knowledge on crop diversification are yet to have much impact on these communities. In other words, the government has not given due importance to these special micro-projects that was planned in the Tribal Sub-Plan approach.

ORISSA TRIBAL DEVELOPMENT PROJECT, KASHIPUR

The Orissa Tribal Development Project (OTDP) in Kashipur aimed to achieve sustainable economic progress for the tribal population of the region through an integrated programme which includes investment in agricultural production and natural resources development. The project covered around 12,500 tribal households and 4,000 non-tribal households. The total project cost was US $24.4 million, of which IFAD provided a $12.2 million loan at a highly concessional rate, the WFP granted $1.4 million, while the balance was met from domestic contributions. The United Nations Office for Project Services (UNOPS) was the co-operating institution, while the Harijan and Tribal Welfare Department of the GoO was the executing agency.

The project ran from May 1988 to December 1997, followed by 21 months of extension. Around 84 percent of IFAD's loan was disbursed, although by June 1998 all remaining funds had also been disbursed (Orissa Tribal Development Programme, 1998). The project adopted an integrated programme of investments. Forty-two percent of the loan was spent on agricultural production and natural resource development; human resource development was allocated 6.5 percent, rural infrastructure 10 percent, land survey and settlement 5.5 percent and implementation/management support received eight percent.

Around 26 percent of the loan was used as price contingency, while only two percent was used for physical contingency. IFAD undertook an evaluation of the OTDP in November-December 1998. This evaluation has contributed a diverse range of knowledge about the project which provides guideline for implementing TD projects.

Infrastructure developed under the project included upgrading or construction of rural roads and bridges, which provide a vital lifeline for transport and communications in the interior villages of Kashipur. This generated sizeable wage employment. However, there was lack of participatory decision making and lack of maintenance and management of the assets in the later period by the project. Wage employment and payment, both in cash and kind, were not carried out on the same scale in post-project periods. On one hand, the project gave the tribals an opportunity to get to know the use of a money economy and also supplemented their income.

However, in subsequent periods, because of a lack of sufficient wage employment provisions, many of them were forced to revert to moneylenders and this aggravated their indebtedness status. The process was unable to build any institutional mechanisms oversee the subsequent processes. The allotment of funds for human resource development was six percent and was less than the project management component (eight percent). The programme basically aimed to build awareness and self-reliance with the help of NGOs. It was observed that the project was over reliant on establishment of physical infrastructure, agricultural development, land development, etc. and gave little importance to identifying an NGO alternative to Agragamee, a local NGO.

Agragamee left the project after the initial period, following a power struggle with the project management unit (International Fund for Agriculture Development, 1998). At one level this reflects the failure of the project to recognise the importance and contribution of human resources development for meeting the overall project objectives and related development processes. Limited success in HRD was the one of the major shortcomings of the project, because the target group did not feel included and sufficiently integrated in it. In other words, participation, training, empowerment and education of the target populations, which are essential for the success and sustainability of any programme, were not given due importance. As a result, the project could not be people-centred and was unable to establish a sense of trust and confidence among the intended beneficiaries of the project.

The project claims that it has placed more emphasis on the role and importance of the indigenous knowledge system and tried to make use of this in the design and implementation of the programmes. However, many instances have been observed where the knowledge of rural people has not been given due importance. For example, the project did not consider the sites suggested by the villagers for constructing a few water harvesting structures on the grounds that they did not fit the engineering requirements.

Similarly, the coffee plantations promoted by the project as a cash crop have never been traditionally favoured by tribal people for cultural and economic reasons (Industrial Management Consultants of Orissa, 1998).

The development processes adopted in the project did not place much importance on the valuable knowledge system and problem-solving strategies in the farming system, on natural resource management, biodiversity, health, education, social organisation or mobilisation. The project could not incorporate the traditional knowledge resources with technical knowledge suitable to the context and environment of the tribal people. In other words, a land-to-lab approach should have been used as a catalyst in accelerating the development process, while adopting new knowledge-transferring technologies to the tribal people.

Illegal cultivation of podu land is a common practice in many tribal-dominated regions of the state. Tribal people in Kashipur region observe this as an age-old practice. From an agricultural point of view the project conferred land titles on these shifting patches, promoting sound environmental management practices, and helped tribal people restore the agro-ecological balance. From a socioeconomic point of view the initiative of providing land titles in the names of both spouses enhanced the social status, security and confidence of the tribal people and provided opportunities for income generation.

However, this manner of privatising landed property imposed on tribal villages partially upset the existing communitybased social security networks. In such a situation the land reform programme could not be accompanied by opportunities for employment, marketing, and access to rural financial services or institutional support.

The Project Management Unit (PMU), headed by a project manager and officials deputed from line departments, managed the project poorly. This was the result of frequent changes of project managers, adoption of a top-down approach in administration with limited scope for participatory management, lack of an appropriate monitoring and evaluation system, low take-up of key positions and poor co-ordination among key functionaries located at Bhubaneswar and Rayagada. Staff were not adequately technically equipped. The PMU was not sufficiently prepared for a participatory approach in implementation, which greatly marginalised their performance.

The project could establish that, without the adequate participation of different shareholders and more particularly the target groups at different stages of the project, like design, decision making and implementation, post-project sustainability would be of major concern.

In the IFAD project the involvement of tribal people in the preparation of action plans programmes and budget was minimal. This created mistrust and discontent between the tribal people and the development agencies, which were reflected when the state entered the region through the corporate sector to explore bauxite minerals in the Kashipur region.

REVISED LONG-TERM ACTION PLAN (LTAP) FOR KBK DISTRICTS

The LTAP and KBK7 programme was launched by the then prime minister on 18 August 1995 for an initial period of seven years, with an objective to pool the available resources and integrate them scientifically to effect the speedy development of the extremely backward KBK districts of Orissa. Over time the undivided KBK districts have been divided into eight districts, comprising 14 subdivisions, 37 Tehsils, 80 CD Blocks, 1437 GPs, and 12,293 revenue villages. The total geographical area of the KBK region is 47,810.2 squre km2. The average density of population per square kilometer in this region varies from 69 in the case of Malkangiri district to 188 in the case of Bolangir district, with an average of 13 people per square kilometer in the whole KBK region. The basic objectives behind this reformulation are to give people greater access to welfare services.

The demographic strength of the KBK districts lies in their differences in ethnic composition, which includes SCs, STs and many other caste communities, who, despite their similarities, maintain cultural specificity, distinct practices, values and customs. Tribal communities like the Bonda, Didayi, Dangaria Kondha, Chuktia and Bhunjia, as well as the Kutia Kondha, still express their identities in their backwardness and development features.

Looking at the gaps in the envisaged achievements of the LTAP, the Government of Orissa submitted and has been implementing its revised LTAP (RLATP) for the period 1998-99 to 2006-07, consisting of Central Plans and Centrally Sponsored Schemes in various sectors. The RLATP envisages drought proofing, poverty alleviation, and improved quality of life in the region through strategies like building a productive rural infrastructure, income generation on a sustainable basis, mobilising and energising the rural poor and restructuring and energising the social security system.

The major programmes covered emergency feeding for 2,00,000 elderly people, nutritious food for 9,42,000 children up to the age of six, provision of health services to 130,000 patients through 90 Mobile Health Units, irrigation of 39,520 hectares of agricultural land through 314 watersheds, and of 16,480 hectares of land by 645 lift irrigation points and 26 medium irrigation projects, planting of 1,25,000 hectares of land and creation of person days of employment for the poor, provision of drinking water from 13,151 hand pumps and the establishment of 400 tribal girls' high schools, each with a 40-bed hospital, for educational expansion among the tribals.

Various educational programmes, like mid-day meals for the students and free distribution of books and clothing, amply reflect a positive impact on the drop-out rates, which fell from 75.89 percent during 1996- 97, to 28.93 percent in 2004-05 (Government of Orissa, 2004). Similarly women's literacy was 15.87 percent during 1991, which increased to 29.10 percent during 2001 (Government of Orissa, 2005). Despite many claims for the achievements of this special programme, many studies have demonstrated the realities on the ground in the KBK districts and the programme's deficiencies in affecting the different areas of life and livelihood of this region. These may include problems with primary education and the primary health service delivery system, and the increase in planting and reduction in the coverage of shifting cultivation. That apart, deaths from starvation in Kashipur and Nawarangpur, of children in Rayagada, due to anthrax in Koraput and Rayagada, the eating of mango kernels in Kandhamal and Rayagada, bonded labour, child labour, the selling of children and, migration of the poor from this region are still featured in the media, and in the reports of various committees and commissions. The poor growth of infrastructure, most particularly communications, in highly inaccessible regions like Malkangiri, Koraput and Rayagada has substantially affected the delivery of basic life-support systems to the villages. This has partly encouraged the growth of the Naxalite movement in these regions, which has become a constant headache for the state.

TRIBAL DEVELOPMENT APPROACHES FOR THEIR ALL ROUND DEVELOPMENT

The tribal population of India constitutes around 8 per cent of total population over 94,000 tribal villages. Tribals are mainly concentrated in Andhra Pradesh, Chattisgarh, Odisha, Jharkhand, Gujarat, Madhya Pradesh, Rajasthan, Maharashtra, West Bengal, North-Eastern States and North-Western Himalayan States.

The small, marginal, fragmented, unirrigated and mono crop agriculture holdings and low productive livestock population do not offer adequate opportunitiesto to the tribals. Tribals in remote areas are still devoid of common infrastructure facilities of road and communication, health and education and safe drinking water, which do not allow them to absorb technological and financial facilities provided by government.

So for their All Round Develpment, In 1972, Tribal Development Directorate established for effective implementation of Tribal Welfare Schemes. In 1976 Tribal Development Commissionerate was established for All Round Development of Tribal. In 1984 separate Tribal Development Ministry was established to strengthen the Tribal Development Department, Directorate was merged into Commissionerate in 1992.

The comprehensive Tribal Development Approach involves the following components:

- Orchard development (fruit/ plantation/herbal crops and forest plants) as the core componen

- Soil conservation in the wadi
- Water resources management (conservation and use)
- Sustainable agriculture
- Human resource development (community development)
- Women development - A special emphasis is given for involvement of women in all spheres ofthe programme.
- The components include drudgery reduction measures, on-farm and non-farm income generating activities and self help groups for inculcating thrift and credit habits.
- Community Health
- Micro-enterprises for landless people
- Processing and marketing
- Other auxillary components to dovetail with above activities.

Objectives of Tribal Development Approach:

- To promote sustainable participatory livelihood programmes
- To take up promotional efforts such as capacity building, exposure visits, training, developing literature, sensitization programmes etc.
- To implement sustainable livelihood programmes
- To support promotional activities for micro-credit, promotion of SHGs, Income
- Generating Activities for land-less, SC/ ST communities and other weaker sections of the community
- To support activities related to development of tribal market
- To support other relevant activities as approved by NABARD

PARTICIPANT GROUPS (PGS)

The core activity will be a family based programme and will be undertaken by the member of tribal family. For better planning and management, the individual project participant will come together as small groups of about 10 members each.

It is necessary for people to understand the relationship between their poverty and the degraded environment in which they live in. They must also be provided with an equally good, if not better, economic alternative.

Social empowerment, improvement in quality of life including health and women development, in tribal predominant areas of the country through demonstration projects supported through Non-Government Organisations (NGOs)/ Community Based Organisations (CBOs)/ GOs.

DEFINITION

The tribal situation in the country presents a varied picture. Some areas have high Tribal concentration while in other areas, the tribals form only a small portion of the total population. There are some tribal groups, which are still at the food gathering stage, some others practice shifting cultivation, yet other may be pursuing primitive forms of agriculture.

The Constitution of India provides for a comprehensive framework for the socio-economic development of Scheduled Tribes and for preventing their exploitation by other groups of society. A detailed and comprehensive review of the tribal problem was taken on the eve of the Fifth Five Year Plan and the Tribal sub-Plan strategy took note of the fact that an integrated approach to the tribal problems was necessary in terms of their geographic and demographic concentration.

If a faster development of this community is to take place. Accordingly, the tribal areas in the country were classified under three broad categories:

- States and Union Territories having a majority scheduled tribes population.
- States and Union Territories having substantial tribal population but majority tribal population in particular administrative units, such as block and tehsils.
- States and Union Territories having dispersed tribal population.
- In the light of the above approach, it was decided that tribal majority States like Arunachal Pradesh, Meghalaya, Mizoram, Nagaland and U.Ts. of Lakshadweep and Dadra and Nagar Haveli may not need a Tribal sub-Plan, as the entire plan of these States/Union Territories was primarily meant for the S.T. population constitutioning the majority. For the second category of States and Union Territories, tribal sub-Plan approach was adopted after delineating areas of tribal concentration. A similar approach was also adopted

in case of States and Union Territories having dispersed tribal population by paying special attention to pockets of tribal concentrations, keeping in view their tenor of dispersal. To look after the tribal population coming within the new tribal sub-Plan strategy in a coordinated manner, Integrated Tribal Development Projects ere conceived during Fifth Five Year Plan and these have been continued since them. During the Sixth Plan, Modified Area Development Approach (MADA) was adopted to cover smaller areas of tribal concentration and during the Seventh Plan, the TSP strategy was extended further to cover even more smaller areas of tribal concentration and thus cluster of tribal concentration were identified.

- At the time of delineation of project areas under the Tribal sub-Plan strategy, it was observed that the ITDPs/ITDAs are not co-terminus. Areas declared under Fifth Schedule of the Constitution. The Scheduled Areas as per the Constitutional orders have been declared in eight States viz A.P., Bihar, Gujarat, H.P., Maharashtra, M.P., Orissa and Rajasthan, As per the provisions contained in the Fifth Schedule of the Constitution, various enactment in the forms of Acts and Regulations have been promulgated in the above states for the welfare of scheduled tribes and their protection from exploitation.

Since TSP strategy also has twin objectives namely Socio-economic development of Schedule tribes and protection of tribal against exploitation, the Govt. of India in Aug., 1976 had decided to make the boundaries of Scheduled Areas co-terminus with TSP areas (ITDP/ITDA only) so that the protective measure available to Sch. Tribes in Sch.

Areas could be uniformly applied to TSP areas for effective implementation of the development programmes in these areas. Accordingly, the TSP areas have been made co-terminus with Sch. Areas in the State of Bihar, Gujarat, H.P., Maharashtra, Madhya Pradesh, Orissa and Rajasthan.

The State of A.P. where the TSP areas are not co-terminus with sch. Areas has also furnished a proposal to this effect which is under examination.

NEHRU AND ELWIN ON TRIBAL DEVELOPMENT: A CONTRASTING PERSPECTIVES

Verrier Elwin, a citizen of Great Britain, came to India in 1927 as a Christian missionary. Exactly a year later he got the chance to meet Mahatma Gandhi and become attracted to his philosophy, woven around the reformation of grassroots society in India. Gandhi's vision on emancipation of the oppressed was so persuasive and practical that it worked like magic in transforming Elvin from a religious man to a 'phi anthropologist'. At the beginning of his career he was tempted to work among the untouchables, but he could not stick to this decision for long. Once, in an interaction, Jamnalal Bajaj mentioned tribes and hinted their unique social system and economic life. Elvin now become fascinated by tribes and shifted his interest from the untouchables to the tribes, from the people suffering from hierarchy-based inequality to the people facing disadvantage of isolation. From then he never deviated from this focus, rather he went on studying tribes throughout his life, first in central India and then in the North-East. In the course of his study he was able to understand many aspect of the tribal life, ranging from the socio-cultural domain to their poverty and depletion of their livelihood. He took Indian citizenship in 1954. Jawaharlal Nehru, then prime mister of India, appointed him Anthropological Advisor to the government of India and assign him the task of implementing the tribal welfare programme, particular in the North-East. Both Nehru and Elwin, one as an architect of modern India and other as an anthropologist-cum-philanthopolist, contributed diversely to the discourse on tribal development.

To develop the proper understanding about the tribal development in India, we need to understand these negative and positive experiences which will provide a complementary view of the development process. So that here we are focusing and analyzing the Nehruvian and Elwin approaches in the context of tribal development in India. The debate between Nehru and Elwin on tribal development gained grounded after independence, and, therefore, claimed an intrinsic link with the national development discourse. To the extent that Nehru was an extreme nationalist, Elwin was the moderate nationalist; the trend of national development was more pronounced in Nehru's approach whereas

Elwin's concern was confined to the welfare of the tribes, a segment of the nation. In other world, Nehru modeled his approach on the lines of the western paradigm and unequivocally proposed uniform application on this model for the development of all section of people, irrespective of gender, cast, tribe or religious background. The areas of his vision of development were wider and more diverse from fostering human dignity, world peace, democracy, planning and development, socialism, secularism, Indian national hood, science and technology to overall change through consent and non-violence. In specific context of tribes, he recognized the importance of education, health and stable subsistence as the important means for their development.

Elwin more or less referred the same things, but differ with Nehru in approach. In his disputed isolationist approach, Elwin insisted that the tribes should maintain a selective distance from the mainstream socio-political-economical system, which was, however, not accepted to Nehruvian patriotism. It might be possible that Elwin had changed his approach from isolationist to integrationist under the influence of a Nehru.

Regarding tribal development, Nehru said " I have no doubt that development and changed so-called progress will come to them, because it is becoming increasingly difficult for any people to live their isolated life cut off from the rest of the world. But let this development and change be natural and be in nature of self development with all the help one can give in the process". To active this ideology of development, Nehru borrowed the western paradigm and set it in a tribal context. He was, however, against understanding tribal social and cultural identity in this development process. It is noticeable that by exposing colonial rule as responsible for the misery and backwardness of the tribes, Elwin initiated decolonization of the tribal development approach earlier than Nehru. Nehru later reshaped the decolonization process with the inclusion of modern technology, market forces and scientific outlook as added means for their development.

Nehru aimed to wipe out the gap between the rich and the poor, to offer equal opportunity of development to all, and ensure equal participation in the development process. Elwin did not pay attention to the persisting discrepancy among classes, his concern was confined to the gap between the 'savage' and 'civilized' between the so called modern people and innocent tribes. Elwin discarded the theory about the threshold of pain; that the 'savage' are internally stronger and better able to bear pain that the civilized that are more delicate and wound be hurt more.

The Nehruvian approach could not retain it uniformity in ideology and practice. Nehru subscribed to principle to the principles of not interfering and not uprooting tribes during the introduction of new development prorgammes, but in practice almost all the large scale industries and big dams planned during his lifetimes were established in tribal areas, causing massive displacement. Nehru may have been right in introducing such development programmes from the larger perspective of national development, but he was equally wrong for not devising an acceptable mechanism to confirm tribal participation in that development process.

The approaches of both of these stalwarts were not free from their respective political interests. Nehru showed special political favours for NEFA tribes, more than for tribes of living in the rest of India.

Nagaland became full state in 1963 on his approval. After his death, his successor Indira Gandhi offered separate statehood to Manipur and Meghalaya and raised the status of Arunanachal Pradesh and Mizoram to full-fledge states. Till this period, none of the central or southern tribal regions ever got such a privilege, either in the form of separate statehood or as autonomous councils, although they had tribal populations about four times higher than in the north-east.

The political maneuvering in Elwin's approach is evident in the shifting of his concerns from the central tribal region to the north-east in the later part of his life. He gained his first hand experience of vulnerability of tribes after his studies in central region and also developed his isolationist approach on this basis; but he applied it in north-east, not in the central tribal region. One could not blame Elvin for this, because he did seek the support of Gandhi to apply this approach to the tribes of central region, but Gandhi never acceded to his appeal. He shifted to the north-east when Nehru provided a political base to apply his ideas.

The major drawback in Elwin and Nehru's approaches was that they were confined to certain region and particular tribes; they could not provide an all India framework for the development of tribes. At the same time, they left enormously valuable feedback for tribal policy for the 21st century in that they showed that neither complete isolation nor large scale and sophisticated development programme minus tribal participation was feasible. We need a revised formula of decentralization and lager participation of the tribes in development policy and implementation.

Chapter 2

Tribal Communities in India

Tribes are relatively isolated from larger cultural influences, have a relative cultural homogeneity and a simple technology. They believe in spirits, magic and witchcraft. They have their own taboos which prohibit certain actions that are punishable by the community, by the supernatural, or by magical consequences. Large number of the tribes believe in animism, according to which all objects—both animate and inanimate— are permanently or temporarily inhabited by spirits or souls.

Often, an activity is believed to be caused by these spirits. Some spirits are worshipped and treated with fear and respect. Some scholars have maintained that animism was the earliest form of religion of the tribes.

Many tribes believe in ancestor worship too:

- *Common name:* Each caste has a distinct name of its own through which it is distinguished from others.
- *Common territory:* Tribes generally occupy common geographical areas.
- *Common language:* Members of one tribe speak the same language. Each tribe has its own dialect, if not the script.
- *Common culture:* Each tribe has prescribed patterns of behaviour and festivals and deities to worship.
- *Endogamy:* Each tribe has the practice of marrying members within their own tribe.
- *Political organisation:* All tribes have their own political organisation. They have councils of elders which control members.
- As against the national average of 43 per cent, 57 per cent of the tribals are economically active.

- As regards the nature of work, against 73 per cent national average, 91 per cent tribal workers are engaged in agriculture. About 3 per cent tribals are engaged in manufacturing (against 11 per cent of general population) and 5 per cent in servicing (tertiary) sectors (against 16 per cent average of general population). About 1 per cent tribals are engaged in forestry and food-gathering.

Some other features of the tribals are: most of them live in isolated terrains; the main sources of their livelihood are agriculture and gathering of forest produce; they do not cultivate for profit; they still largely rely on barter system; they spend a greater part of their earnings on social and religious ceremonies; and a large number of them are illiterate and are victimised by unscrupulous forest contractors and moneylenders.

PROBLEMS OF TRIBAL COMMUNITIES

LAND ALIENATION

The history of land alienation among the tribes began during British colonialism in India when the British interfered in the tribal region for the purpose of exploiting the tribal natural resources. Coupled with this tribal lands were occupied by moneylenders, zamindars and traders by advancing them loans etc. Opening of mines in the heart of tribal habitat and even a few factories provided wage labour as well as opportunities for factory employment.

But this brought increasing destitution and displacement. After the British came to power, the Forest policy of the British Government was more inclined towards commercial considerations rather than human. Some forests were declared as reserved ones where only authorized contractors were allowed to cut the timber and the forest -dwellers were kept isolated deliberately within their habitat without any effort to ameliorate their economic and educational standards. The expansion of railway in India heavily devastated the forest resources in India.

The Government started reserving teak, Sal and deodar forests for the manufacture of railway sleepers. Forest land and its resources provide the best means of livelihood for the tribal people and many tribes including the women engage in agriculture, food gathering and hunting they are heavily dependent on the products of the forest. Therefore when outsiders exploit the tribe's land and its resources the natural life cycle of tribal ecology and tribal life is greatly disturbed.

POVERTY AND INDEBTEDNESS

Majority tribes live under poverty line. The tribes follow many simple occupations based on simple technology. Most of the occupation falls into the primary occupations such as hunting, gathering, and agriculture. The technology they use for these purposes belong to the most primitive kind. There is no profit and surplus making in such economy. Hence there per capita income is very meagre much lesser than the Indian average. Most of them live under abject poverty and are in debt in the hands of local moneylenders and Zamindars.In order to repay the debt they often mortgage or sell their land to the moneylenders. Indebtedness is almost inevitable since heavy interest is to be paid to these moneylenders.

HEALTH AND NUTRITION

In many parts of India tribal population suffers from chronic infections and diseases out of which water borne diseases are life threatening. They also suffer from deficiency diseases. The Himalayan tribes suffer from goiter due to lack of iodine. Leprosy and tuberculosis are also common among them. Infant mortality was found to be very high among some of the tribes. Malnutrition is common and has affected the general health of the tribal children as it lowers the ability to resist infection, leads to chronic illness and sometimes leads to brain impairment. The ecological imbalance like cutting of trees have increased the distances between villages and the forest areas thus forcing tribal women to walk longer distances in search of forest produce and firewood.

EDUCATION

Educationally the tribal population is at different levels of development but overall the formal education has made very little impact on tribal groups. Earlier Government had no direct programme for their education. But in the subsequent years the reservation policy has made some changes. There are many reasons for low level of education among the tribal people: Formal education is not considered necessary to discharge their social obligations. Superstitions and myths play an important role in rejecting education. Most tribes live in abject poverty. It is not easy for them to send their children to schools, as they are considered extra helping hands. The formal schools do not hold any special interest for the children. Most of the tribes are located in interior and remote areas where teachers would not like to go from outside.

CULTURAL PROBLEMS

Due to contact with other cultures, the tribal culture is undergoing a revolutionary change. Due to influence of Christian missionaries the problem of bilingualism has developed which led to indifference towards tribal language.

The tribal people are imitating western culture in different aspects of their social life and leaving their own culture. It has led to degeneration of tribal life and tribal arts such as dance, music and different types of craft.

SUSTAINABLE LIVELIHOODS FOR TRIBAL COMMUNITIES

Twenty-five year old Gobardhan Munda's income has doubled, he now has a bank account and a Kisan Credit Card. He grew up juggling several jobs to support his seven member family. Barely able to eke out a living from his small plot of land, he would work as daily wage earner, loading construction material on trucks that passed through the city.

He earned INR 100 a day. Two years ago, he volunteered to participate in a pilot to test the impact of drip irrigation on productivity of small holdings. On a small plot of land that received just about enough water supply to cultivate one season of potato, he now grows tomatoes, cauliflower and cucumber. Today he says, "Our village sends truckloads of vegetables to nearby markets, this has never happened before because of the acute water shortage".

Highlights:

- A drip irrigation prototype developed in Jharkhand is providing small and marginal farmers with sustainable income and livelihoods

- The prototype has helped farmers adopt innovative technology best suited to vegetable cultivation on small and marginal landholdings
- The technology has also helped empower women farmers to extend vegetable cropping to fallow land
- The prototype, demonstrated in five districts of Jharkhand, has now been upscaled across the state by the Rural Development Department
- The prototype was developed in Jharkhand as part of a livelihood generation project supported by UNDP
- The project, in partnership with the government of Jharkhand, aims to strengthen the state government's capacity to implement livelihood programmes in the state

The prototype has helped many farmers in the Angara Block of the east Indian state of Jharkhand adopt an innovative technology best suited to vegetable cultivation on small and marginal landholdings. For Gobardhan Munda, who never finished school, it has opened other doors. He now regularly operates a savings account with a bank in his village. The bank has sanctioned him a kisan or farmers credit card which enables him to access adequate, reasonably priced and timely credit. He now puts away nearly INR 18,000 annually in insurance and long term savings schemes.

Recognizing the success of the drip irrigation prototype for individual small and marginal land holdings demonstrated in five districts with more than 300 farmers, has now been upscaled by the Rural Development Department across the state. Jharkhand is one of India's most resource rich states. However, inequality remains widespread, and a significant proportion of the population is unable to benefit from government schemes or programmes to reduce poverty.

The state's population is predominantly tribal with high levels of poverty. More than 50 per cent of the scheduled tribe population and scheduled caste population in rural areas live in poverty. This is significantly higher than the national average. In tribal dominated areas such as Angara where Gobardhan lives, more than two-thirds of the population lives below the poverty line and over 50 per cent subsist as marginal farmers with land holdings of between 0.25 – 1 acre. Since 2009, UNDP has partnered with the state government of

Jharkhand to strengthen governments' capacity to effectively deliver livelihoods schemes and programmes. This resulted in the creation of the Jharkhand State Livelihood Promotion Society (JSLPS) to spearhead sustainable livelihoods for the rural poor, in particular, for persistently excluded communities. JSLPS is now the nodal agency for the implementation of the national flagship programme - National Rural Livelihoods Missions in Jharkhand.

For women, drip irrigation prototype has meant that many of them see agriculture as a viable livelihood option. Shiela Devi, farmer from Sikiddri volunteered to be a part of the pilot. Family income has doubled and Shiela plans to cultivate multiple crops in 2012, in an area where acute water shortage had meant that only half the family's land could be cultivated. The technology has helped empower women farmers to extend vegetable cropping to fallow land and consider scaling up further.

As India tackles the challenge of "jobless growth", and strives to secure livelihoods for the poor, the prototypes in Jharkhand demonstrate the possibilities of enabling tribal communities to generate sustainable livelihoods and self-employment for their families.

PROTECTING FORESTS AND TRIBAL COMMUNITIES

The Environmental movement in India is usually associated with the "chipko" movement, the fight against the silent valley "project" or more recently the Narmada Bachao Andolan (NBA). Little attention is given to the myriad little organizations and movements across the country that have been responsible for the protection of forests and tribal communities all across the country. One such organization that we encountered recently is SAKTI (Search for Action and Knowledge for Tribal Initiative), an organization that has been working to protect the forests and the tribal people in Andhra Pradesh for over 15 years.

Based in Hyderabad, SAKTI operates in the East and West Godavari districts and the Nallamalai hills near Srisailam. Both areas have rich forest lands and are home to several tribal communities like the Koyas, the Kondareddies, the Valmikis and the Chenchus (The East and West Godavari tribals are well known for their uprising against the British Empire in the early 20th century). SAKTI is headed by Dr. Sivaramkrishna, a school teacher turned cultural anthropologist turned social activist. Simple and unassuming and yet very passionate, Dr. Sivamkrishna is very well respected in Andhra Pradesh administrative circles because of his work with SAKTI.

Dr. Sivaramkrishna began his work with the tribals in the East Godavari district while researching on his doctoral thesis. In the process of documenting and interpreting the tribal cultures through their music, dances and folklore, he was exposed to the plight of the tribal people and their exploitation by government officials, bureaucrats and big businesses. He soon founded SAKTI and with the help of his colleagues started mobilizing the tribals to fight for their rights.

One of the first issues addressed by SAKTI was tribal land rights. A notion alien to the tribals, property rights was introduced to the tribals by the British. Early in the 20th century, the British Administration assigned land to individual tribals. But over time, land was stolen from the tribals by conniving non-tribals and corrupt government officials. One of the biggest obstacles the tribals face when fighting for their rights is their lack of understanding of the judicial system and the administrative machinery. To overcome this barrier, SAKTI volunteers not only taught the tribals to read and interpret land records but also trained them to handle legal issues themselves.

Krishnaveni is one of the tribal women trained by SAKTI. She belongs to the Koya clan and is educated only till class V. But armed with skill of reading and interpreting land records, she has confidence to question government officials like the Mandal Revenue officer and the District Collector. She leads the fight by tribals in her village and a few neighouring villages to regain land which was illegally usurped from their forefathers around 1902. Krishnaveni is just one of the many whose lives have been transformed by the efforts of SAKTI volunteers.

In 1984 SAKTI won a public litigation case against the Godavari Plywood factory, an industry that was threatening the livelihood of the tribal people by cutting mango and jackfruit trees in the tribal forests. While Sunderlal Bahuguna and Chandni Prasad Bhat were advocating tree hugging to protect the trees in the north, and while the naxalites in A.P were taking extremist measures to fight for the rights of the poor, SAKTI had adopted an entirely different approach using the democratic machinery and judicial system to fight for tribal rights and the environment.

Since then SAKTI has filed numerous other public litigation cases against development projects that threaten the environment and the survival of the tribal people. Recently, SAKTI won a case against the construction of Bhupatuphalem reservoir in the East Godavari district. The reservoir project, if implemented, would submerge 6 tribal villages and thousands of acres of fertile forest land that provides livelihood for the tribal population.

THE WATER PURIFICATION PLANT IN MAREDUMILLI

SAKTI has also been involved in various developmental activities in tribal as well as non-tribal areas. In Renchumettu near Rampachodavaram in the East Godavari district, its volunteers have helped the Kondareddy tribe implement a watershed development project. The check dams and irrigation tanks built with the help of SAKTI engineers have vastly increased the productivity of this tribal community. In Maredumilli, another village consisting mainly of people from the Valmiki tribe, SAKTI engineers have built a water purification plant to remove the excess dissolved iron in the ground water.

To help the tribals increase their cash income, SAKTI has provided training to the tribals in income generation activities like making cane and bamboo furniture. SAKTI is also promoting renewable energy technologies in the tribal areas. In Maredumilli, SAKTI engineers installed solar street lamps. SAKTI is now planning to implement a micro-hydel power generation project to provide electricity to the remote tribal villages.

SAKTI got involved with the weaver community in Amalpuram after a devastating cyclone that struck the Andhra Pradesh coast in 1996 washed away their neglected colony. Its volunteers helped the weavers rebuild their lives by providing them with low-cost retrofitted houses, handlooms, spinning yarn and sanitation facilities such as drains and community toilets. SAKTI has trained the weavers in the area of disaster management. Currently, SAKTI is trying to assist the weavers in adapting their skills to the new market requirements and is also actively seeking to market the woven products.

SAKTI has also assisted the scheduled caste villages near Amalapuram. Like the weaver colony, their villages have also been long neglected by the government. In spite of being close to the Godavari river, these people did not have access to clean drinking water. SAKTI helped the villagers build their own water tanks for storing clean and safe drinking water.

Despite all its accomplishments, SAKTI faces many obstacles. With the globalization/liberalization policies adopted by the Indian government, tribal populations face the threat of extinction. The livelihood of the poor and marginalized sections of the Indian society as a whole is threatened by these policies. The judicial system has not been of much help, partly because of corruption and partly because the laws are being manipulated in favour of the rich and the powerful.

As we write this article, some volunteers from SAKTI, Shyam, Chinnarao and Someswara Rao languish in an Indian jail. Shyam is a civil engineer who was responsible for implementing the engineering projects we listed earlier. Chinnarao who belongs to the Valmiki tribe and has completed high school, has been researching the tribal culture, flora and fauna in the Ramapchodavaram area in East Godavari district along with Srinu, a Koya tribal who has a degree in social service and is also the driver and photographer for SAKTI. Somesawara Rao is a Koya from West Godavari who like Krishanveni has been involved in the land rights movement. All three were arrested on baseless allegations in February 2001 when they were visiting the Tenkalagadda village in East Godavari district. Three tribal boys were also arrested in the same context. Krishnaveni, the Koya woman we mentioned earlier in the chapter, was arrested a few weeks back, again on flimsy grounds.

The future of organizations like SAKTI depends to a large extent on ordinary citizens like us. The social change that these organizations aspire for is not possible without our participation and our support. We could turn a blind eye to the increasing marginalization of the poor, the exploitation of the weak and the destruction of our natural heritage. Or we could join their endeavor to create a just and sane world by actively supporting their cause. The choice is ours.

LAW AND THE CONSTITUTION: EVICTION OF FOREST COMMUNITIES

The move to evict forest dwellers and forest dependent communities from the forest is an unsubtle attempt at re-imagining their role as a foe of the forest and of wild life, and as a threat to national, and global, environment.

This is based not on empirical fact, but on what may be termed 'institutionalised prejudice'. A version of environmentalism has been foisted on forest communities, conspicuously through the court, by which forests become a bureaucratic enterprise to the exclusion of those who, over generations, have been part of forest life, and whose fate and future are linked inextricably with the forest. In one sense, this is a continuation of the legal regime that was imprinted into the statute books, such as the Indian Forest Act 1927 (which had a predecessor in the Indian Forest Act 1878). But even this colonial attempt to control and commercialise forests did not go as far as the exiling of forest communities that is presently being ruthlessly executed.

The Indian Forest Act 1927 sanctions the state to exercise of control over the forests, and to assert a species of ownership. Forests were classed as reserve forests, village forests and protected forests. Enacted to assert state proprietorship, and ownership, over forest resources, the Forest Act 'reserved', 'protected' and declared forests in which it then shrank the rights of the forest communities as the state deemed apt. In this process, notions of common property, and use, were forced aside, and replaced by state control to serve the interests, then usually commercial and expansionist, of the state. The relationship of forest communities to the forest were reductively perceived as interests and rights that could be 'settled'. In the process of settling forest rights, forest communities were reduced to claimants. Even as the Forest Act spells out the many things that the state may prohibit forest communities from doing in relationship to the forest, there were no such limitations placed on the state. The denuding of forest resources may be traced in part to this absence, and in further part to the rapacious nature of industries' needs and use of forest resources. Despite this, it is the forest communities, who are not outsiders and whose lexicon has not altered from 'use' to 'exploitation' of forest resources, who are being sent into exile. This is the illogic of the law.

Forest communities have had to wage a continuing battle against being illegalised, and against their forest-related activity being criminalised, even as the Forest Act 1927 ensured this entrenching of state control as also of the reductionist approach to the rights of forest communities. Yet, when the Constitution of free India was promulgated in 1950, the 'continuity' that was accorded an importance so that there would be no vacuum where the law had been, allowed the Forest Act to continue as it was. This happened because Art. 372 of the Constitution declared that 'all the law in force in the territory of India immediately before the commencement of this Constitution shall continue in force therein until altered or replaced or amended'.

In the 1950s and 1960s, the colonial agenda of commercial exploitation of forest by the state for its expansionist projects, was refashioned to include an emphasis on industrial growth as development. So it is that industry was allowed access to forests, at pitifully low rates, to clear forest growth for its purposes.

It was not until the UN Conference on the Human Environment held in Stockholm in June 1972 that 'environment' came on to the policy makers' agenda. In 1981, Parliament enacted the Air (Prevention and Control of Pollution) Act. Earlier, in 1974 the Water (Prevention and Control of Pollution) Act had been enacted by Parliament.

It is instructive to read the Statement of Objects and Reasons for these two legislations: both categorically trace the problem of pollution and deterioration of air, and of water sources, to 'the growth of industries and the increasing tendency to urbanisation' (Water Act) and 'the increasing industrialisation' (Air Act). Yet, when the depleting forest cover was under scrutiny, the predominant role played by industry in the loss of forest was not given centrality.

There is no other way that the handing over of forest land to Harihar Polyfibres, after the importance of forest conservation had been set into the statute in the Forest (Conservation) Act 1980 - can be explained.

The Forest (Conservation) Act 1980, enacted to shift, and centralise, the power over forests was intended to check deforestation which, the Statement of Objects and Reasons states, 'had been taking place on a large scale in the country'. The Act, like the Ordinance that preceded it, 'made the prior approval of the Central Government necessary for dereservation of reserved forests and for use of forest land for non-forest purposes.' The Act also provides for the constitution of an advisory committee to advise the Central government with regard to grant of such approval. Since the Act came into force, it is mining interests that have been liberally represented in the cases before courts asking for permission to continue with mining despite the devastating effect mining has on land. Increasingly, the large scale displacement that 'development projects' such as dams engender, have had the consequence of state governments seeking the central government's permission to dereserve forest areas so as to provide rehabilitation sites to the displaced: the option of altering the project of what turns out to be 'destructive development' has almost never been considered.

It is in this context of industry, mining interests and 'project development' which last, in the case of dams as an example, invariably drowns forest resources and demands diversion of those forests that escape submergence, in which 'conservation' is being spoken. Yet, it is the people of the forest who have been projected as its arch depredator.

In 1972, the Wild Life (Protection) Act was passed. The Act was amended twice, once in 1982, and again in 1991. Even as the court sanctions, even directs, the forced eviction of forest communities, it is instructive to recall what the Statement of Objects and Reasons to the 1991 Act said: '... 6. While making the provisions of the Act more effective and stringent due regard has also been given to the rights of the local people, particularly the tribals. It is being provided that except for the areas under reserve forests, (where the rights of the people have already been settled) and the territorial waters, no area can be declared as sanctuary unless the rights of the people have been settled. State Wild Life Advisory Boards are also being made responsible for suggesting ways and means to harmonise the needs of tribals and the protection of wildlife.' Local people, especially tribals, are, according to this parliamentary dictum, to be taken into the reckoning; even if the colonial vestige of 'settling' of rights has been retained. And the effort is to be towards harmonising the interests of the tribals with that of the forest; not tearing them asunder. Yet, when the order of the Supreme Court was interpreted to mean forcible eviction of forest communities, this parliamentary purpose was not even acknowledged.

The 42 nd Constitution Amendment Act, 1976 inserted Article 48A into the Directive Principles of State Policy: 'The State shall endeavor to protect and improve the environment and to safeguard the forests and wildlife of the country.' And Article 51A, also introduced by the 42 nd Amendment, which lists out the fundamental duties said: 'It shall be the duty of every citizen of India - .... (g) to protect and improve the national environment and forests, lakes, rivers, wildlife and to have compassion for living creatures.' In directing that all forest communities be evicted, there has been no attempt to ascertain what the relationship between the forest communities and the forest is. Nor has there been any recognition of the damage to the forest resources that will almost inevitably result from emptying the forest of its dwellers and the forest dependent communities; and of leaving the protection, and the nurturing, of forests to the forest bureaucracy alone.

There is a further aspect to the constitutional treatment of the forest communities. In the late 1970s the judiciary devised a judicial procedure, now widely known as PIL, by which it brought within its ken the lives of classes and communities who had been excluded from constitutionalism thus far. In tandem with this development in judicial process, the substantive content of the 'right to life' in Article 21 was expanded.

The right to dignity, health, clean environment, education, livelihood and shelter were some aspects of this wider meaning given to the law. In S.P. Gupta v. Union of India (1981 Supp SCC 81), the Supreme Court set out in unmistakable terms that PIL had been devised to provide access to justice to the indigent, illiterate and ignorant who were unable to reach rights, and would so remain if there was no intervention to further their cause. In the early years of the `80s, when the degradation of the environment was taken to the court in PIL, it was the pollution of rivers, especially by industrialisation, that was in issue.

The court often ordered temporary closure of the industry involved, and negotiated the setting up of effluent treatment plants and central effluent treatment plants and, upon the installing of these clean-up technologies, the industries were permitted to restart operations (clean-up technologies, it may be added, did not and were not expected to stop the pollution; only to reduce it.) Environmentalism has, however, since captured the imagination of the court. In turn, this has resulted in a prioritisation of interests and rights, displacing altogether concerns about the lives of those who live on law's margins such as the forest communities.

Increasingly, with a strident environmentalism that is exclusive and excluding, the inter-dependence between the forest communities and the forests is being drowned out. So are the various constitutional injunctions that would require respect for the forest communities. For instance, a significant proportion of the forest communities are scheduled tribes. Scheduled tribes have a special status in the Constitution. Recognising the importance of protecting the habitat from incursions and being taken over, the Constitution carves out 'scheduled areas' which the President will notify for special protection.

The 5 th Schedule and the 6 th Schedule to the Constitution provide a different dispensation in the matter of administering Scheduled Areas. Embargoes on alienation of land by a tribal to a non-tribal have been enacted in relation to scheduled areas, to reduce the potential for exploitation of tribals. In 199_, the Supreme Court ruled, in Samata v. State of A.P., that the prohibition of alienation meant that the state too could not acquire land from a tribal to hand it over to a non-tribal. And that ruling continues to be the law despite attempts by a range of vested interest to change this situation, by amending the 5 th Schedule to the Constitution, if necessary. In the directive principles of state policy, in Article 46, there is a specific provision directing that 'the state shall promote with special care the educational and economic interests of the weaker sections of the people, and in particular, of the scheduled castes and scheduled tribes, and shall protect them from social injustice and all forms of exploitation.'

Despite all these constitution mandates that have been spelt out, there are moves afoot to send communities into exile. That this is both unconstitutional and unconscionable is evident, and cannot be ignored.

The process of exiling forest communities from their habitat and livelihood has a way of classifying them into:

- The eligibles,
- The ineligibles, and
- The invisibles.

The eligibles are those who are recognised as having interests in the forest that must be 'settled' as part of the displacement process. The ineligible are those whose claim to be recognised as having interests are not accepted. And the invisibles are those who do not feature in any government document or register, and the whole exercise of dispossession and displacement is effected as if they do not exist. The poor state of land and habitation records contributes to this process of systemic denial of rights. That many forests dwellers have remained uncounted, they have not been given pattas, and they have been forced by the law into various states of illegality, also lends itself to creating this unjust situation. It is also significant that those least dispossessed in the working of the law, *i.e.*, the eligibles, have only the right to reduce their interests to a claim-and they may then receive compensation which will then be seen as 'settling' their rights. The inevitable impoverishment that results is not accounted for anywhere. It is a steep decline in policy-from special protection to exile and disarray-that this move portends. This also negates, in totality, the letter and the spirit of the Panchayats (Extension to Scheduled Areas) Act, 1996 which was a stride towards recognising the autonomy of communities in scheduled areas over the resources in their region, including water, forest produce and minor minerals.

These moves to empty the forest of forest communities finds no tolerance in the international law either. India is a signatory to the International Covenant on Economic Social and Cultural Rights, and acting contrary to the Covenant represents a violation of international law. The Covenant sets out the rights, including 'the right of everyone to an adequate standard of living for himself and his family, including adequate food, clothing, and housing, and to the continuous improvement of living conditions.'

The Maastricht Guidelines on Violation of Economic, Social and Cultural Rights explains that states are obligated to 'respect, protect and fulfil' the rights set out in the Covenant. 'The obligation to respect requires states to refrain from interfering with the enjoyment of economic, social and cultural rights. Thus, the right to housing is violated if the state engages in arbitrary forced evictions. The obligation to protect requires states to prevent violation of such rights by third parties...The obligation to fulfil requires states to take appropriate, legislative, administrative, budgetary, judicial and other measures towards the full realisation of such rights.' (Maastricht Guidelines, para 6)

In setting out the 'violations through acts of commission', the Maastricht Guidelines illustrate it thus:

'14. (b) The active denial of such rights to particular individuals or groups, whether through legislated or enforced discrimination;.

(d) The adoption of legislation or policies which are manifestly incompatible with pre-existing legal obligations relating to these rights, unless it is done with the purpose and effect of increasing equality and improving the realisation of economic, social and cultural rights for the most vulnerable groups;

(e) The adoption of any deliberately retrogressive measures that reduces the extent to which any such right is guaranteed;

(f) The calculated obstruction of, or halt to, the progressive realization of a right protected by the Covenant, unless the State is acting within a limitation permitted by the Covenant or it does so due to a lack of available resources or force majeure;'

General Comment 4 of the Committee on Economic, Social and Cultural Rights on the Right to Housing denounces forced evictions when it says:

18. In this regard, the Committee considers that instances of forced eviction are prima facie incompatible with the requirements of the Covenant and can only be justified in the most exceptional circumstances, and in accordance with the relevant principles of international law.

The Committee on Economic Social Cultural Rights, in General Comment 7 on forced evictions recognised the burden of suffering placed especially on particular populations when it said:

' Women, children, youth, older persons, indigenous people, ethnic and other minorities, and other vulnerable individuals and groups all suffer disproportionately from the practice of forced evictions.' And proposed that the least that needed to be done was to provide a procedure to precede forced evictions, where forced eviction cannot be avoided. These procedural protections include:

- An opportunity for genuine consultation with those affected;
- Adequate and reasonable notice for all affected persons prior to the scheduled date of eviction;
- Information on the proposed evictions and where applicable, on the alternative purpose for which land or housing is to be used, to be made available in reasonable time to those affected;
- Especially where groups of people are involved, government officials or their representatives to be present during an eviction;
- All persons carrying out the eviction to be properly identified;
- Evictions not to take place in particularly bad weather or at night unless the affected persons consent otherwise;
- Provision of legal remedies; and
- Provision, where possible, of legal aid to persons who are in need of it to seek redress from the courts.

And the obligation of State was spelt out:

Evictions should not result in rendering individuals homeless or vulnerable to the violation of other human rights. Where those affected are unable to provide for themselves, the State party must take all appropriate measures, to the maximum of its available resources, to ensure that adequate alternative housing, resettlement or access to productive land, as the case may be, is available.

None of this is respected in the mass eviction of forest communities. Instead, a language is being developed which dispossesses and disenfranchises forest communities by referring to then as 'encroachers' and foisting 'illegality' on them.

Chapter 3

Tribal Socio-economic Transformation and Development in India

SOCIO-ECONOMIC PROGRAMMES FOR SCHEDULED CASTES AND SCHEDULED TRIBES

One of the major concerns of Indian planning has been the welfare and development of the weaker sections of society, and among them more especially that of the scheduled castes, the scheduled tribes and the denotified, nomadic and semi-nomadic tribes who constitute nearly one quarter of the total population. These groups have, for historical reasons, remained socially and economically backward, and hence concerted efforts have been made under the plan to raise their social and economic status, as required by the Directive Principles of Article 46 of the Constitution.

In the first two plans, welfare programmes were drawn up and implemented for improving the educational and economic status of the scheduled castes, scheduled tribes and other backward classes. In addition, in the tribal and the scheduled areas, an area development approach was adopted. By the end of the Fourth Plan, however, it was evident that the strategy for the development of these disadvantaged groups would have to be based on comprehensive economic and human resource development efforts so that these sections of the population would acquire the ability to utilise the fruits of general economic development arising from the various sectoral development programmes. The Tribal Sub-Plan approach was adopted in the Fifth

Plan and the Special Component Plans (for SCs) formulated in the Sixth Plan and these resulted in earmarked allocations for the Tribal Sub-Plans and scheduled castes' socio-economic development, apart from the general programmes of economic development undertaken by the Central and State Governments. In the Sixth Plan, the emphasis shifted from welfare to family and beneficiary-oriented development schemes within the general framework of socio-economic programmes specifi-cally directed at and designed for the benefit of the scheduled castes and scheduled tribes. In the Sixth Plan, a definite target of assisting 50 per cent of the scheduled caste anoscheduled tribe families to cross the poverty line was adopted for the first time.

Clearly, at the beginning of the Seventh Plan, an assessment is called for in order to ascertain if the major objective of narrowing the socio-economic gap between the general level of economic and social development and that of the scheduled castes, scheduled tribes and other backward classes has been achieved and to know how far the modified strategies have been successful in tackling the historical legacy of their backwardness. Specifically, it is important to know what has been the impact of the programmes undertaken for their benefit in the following areas:

(a) Education, which accounted for over 50 per cent of all expenditure up to the end of the Sixth Plan.

(b) Economic programmes, which accounted for about 28 per cent of expenditure till the end of the Sixth Plan; and

(c) Social welfare schemes, which accounted for about 22 per cent of total expenditure till the end of the Sixth Plan.

The inter-decennial trends in the population of scheduled castes and scheduled tribes, in their occupations and in their literacy percentages are brought out.

Table. Population of Scheduled Castes and Scheduled Tribes

(In millions)

Year	Total population	SC population	SC's as percentage of the total	ST population	ST' s as percentage of th e total
(1)	(2)	(3)	(4)	(5)	(6)
1961	439	65	14.6	30	6.9
1971	548	80	14.5	39	6.9
1981	685	106*	15.5	54*	7.9

• Includes projected estimates for Assam.

Table. Inter-Decennial Trends in Occupation

(Percent)

	Share of total population	Share of SC		Share of ST		
	1971	1981	1971	1981	1971	1981
(1)	(2)	(3)	(4)	(5)	(6)	(7)
Cultivators	43.4	41.5	27.87	28.17	57.60	54.43
Agricultural labourers	28.7	25.2	51.75	48.22	33.00	32.67
Non-Agricultural activities	27.9	33.3	20.38	23.61	9.40	12.90

Table. Literacy Rates among Scheduled Castes/Scheduled Tribes and the Rest of the Population

(Percentage)

Year	Rest of the Population	Scheduled Castes	Scheduled Tribes
1961	27.86	10.27	8.53
	(16.59)	(3.29)	(3.16)
1971	33.80	14.67	11.30
	(17.11)	(6.44)	(4.85)
1981	41.22	21.38	16.35
	(29.51)	(10.93)	(8.04)

The population of scheduled castes as a percentage of the total population was stable over the decade 1961 -71, increasing to 15.5 per cent in the following decade, while the population of scehduled tribes, after remaining static at 6.9 per cent of the total population in the 1961 -71 decade rose to 7.9 per cent in the 1971 -81 decade. It however, needs to be recalled that the population of scheduled tribes went up on account of the removal of area restriction for scheduled communities in 1976.

15.5 The inter-decennial trends in occupational categories among the working population of scheduled castes and scheduled tribes are brought out. It is noteworthy that for the scheduled castes, there is a slight increase in the share of cultivators, while for the secheduled tribes there is a decline. Both the groups show a decline in the share of agricultural labourers, this being marked in the case of scheduled castes. An increasing trend of non-agricultural activities is descernible among both.

As regards literacy, which is one of the major indicators of social advancement, the position. The percentage of literacy among communities other than scheduled castes and scheduled tribes showed an increase from 33.8 in 1971 to 41.22 in 1981; the corresponding, increases for SCs and STs have been less. Then increase in female literacy among the SCs and STs has been very slow. While the enrolment percentage for the total child population in the 11-14 age group was 33.53, for SCs it was 29.3 and STs 15.78.

As regards employment in government service the number of scheduled tribe employees in the Central Government. It will be seen that over the period 1965-83, the employment of persons belonging to the scheduled castes went up by 93 per cent and the employment of scheduled tribes increased by nearly 217 per cent. The employment of scheduled castes in Class I jobs went up by more than 10 times in this period and that in Class II jobs by more than 7 times. The corresponding figures for increase for the scheduled tribe employees are by more than 14 times in Class I jobs and by nearly 9 times in the case of Class II jobs. While these figures indicate that the progress has been made, it is an undeniable fact that the progress has not been fast enough and that neither of these two sections of the population, *i.e.,* scheduled castes and scheduled tribes, are able to make full use of the reservation quotas.

Table. Employment profile of Scheduled Castes, Scheduled Tribes in Central Government

Group	Total number of employees	Scheduled Castes	Percentage	Scheduled tribes	Percentage
(1)	(2)	(3)	(4)	(5)	(6)
1965					
Class-I	19,379	318	1.64	52	0.27
Class-II	30,621	864	2.82	103	0.34
Class-III	10,82,278	96,114	8.88	12,390	1.14
Class-IV (excluding sweepers)	11,32,517	2,01,073	17.75	38,444	3039
TOTAL	22,64,795	2,98,369	13.17	50,989	2.25
1983					
Class-I	52,683	3,536	6.71	741	1.41
Class-II	62,485	6,351	10.16	915	1..46
Class-III	21,28,650	3,10,949	14.61	88,149	4.14
Class-IV (excluding					

sweepers)	13,02,534	2,55,094	19.58	71,812	5.51
TOTAL	35,46,352	5,75,930	16.24	1,61,617	4.56
	(57)	(93)		(217)	

REVIEW OF THE SIXTH PLAN

The Sixth Plan strategy for the socio-economic development of scheduled castes, scheduled tribes and other backward classes was designed to ensure a higher degree of devolution of funds through the Special Component Plans and through special Central assistance than in the earlier plans, with the overall objective to see that at least half of them were provided substantial assistance to enable them to cross the poverty line. The total outlays contemplated in the Sixth Plan and the amounts actually spent.

TRIBAL AREAS UNDERGOING SOCIO-ECONOMIC TRANSFORMATION

Some of the tribal areas in Himachal are undergoing significant socio-economic development changes in terms of literacy, educational patterns, societal structure and other aspects according to a study, 'Socio-economic development in tribal areas of HP since inception of tribal sub-plan 1974', conducted under the aegis of Indian Council of Social Science Research (ICSSR) by a geographer of Himachal Pradesh University (HPU) Dr B R Thakur in the five notified tribal regions of Kinnaur, Lahaul, Spiti, Pangi and Bharmaur.

Thakur said, "Anthropologically HP cannot be termed a tribal state, yet it is inhabited by significant tribes which constitute nearly 4 per cent of the total population. The tribal socio-cultural milieu in Himachal is unique in terms of certain cultural aspects. Facing hostile topographical conditions, extreme cold and dry agro-climatic conditions, a non-industrialized economy and limited basic infrastructural facilities, the tribes are not homogenous groups and some continue to be backward despite development programmes having been implemented."

Polyandry and polygamy marriage practices are on the decline and the incidence of child marriages has declined in almost all the tribal areas. About 64 per cent of the residents of these sample households talked in Hindi despite having their own tribal dialects. The proportion of nuclear families was higher than joint families, indicating a changing social milieu within the tribal region. Overall literacy rates of the region have increased and female literacy has also increased significantly from 7.31 per cent in 1971 to 50 per cent in 2001 and gender disparity in this regard has declined. Enrollment in primary education has increased but it has not increased at the same pace in secondary and higher education.

The housing and sanitation conditions have improved, particularly in Kinnaur, Lahaul and Spiti. There has been a continuous increase in the proportion of people living in 'pucca' houses, having toilets and in-house water connections in all the areas. There has been growth in LPG connections, TV sets, newspaper and cell phones. More people are exposed to communication and media facilities in Lahaul, Kinnaur and Spiti than Bharmaur and Pangi blocks, according to the study. The cropping pattern has changed in these areas and traditional crops including small millet have been replaced by pulses and non-food grain crops like apple.

The pace of transformation in the tribal region is higher in Kinnaur, Lahaul and Bharmaur due to suitable agro-climatic conditions and better accessibility. The cropping pattern of the region is still dominated by food grains except Kinnaur district where apple cultivation continues to dominate the cropping pattern.

Thakur said, "The study was conducted to assess social transformation of tribal people, social and demographic characteristics, economic transformation, modernization of agriculture, changing occupational patterns, work participation rates, workforce structure, physical and social infrastructural development in education, health care, drinking water, electricity, roads and communication facilities, besides other aspects." A total of 1,132 households were surveyed in the five regions for the study taking samples of villages from each region and the sampling criteria included one community block headquarter, the largest populated but accessible village and the largest populated but inaccessible village as per census 2001.

SOCLO-ECONOMIC PROGRAMMES FOR SCHEDULED CASTES AND TRIBES

The aim of the Seventh Plan is to continue the thrust towards the socio-economic development of the scheduled castes and to give them occupational mobility and economic strength. Programmes will have to be designed in order to fulfil their minimum needs together with emphasis on the integration of different sectoral development programmes, with a clear recognition of the needs of the scheduled castes. Special attention will be given to assist this segment of the population to cross the poverty line.

The emphasis on beneficiary-oriented programmes and schemes for the socio-economic uplift of the scheduled castes will continue, but it is necessary to recognise that the strategy has to cater to two broad occupational categories which can be distinguished namely, (a) those engaged in land-based activities and (b) those engaged in non-land based activities. In the first category would be included landless agricultural labourers and marginal cultivators, while the second category would include leather workers, weavers and other artisans, fishersmen, scavengers, etc. It is possible that these occupational categories are not mutually exclusive and that many families might be engaging themselves in activities belonging to both categories.

In the first category, the main problem is lack, or inadequacy, of assets. Allotment to the landless of ceiling surplus land, Government wasteland and other lands found surplus, will be undertaken. Implementation of ceiling laws will be speeded up. Plugging of loop-holes in the ceiling laws and pursuit of time-bound programmes can lead to substantial allotment of surplus land to scheduled caste families. Land-holding families will be helped in the development of their land, through provision of agricultural credit, inputs, irrigation, etc. under the Small and Marginal Farmers Schemes.

Where irrigation becomes available, enforcement of wet-land ceiling can make available surplus land which can then be distributed among the scheduled castes. The programmes of provi- sion of irrigation to land owned by the Scheduled castes in compact blocks will be continued. For agricultural labourers, enforcement of the statutory minimum wages is important; the enforcement machinery will be mobilised for the purpose, particularly in major wage-employment areas. Programmes of animal husbandry, handicraft, village and cottage industries and inculcation of skills for induction into the tertiary sector will also be taken up for them.

Efforts will be made to properly organise and modernise all stages of activities of weavers, leather workers and other artisans. The necessary infrastructure and other facilities will be created for those engaged in fisheries. For all these occupational categories comprehensive schemes for common facilities, skill improvement, supply of raw materials and marketing of products will be formulated and implemented. Formation of co-operatives of brick-kiln workers would prove useful for organising their work on a proper footing. Steps will be taken to make the unorganised labour in the urban sector, comprised of rickshaw pullers, cart pullers, etc., owners of their vehicles. The number of scheduled caste families in each occupational group needing assistance, the quantum of assistance required by each family and the manner in which it should flow to them will be worked out by each State and UT Adminstration. All these schemes will form an important component of anti-poverty programmes aimed at raising the families above the poverty line.

The Scheduled Castes Development Corporations which constitute one of the instruments of economic development of SC families have been acting as catalysts, promoters and guarantors in respect of beneficiary-oriented programmes. However, for lack of clear-cut agreement on procedures with other financial insitutions, their full potential has not been realised in the Sixth Plan period. Moreover, there have been deficiencies in the working of some of the corporations. The functioning of the corporations will be thoroughly evaluated and the short-comings rectified. The identification, release and rehabilitation of bonded labour will continue to be given priority attention. In reality, the per family requirement of funds for rehablitation does not amount to much, and hence, the total outlay might not be very large; in any case this can be provided for fully. In fact, if funds available from all relevant sources for the rehabilitation of bonded labour are pooled, they will be adequate. A concerted effort and coordination between the different agencies are essential.

In most parts of the country, scheduled castes live in separate localities lacking essential services. In towns, they live in slums devoid of basic amenities. Basic facilities like drinking water, housing, health facilities, electrification, link roads, and fair price shops will be provided for in the bastis by the end of the Seventh Plan.

In the matter of sources of drinking water supply and other village-level amenities, social accessibility will be borne in mind, new sources will be located in SC bastis, which would be meant for all communities.

Total elimination of scavenging is one of the objectives of the Seventh Plan. For this purpose, lowcost sanitation and whole-town approach for conversion of dry latrines into waterbome latrines will be adopted. New latrines need to be provided where none exists now. Sanitation workers of municipal bodies liberated from scavenging will be redeployed in other civic activities. The small number of those employed privately have to be trained for, and provided with, alternative avocations. Financial provision for elimination of scavenging, training of liberated scavengers and their employment will have a, priority claim on the Special Central Assistance to the States' Component Plans. A major task in the Seventh Plan will be the removal of deficiencies in the implementation of programmes. Reform measures in relation to administration, implementation, monitoring and evaluation of programmes will be undertaken. These include assignment of specific responsibilities to Collectors in the implementation of SCP programmes, communication of disaggregated physical and financial targets to district and block-level authorities, strengthening of implementation machinery, regualr inspection, preparation of a check-list, for each programme, avoidance of multi-counting of beneficiary families, and review of programmes at the level of the Chief Secretary and the Chief Minister. In the field of personnel policies selection of dedicated and competent persons and their posting with reasonable security of tenure is most important. To sum up, in the Seventh Plan period, linkages between different sectors and programmes, back-up services organisational structures and personnel coordination will receive close and continuing attention.

The programme of scheduled castes development is not likely to succeed without public participation. Decentralisation will be carried through to the last rung. The role of non-government voluntary organisations in activising the systems, training cadres of grass root workers, mobilising the resources of the community and providing professional and managerial expertise will be valuable. Even more important will be their attempt at raising the awareness of the people through non-formal and informal educational methods. The media can render extremely useful service here.

As part of the strategy of the Special Component Plan earmarking of outlays in the State plan sectors has helped to galvanize larger flow of funds for scheduled castes' development. In the Seventh Plan, the States will set apart as large a proportion of the total State plan outlay as is feasible for the SCP. Schemes and programmes will be formulated to the extent of this amount in accordance with the object and priorities of SC development and corresponding outlays will be distributed sector-wise. In the Sixth Plan, special Central assistance was introduced as an additionality to States' SCP with a view to creating a multiplier effect and to help fill gaps which financial flows from the Central and State plans were not able to fill.

To make the maximum possible impact, the Special Central assistance was to be pooled with the states' own resources. The ortly condition imposed was that it should be used for programmes of economic development, including relevant training, back-up services, institutional build-up and arrangements for implementation, supervision, monitoring and evaluation. The versatility of the Special Central Assistance is yet to be fully exploited and overall planning for its use has to be done. The Special Central Assistance for Socio-economic programmes for SCs in the Seventh Plan will be Rs. 930 crores.

SCHEDULED TRIBES

The tribal areas present a considerable degree of environmental and ethnic diversity. Tribal communities differ in their socio-economic levels, educational attainments and cultural milieus. The Tribal sub-Plan (TSP) strategy adopted comprises; (a) identification in a State of development blocks where tribal population is in a majority and their constitution into integrated tribal development projects (ITDPs) with a view to adopting therein an integrated and project-based approach for development; (b) earmarking of funds for the TSP and ensuring flow of funds from the Central and State Plan sectoral outlays and from financial institutions; and (c) creation of appropriate administrative structures in tribal areas and adoption of appropriate personnel policies. The TSP has, overall, a two-fold thrust, firstly, socio-economic development of tribal areas and secondly, that of the tribal families. Thes basic premises will continue to be operative in the Seventh Plan.

The majority of tribal areas have remained isolated and backward. With their low levels of training, skills and technology which have remained largely traditional, the natural resources of tribal areas have remained unexploited for the development of tribals. Tribal areas are, further, characterised by socio-economic exploitation by non-tribals. One of the major tasks in the Seventh Plan will be to create an awareness of these factors among the tribals, and stringent anti-exploitative measures under-taken along-side socio-economic development programmes. Particular care needs to be taken of the small primitive tribal groups, some of which face extinction. One of the causes which has given rise to discontent among tribals is the loss of their lands, and remedial measures against this need to be given priority- Also, tribal families displaced as a result of location of projects like power, irrigation, industries, mining etc., in tribal areas will need to be properly rehabilitated.

The planning process in tribal areas has to be a judicious mix of beneficiary-oriented programmes, human resource development and infrastructure development the bias being towards the first two 30 lakh tribal families in TSP will be assisted in the Seventh Plan to build to build up their economic base.

In the protective Sphere, legislative measures already in force will be implemented stringently, as in the fields of agricultural tenancy, money-lending, debt-relief, bonded labour, forestry, excise and trade, as well as in respect of socio -cultural exploitation etc. Also, codification of customary laws still prevalent among the tribals will be attempted.

Large agricultural multi-purpose societies (LAMPS) in tribal area will be strengthened through broadening of their popular base in the board of directors and/or other executive bodies to make them effective instruments for the elimination of exploitation in the sale and marketing of tribal produce, consumer necessities and credit. To coordinate the activities of State-level Tribal Development Corporations, the national level Tribal Marketing Organisation already set up needs to get into full gear. Plan formulation and project reports will be made in close consultation with beneficiary-participants. Scientific project reports will be prepared for ITDPs, tribal concentration pockets and primitive tribal groups with reference to the natural resource endowment, the traditional occupations and skills of the people and a properly drawn-up development perspective.

A balance will be struck between subsistence and commercial production, keeping in view the state of infrastructural development, the type and extent of marketing network and the efficiency of public delivery systems, and eco-systems oriented towards the needs of the weaker sections.

As regards tribals practising shifting cultivation, first of all no viable alternative programmes have been presented so far to the shifting cultivators for directing them away towards alternative means of livelihood. Without such alternatives being available, it is difficult to envisage how this practice, so destructive in its impact on the environment and the ecology of fragile areas, can be curbed or eliminated. Secondly, even where the semblance of a viable programme has been in sight, it has suffered through faulty formulation and subsequently in implementation; the programmes impinged on several sectors Jike land, agriculture, irrigation, marketing and there was lack of coordination among the concerned authorities. Particularly in relation to shifting cultivation, an inter-disciplinary approach is a 'sinequanon' for a successful programme. At present, this is conspicuous by its absence. Wherever shifting cultivation is a major problem, there is need for each concerned State Government to examine the matter in-depth and develop such an approach towards tackling this urgent problem of environmental degradation.

About 2 lakh tribal families of about 5,000 forest villages do not possess even now any rights to the Appropriate remedial measures are required to be taken up by the State Governments.

A policy for the rehabilitation of project displaced persons has to be formulated at the national level, prescribing the general policy for the rehabilitation of persons displaced by large-scale land acquisition for projects and the special measures to be taken in the interest of scheduled tribes in such cases. Among other things, the policy will have to enjoin that rehabilitation of displaced persons, particularly the tribals, will form an integral part of the investment costs of projects relating to industries, irrigation, power, mining and forestry and wild life, of more than a certain magnitude, whether taken up in the Government corporate, joint or private sectors.

Integration in administration in tribal areas at ITDP levels has been the aim, but there are several programmes operataing in these project areas, like IRDP, DPAP, RLEGP and NREP, in respect of which the tribal area administration headed by the Project Administrator of the local ITDP has not been kept in the picture. This has had consequential effect on coordination.

Greater attention will be paid during the Seventh Plan to concurrent monitoring and evaluation through the existing field functionaries in the tribal areas on the principle of checks and balances. Further, independent academic and research organisations will be deployed for evaluation studies on the impact of various development projects meant for the socio-economic uplift of tribals.

For removing the backwardness of tribal women, adequate stress on economic development schemes aimed at them, or in which they can participate, needs to be given. While executing the programmes it has to be ensured that tribal women are assisted under income- generating programmes of IRDP and SCA. Mahila Samities and other Women's organisations in tribal areas which are identified for the implementation of economic programmes for tribal women may be considered for being assisted on a selective basis. The Madhya Pradesh Government have established a Kanya Shiksha Parishad at Chhindwara where education and training is imparted to tribal women in a unified manner. Such centres could be considered for establishment by other States. Inclusion of tribal women representatives in the project implementation committees meant for development of tribal people would go a long way towards integrating specifically into the socio-economic programmes for their uplift.

The process of plan formulation generally and also the planning of specific projects need to attach importance to the ethos, needs and aspirations of specific tribal groups, while keeping the State and national priorities in view. The concept of planning from below needs to be given concrete shape in tribal areas by taking up re-formulation of the existing ITDP project reports/ plans. The State Tribal Sub-Plans are not to be merely a compendium of tribal areas project plans and the tribal componenl,of the programmes of individual development departments, but should also include programmes and outlays under imprtant non-plan sectors having a developmental thrust.

The role of institutional finance in the beneficiary oriented programmes is vital. Financial institutions need to make an assessment of the role played by them so far and take the necessary steps for more active involvement. The plans of institutional finance have to be compatible with the partially-monetised economy of the tribals.

The Fifth Schedule of the Constitution provides a legal and administrative framework for the Scheduled Areas. Even this schedule in not fully operational as yet and this lapse has to be rectified. Further, the design support of the Fifth Schedule will have to be meaningfully combined with the self-management thrust of the Sixth Schedule to lend emphasis to endogenous growth. Non-government voluntary organisations can make significant contributions by catalysing the involvement of and the "active participation by, tribals, approaching the tribal problems from a closer perspective and taking up development programmes for primitive tribal groups in relatively inaccessible areas. The right type of voluntary organisations, depending on local sources of funds, would be encouraged. Coordination among governmental and non-governmental agencies would need to be fostered. On the whole, the existing preponderant reliance on official agencies has to be replaced by the participation of the beneficiaries in the planning and implementation process through elective, nominated and traditional institutions, as well as voluntary organisations. In order that the dynamics of development does not directly or indirectly conflict with the custorhary modes and usages prevalent in tribal areas, it is necessary to codify the laws, coventions and usages, particularly in the developmental and functional areas. For want of adequate knowledge on the part of the planning personnel it is possible that by taking a wrong direction, the development process makes no headway at all.

To avoid this, phased programme of codification of customary laws relating to property (particularly land), Inheritance, family and kinship, traditional tribal institutions, traditional village officers, etc., will be taken up.

Earmarking of portions of funds allocated to various sectors of State and Central Plan has been a part of the tribal sub-plan strategy. In the Seventh Plan period, of the total Plan outlay of a State/Ministry a reasonable proportion needs to be reserved for the TSP. The Special Central Assistance for TSP has been fixed at Rs. 756 crores for the Seventh Plan.

SOCIO-ECONOMIC PROFILE OF THE FAMILIES OF TRIBAL MIGRANTS IN THE SELECTED STATES

This chapter assesses the social and economic situation of the tribal women and the specific factors responsible for migration of tribal women from the tribal areas to various towns and cities in search of employment.

CHHATTISGARH STATE

Chhattisgarh State was carved out of the erstwhile Madhya Pradesh State on 1st November, 2000 and has a total area of 1,35,194 square kilometers comprising of 16 districts, 146 Blocks and 19,744 inhabited villages. According to the 2001 Census, the total population of Chhattisgarh is 2.08 crore out of which 79.9 per cent is rural in nature.

The density of population in the State is 130 persons per square kilometer. The State has a predominant ST population accounting for 31.8 per cent, SCs 11.6 per cent and the rest other communities including Backward Classes. The sex ratio of the State is 989 females per 1000 males. The state is broadly divisible into three agro-climatic Zones – the central belt, the northern belt and the southern belt.

The state has about 44,746 lakh hectares of forest area, which is 32.5 per cent of the total geographical area of the state. Work participation rate in the State is around 46.5 per cent and 44.5 per cent have returned as cultivators, 31.9 per cent as agricultural labourers and 2.1 per cent as household industry workers.

The State is endowed with rich mineral resources like Iron, Coal, Bauxite, Tin, and Dolomite. The decadal growth rate of the State is 18.6 per cent against the national average of 21.01 per cent and the literacy rate is 64.7 per cent which is equivalent to the national average.

TRIBAL SCENARIO

The population of the STs in the state is 66.17 lakh (2001 Census) accounting for 31.76 per cent of the total population of the state and 94.7 per cent of which is rural in nature. The sex ratio among STs is 1012 females per 1000 males which is more favourable towards males. In terms of the concentration of ST population, the State occupies 6th position with 7.85 per cent STs in the country.

There are 42 different tribes including five Primitive Tribe Groups (PTGs) comprising about 12 lakh tribal families. The ST population is spread over the entire state with Kanwar tirbe predominantly in the north while the Gonds are the majority tribe in south. About 33 per cent of the state's population is estimated to be living below poverty line (BPL) and the majority of it is STs. As per the 1997 BPL survey, 5.89 lakh tribal families are below the poverty line. The primitive tribe population is 1.11 lakh and their entire population is under BPL category.

The central belt covers more than one-third area, consisting of 11 districts of the state and partial sub plan area belongs to this region. The northern and southern belts comprise major tribal populated districts of Bastar, Dantewada in the south and Koriya, Surguja and Jashpur in the north. The literacy rate among the Scheduled Tribes in the State is 52.10 percent that is almost double than in the 1991 which was 26.70 percent. It is higher than the national average of 47.10 percent for Scheduled Tribes population. Similarly, the male and female literacy rates are also higher than the national average in this regard; which are 65.00 and 39.30 percent respectively. The Work Participation Rate (WPR) of the Chhattisgarh Scheduled Tribe population is 53.40 percent that is slightly lower than the national average of 49.10 per cent. The WPR for male and female tribal population is 56.70 and 50.20 percent respectively.

The majority of the Scheduled Tribe population in the State, i.e. 56.60 percent, is categorized as 'cultivators' while 'agricultural labourers' category constitutes 32.70 percent. The national average for 'cultivators' and 'agricultural laborers' 44.7 per cent and 32.7 per cent respectively. 'Other workers' are about 9.70 percent while the 'house hold industry (HHI)' category constitutes about 1.20 percent of the WPR of the State. In the present study, two districts namely, Jashpur and Sarguja were selected and 4 blocks; Bagicha,

Kunkuri, Batouli and Sitapur covering 51 villages and 396 families were covered.

JHARKHAND STATE

Jharkhand state has come into existence in 2000 out of the bifurcation of Bihar state and comprises 22 districts. With an area of 74,677 sq.km, the state has 35 per cent of the population of the erstwhile Bihar state. The state accounts for 36 per cent of country's coal, 40 per cent of copper, 22 per cent of iron and 90 per cent if mica, bauxite, quartz and ceramics. The literacy rate is 54.13 per cent (2001census). The total ST population of Jharkhand is 7,087,068 as per the Census 2001. It is about 26.70 percent of the total State population of 26, 94,589 persons. The average growth rate of the ST population is 17.30 percent that is lower by 6.00 percent than the average population growth rate in the State. There are 30 STs in Jharkhand and the major among them are Santhal, Oraon, Munda, Ho, Kharia, Bhumji, Lohra, Kharwar, Chero, Bedia, Mal Paharia and Mahli are the main STs in Jharkhand. The majority of the ST population, about 91.7 per cent., lives in rural and forest areas. Gumla, Purbi Singhbum, Lohardaga, Pashchimi Singhbhum, Dumka, Giridih, Ranchi, Sahibganj, Gumla and Pakur are the main districts with higher concentration of the Scheduled Tribe population. The sex ratio of the ST population in Jharkhand is 987 females per 1000 males that is higher than the national average of 978 for the same population category. Compare to the literacy rate of 27.50 percent in 1991 it has increased up to 40.70 percent in 2001 among the ST population in the State. It is significantly lower than the average national literacy rate of 47.10 percent for the ST population. The male and female literacy rates are 54 per cent and 27.2 per cent in 2001.

The Work Participation Rate of the ST population in Jharkhand in 1991-2001 is 46.30 percent that is lower by about 3.00 percent than the national average of 49.10 percent. Similarly, the main workers in the State constitute 59.40 percent of the total workers which too is lower than the national average of 68.90 percent for the overall ST population. It is interesting to see that the male WPR shows a decline from 53.40 percent to 51.90 percent while the female WPR for the same period shows an increase from 38.30 percent to 40.60 percent.

About 50.00 percent of the ST population in Jharkhand is categorized under the 'cultivators' category which is significantly higher than the national average of 44.70 percent while the other 31.00 percent comes under the 'agricultural labourer' category which is lower than the national average of 36.90 percent. 'Other workers' category constitutes 13.50 percent of the total Scheduled Tribe workers in Jharkhand which is again lower than the national average of 16.30 percent. The work force percentage involved in household industries (HHI) is 3.00 percent, a bit higher than the national average of 2.10 percent. In the present study, two districts namely, Gumla and Simdega were selected and 4 blocks; Chainpur, Sisai, Kurdeg and Thethaiangar covering 49 villages and 402 families.

ORISSA STATE

Orissa state with a geographical area of 4.74 per cent of the country and comprising 36.7 million people of India's 3.57 per cent population is a low income state. The state has 30 districts and is rich in natural resources, inland water with 11 major rivers Mahanadi being the major one, many big and small water bodies with the famous Chilka lake, a big stretch of coastal line with a good potential for fisheries, a good forest cover of about 30 per cent surface area and endowed with rich mineral deposits of coal, Iron, Bauxite, Lime stone, Dolomite.

Scheduled Tribes socio-economic profile

ST population in Orissa is 8.15 million comprising 22.13 per cent of the total population of the state and 9.7 per cent of the total tribal population of the country. Orissa has the third largest concentration of tribal people in the country. There are 62 tribal communities including 13 Primitive Tribal Groups (PTGs) in the State. Khond is the most populous (17.1 per cent) ST followed by Gond, Santal, Kolha, Munda, Saora, Shabar and Bhottada.

ST households are about 1.8 million and 94.5 per cent of them are rural based. About 44.7 per cent of the State's geographical area has been declared as Scheduled Area which covers 12 districts and is inhabited by about 68.1 per cent of the STs in the State comprising the districts of Mayurbhanj, Koraput Sundargarh, Kandhamals, Sambalpur, Keonjhar, Kalahandi and Balasore districts. In 7 districts namely Malkangiri, Nabarangpur, Rayagada, Sundargarh, Kalahandi, Koraput and Gajapati, STs are more than 50 per cent of the total population in the district. Majority of STs live in hilly and forest areas, which are mostly inaccessible and isolated. 62 STs in Orissa speak as many as 74 dialects and their cultural heritage is rich and varied.

Their economy is largely subsistence oriented and non-specialised. At one end of the spectrum we find nomadic food gatherers and hunters and at the other end, agriculturists and horticulturists. The literacy rate among the STs is 37.36 per cent against the overall literacy rate of 63.1 per cent of state (2001 census). The ST male and female literacy rates are 51.5 per cent and 23.4 per cent respectively. As per 2001 Census, 57.4 per cent STs are main workers and the remaining 42.6 per cent are marginal workers. Cultivators account for 33.4 per cent of total workers, whereas agricultural labourers constitute 46.8 per cent and workers engaged in household industries constitute 4.8 per cent of the total workers. Most of the cultivators among the STs are small and marginal farmers. In the present study, two districts namely, Sambalpur and Sundargarh were selected and 4 blocks; Bamra, Kunchinda, Kaumunda and Rajgangapur covering 48 villages and 403 families.

MADHYA PRADESH STATE

According to the Census 2001 the total ST population of Madhya Pradesh is 12,233,474, the largest tribal population in any state in India. This is 20.30 percent of the total State population consisting 60,348,023 persons. The growth of the tribal population in Madhya Pradesh during 1991-2001 has been 26.4 percent, higher by 2.1 percent by overall growth of the total population which was 24.3 percent for the same period.

There are about 46 STs in the State. Bhil, Gond, Kol, Korku, Sahariya and Baiga are the major tribes in the State, consisting about 92.2 percent of the total tribal population. Meanwhile, though small population wise, but historically and socially significant, Pradhan, Saur, and Bhariya, Bhumiya, along with Majhi, Khairwar, Mawasi and Panika, are other important tribes of Madhya Pradesh. Mina, Andh, Birhul, Parja and Nagesia tribes have less than a population of 500 persons.

The majority of the ST population, about 93.6 percent, in the State lives in rural and forest areas. Jhabua, Barwani, Dindori, Mandla, Badwani, Dhar, Shahdol, Sheopur, Balaghat, Baitul, East Nimar, West Nimar and Seoni are the main districts with tribal populations. The overall sex ratio among the tribes in Madhya Pradesh is 975 females per 1000 males which is lower than the national average sex ratio of 978 for the overall national tribal population.

As far as literacy among the tribal population of Madhya Pradesh is concerned, it was 41.2 percent in 2001 against of 18.4 percent in 1991 which shows a significant increase. But yet it is lower than the national average of 47.1 percent for the total national tribal population. In spite of increase in the average literacy rate of the tribal population of Madhya Pradesh the female literacy rate was only 28.4 percent against the male literacy rate of 53.5 percent.

The Work Participation Rate of the total ST population in Madhya Pradesh is 50.5 percent. In this order the male and female work participation rates were 53.2 and 47.6 percent respectively. Cultivators and agricultural labourers constitute 89 percent of the WPR together while 'Other Workers' constitute about 10 percent (including household industry category of 1.1 percent workers) of the WPR in the State. In the present study, two districts namely, Jhabua and Mandla were selected and 4 blocks; Jhabua, Meghnagar, Bichia and Mavai covering 48 villages and 403 families.

SOCIAL AND ECONOMIC STATUS OF TRIBAL WOMEN IN INDIA

The tribal population in India numerically constitutes a small segment of the total population of the country but is a significant part of the population. According to 2001 census data, total population of Scheduled Tribes constitutes 8.2 per cent of the total population of the country. Most of the Scheduled tribe people lives in rural areas and their population comprise

10.4 per cent of the total rural population of the country. The term 'scheduled tribes' first appeared in the Constitution of India, to confer certain constitutional privileges and protection to a group of people who are considered disadvantaged and backward. In the Constitution of India, Article 366 (25) defines Scheduled Tribes as "such tribes or tribal communities or part of or groups within such tribes or tribal communities as are deemed under Article 342 to the scheduled Tribes (STs) for the purposes of this Constitution"The Scheduled Tribes, who are also referred to as 'Adivasis', meant original inhabitants. For long periods of history, they were always socially and geographically isolated.

They belonged to different races with diverse cultural characteristics, speaking varied languages, following a variety of religions and spread across various ecological zones. Process of Sanskritization has affected them culturally, and other processes of displacement have made them a marginalized segment of the society. Since independence, various measures have been taken up at the national level for protecting the interests of the scheduled tribes of the country and particular attention has been given to tribal development in the different plan periods. Out of the total tribal population, tribal women add up to almost half. Like all other communities, development of status of tribal communities also to a large extent depends on the upliftment of the status of tribal women. The popular perception of the tribal women indicates two differing views. Some researchers are of the opinion that the tribal women enjoy higher social status compared to their non-tribal counterparts and some other studies indicate a low status for the tribal women. In fact, provisions made by the Constitution over the years have not made much difference to the status of tribal women. Their status is found to be lower than that of women belonging to the general population, Scheduled caste women and also lower than that of the status of Tribal men.

OBJECTIVES

The main objectives of this paper are -

1. To find out the social and economic status of tribal women in India.
2. To analyze the challenges faced by tribal women.
3. To suggest some strategies for handling the challenges faced by tribal women in India.

METHODOLOGY

This is a theoretical research paper, where secondary information produced by different authors and researchers has been used.

DISCUSSIONS SOCIAL AND ECONOMIC STATUS OF TRIBAL WOMEN IN INDIA

The term status means position of a person in a society. Status has been defined by R.Linton (1936) as a position in a social system. The term role is closely linked to the notion of status. It refers to the behaviour expected of people in a status. The status of a person or a group in a society is determined mainly by the educational status, health status, employment status and decision making ability. All these factors are closely related to one another. The higher level of education will generate health awareness, employment opportunities and decision making ability among these groups.

The status of women in a society depends to a large extent on the social structure and the type of society. In Indian social context, there is a predominance of patriarchal family structure were males predominate in all settings and social contexts. However, among many tribal communities, predominance of matriarchal families could be found. Contrary to patriarchal societies, status of women is found to be higher in matriarchal families. Various studies have suggested that the Garo and Khasi tribes of the North East India assign relatively higher position to women due to the system of matrilineal descent, matrilocal residence and inheritance of property through the female line. But other tribal communities which follow patriarchal norms, the status of women is not as high as it is in matriarchal societies. For some other tribes, such as, Ho, Gond, the husband does not always enjoy a dominant role. Gond woman enjoys equal status with their male counterparts in many aspects of their social life. A study on the Naga women by Hutton (1921) indicated that they have substantial freedom and higher social status.

This indicates that the status of tribal women are not same in all places, rather they vary according to the tribal group and the social structure. However, in tribal societies, tribal women are more important than women in any other social groups because tribal women are very hardworking and in almost all the tribal communities they participate in economic activities almost equally with men or works harder than men and the family economy and income also depend on women. Status is also determined by health conditions. The tribal groups health status is lower compared to that of the general population.

They have high infant mortality rate, higher fertility rate, lack of awareness regarding diseases and health care, drinking water provisions, hygiene. In many parts of India tribal population suffers from chronic infections and water borne diseases, deficiency diseases. Incidence of infant mortality was found to be very high among some of the tribes. Malnutrition is common among them and it has affected the general health of the tribal children. It increases vulnerability to infection, and leads to chronic illness which sometimes may affect brain.

Their health status is also related to economic and educational aspects. Their lack of ability to participate in the industrial economic activities of modern societies has deteriorated their living conditions. The tribals are mostly engaged in occupations which do not generate much income such as hunting, crafts making, agriculture. Industrialization and urbanization has brought about a change in the life and living of the tribals by uprooting them from their day to day activities and making them dependent on the vagaries of non tribals. The education level of the tribal population is low and formal education has made very little impact on tribal groups. The level of literacy among the tribals in most states in India is very low. Reservation policy of the Government has made some changes in the educational status. One of the main reasons for low level of literacy is their assigning relatively less significance on formal schooling.

The school curriculum and education system do not create much interest in them, rather a much more practical based curriculum would be helpful for them. Moreover, since the tribes live in poverty they do not like to send their children to schools as they are considered to be extra helping hands for generating income. Chowdhuri(1988) attempted to examine the socio – economic condition of the Scheduled tribe women in West Bengal in a comparative setting with scheduled caste and non scheduled women.

The main findings were that only 5.01 per cent of Scheduled Tribe females were noted as literate in comparison to Scheduled Caste women who were 13.70 per cent and non scheduled population was 37.43 per cent. This level was quite low as compared to the overall rate of females who are literate. This study was mainly based on the data collected from Census office and from different studies conducted by the Cultural

Research Institute, Calcutta. Various reasons have been attributed for low level of literacy among the scheduled tribe girls. Work participation rate among scheduled tribe women were higher in percentage as compared to others. Poor economic condition has a direct bearing on the degree of participation. Scheduled tribe workers are engaged in agricultural sector and in non gainful occupations. Considering the education, economic and health of the tribal women, their positions were not at all satisfactory. A study by Singh and Rajyalaxmi(1993), status of tribal women in terms of their demography, health, education and employment have been discussed. Since independence, various protections have been given to the tribal population by the Constitution of India. The study highlighted some aspects of tribal work; tribal women work equally with their male counterparts with lower pay, sexual exploitation. Tribal women don't have property rights, they have lower literacy rate than scheduled caste and general population. Tribal women are not healthy and suffer from malnutrition and various diseases. The study highlighted the need to improve the status of tribal girl, to bring about change in the status of tribal woman.

PROBLEMS FACED BY TRIBAL WOMEN

Most tribals faces a number of challenges which they need to overcome in order to improve their status in society. The researcher intends to discuss here the issues faced by tribal women in particular. Absence of any fix livelihood: Various literature studies reveal that although work participation among tribal women is higher compared to scheduled caste and general population but the livelihoods of the tribal people are neither permanent nor fixed. Most of them do not have a regular source of income, and they live below the poverty level. Tribal people residing in the rural areas pursue diverse low level activities for fulfilling their basic needs. Mostly they are engaged in agricultural activities. Apart from that, they are engaged in pastoral, handicrafts and at times as industrial labourers. Tribal women are mainly not engaged in any kind of continuous work and much like their male counterparts are found to work in agriculture.

A meagre number of tribal men and women are engaged in government services. Economic conditions of households are related to other aspects of their life. Lack of access to education: Most of the tribal women work outside their homes and are engaged in various activities. They work in order to earn money for their family. The women's work involves daily labour, agricultural work. Even young children and girls go for work along with their mothers. Most of the time they do not go to school regularly or become drop outs from school. Even the parents in very poor families don't always want to send the children to school because then their helping hands in work would be reduced.

Effect of patriarchy could be strongly seen in most tribal groups and so whatever money women get from their work they give it to their husband and the husband very often spends the money on activities like drinking. Household works are done by the female members of the family. Household work involves cooking, cleaning, washing utensils and clothes, collecting fuel for cooking. The young girls who are studying in primary level in schools hardly learn anything in school and they don't study at home also. The government has announced free and compulsory education to all children up to the age of 14 years, which nowadays encourage parents to send their children to schools with the hope that if their children receive proper education, then their conditions will improve. The children are given free school uniforms, books and mid day meals. However, the girls don't continue school at a stretch. Sometimes they go to school, some other times they do not go to school and stay at home and go to work with their mothers and help their mothers at household work. As a result, they tend to forget what they have learned in school. After the girl child attains teenage the parents stop sending them to schools. Poor condition of health: Lack of awareness about nutritional requirements mostly leaves the tribal women weak, anaemic and they suffer from various diseases.

During pregnancy, special attention is required to be given to women otherwise that will affect the health of both the mother and child. Educational level, employment status, health status and decision making ability helps to measure the status of women in society. Women's education has to be channelized to employment opportunities. This in turn, will increase the decision making ability of women. Women's ability to communicate with other family members and to be able to convince them indicates a decision making ability of women. When the decision making ability is higher, women can have a higher status in the household.

Chapter 4

A Study on the Tribal Autonomy Movement in India

TRIBAL MOVEMENT IN INDIA BEFORE AND AFTER INDEPENDENCE

After independence, various efforts have been made to improve the socio-economic conditions of the tribals and to sustain the constitutional safeguard given to them The Central and State Governments have made incessant efforts in the direction of tribal welfare and development. Special programmes for their development have been undertaken in the successive Five Year Plans. The aim was to bring them on par with other developed sections of the society. But the results are not encouraging in all cases with an introduction of development plans, some societies have found themselves disintegrated.

The establishment of heavy industries, construction of dams and launching of development plans in tribal zones has necessitated displacement of local population. Thousands of tribal families were displaced from their traditional habitats Contact situations with outsiders have been equally detrimental. Destruction of forests as a consequence of felling of trees for industrial purposes has threatened the small communities of hunters and food-gathers.

Those who could take advantage of new economic and educational frontiers were able to better their lot, while a large sections of the tribals, not adequately prepared to deal with new challenges, gradually depressed into poorer sections of the society.

Against economic and social disparities, they have raised a collective voice. The tribals especially in central India, had reacted against their exploiters. These movements were directed towards freeing their land from all those who exploited them economically and culturally. At the same time, each of these movements put emphasis on revitalisation of their culture, their traditional culture which was swayed under the impact of the outsiders.

TRIBAL MOVEMENT BEFORE INDEPENDENCE

As soon as the British took over Eastern India, tribal revolts broke out to challenge alien rule. In the early years of colonialisation, no other community in India offered such heroic resistance to British rule or faced such tragic consequences as did the numerous Advise Communities of now Jharkhand, Chhattisgarh, Orissa and Bengal.

The fact needs reiteration and highlighting in history that the tribals of Orissa were the first ones in India to wage war against British Colonialism. It should also be noted that contrary to the historians this began as early as 1768 and not in 1820 as opined by them. It was in 1768 that under the feudal king Krushna Bhanja of Ghumsar, the Kondha fought a pitched battle against the British and many lost their lives.

The same year Raja Narayan Deb of Parlakhemundi fought another battle at Jalwara where 30 tribals died. Meanwhile, the British took over Ganjam as part of Madras Presidency and appointed Edward Court as its President. But repeated battles IS the British by the tribals under the leadership of Maharandpata Mahadevi Parala Bikaram Bhanja of and late Srikar Bhanja of Ghumsar led the British to abandon the idea of reigning the area and declare it as 'deserted'.

In 1772 the Paharia revolt broke out which was followed by a five year uprising led by Tilka Manjhi who was hanged in Bhagalpur in 1785. In the next two decades, revolt took place in Singbhum, Gumla, Birbhum, Bankura Monbhoom and Palama, followed by the great Koi Rising of 1832 and Khewar and Bhum.j revolts (1832-34).

The various uprising of the "Kondh meli" and the revolt of the revolt for against their feudal ruler in 1837, the noteworthy militant struggle of the Khonds for a decade from 1846-56 under the leadership of Chakara Biso, and the resistance to British exploitation by the Santhals of Orissa under the Murmu Brothers among many others will go down as momentous events in the history of Onssa's struggle against the British.

The rebellion of 1855-1857 was a great event in history of Santhal. In 1855 the Santhals wage war against the permanent settlement of Lord Cornwallis. On 30th June, 1855 a massive rally of Santhal, over ten thousand, protested against their exploitation and oppression. The 'rally, led by Sidho and Kano, took an oath to end the oppressive rule of the British, Zamindars and money-lenders and, it deeded to set up an independent Santhali Raj.

The money-lenders and Zamindars had flocked into Santhal areas. The crops of the Santhal were forcibly seized, the interests chafed on loans varied from fifty to five hundred per cent. The Santhal uprising (1855-1857) was an attempt to recover the tribal land which was steadily lost to the outsiders and to wipe out the non-tribals from their territory. It is estimated that fifteen to twenty five thousand Santhals were killed in this uprising.

As stated earlier, in 1855 the Santhals waged war against the permanent settlement of Cornwallis and a year later, numerous Advice leaders play a key role in the 1857 war of independence. But the defeat of 1858 only intensified British exploitation of national wealth and resources.

A forest regulation Act passed in 1865 empowered the British Government to declare any land covered with trees or brushwood as Government forest and to make rules to manage it under terms of its own choosing.

The Act made no provision regarding the rights of tribal users, a more comprehensive Indian Forest Act was passed in 1878, which imposed severe restrictions upon Advice rights over forest land and produce in the protected and reserve forests. The Act radically changed the nature of the traditional common property of the Advice communities and made it State property. Advices uprising in the Jharkhand belt were quelled by the British through massive deployment of troops across the region. There was uprising and the B.rsa Munda movement was the most important of the late -18th century struggles against British rules and their local agents. The long struggles led by Birsa Munda were directed at British policies that allowed the Zamindars and money-lenders to harshly exploit the Advises. As he organised a force to fight oppressive landlords,

Christian missionaries and British officials, he was imprisoned. He was released only after two years.

Out of jail, Birsa asked his people to ready their arms to fight injustice He trained his army and became the politician leading his people to their goal of self-rule He was however arrested again and died in jail. Yet the seeds of unrest were sown among his people and they continued to fight against injustice. The Jharkhand movement had its root in this movement.

In 1914 Oraon started what is called Tana Bhagat movement. Tana Bhagat movement is one kind of Bhagat movement which emerged among the Oraon of Chotanagpur, Bihar. The Tana Bhagat movement is essentially religious in nature. Although Birsa Munda movement was started basically as a socio-religious movements latter on his movement assumed quasi-political and militaristic shape.

Among the Oraon the term Bhagat has been applied to a distinct section of tribe which subscribes to the cult of Bhakti. The Bhagat movement is characterized by a large scale incorporation of Hindu practices into its ideology. However the tribal' leaders of both the movements were essentially fighting the foreign exploiters like the landlords and contractors.

All these prepared the ground for the Sepoy Mutiny's impact on Orissa in 1857.The Kolhas, Gonds, Santhals, Birjhals and Khonds joined hands with Surendra Sai in this first revolt for Independence.

Latter the Bhajan meli engaged the British in skirmishes, ambushes, and battles for more than 2 decades from 1868-1891 an experience the British never cherished. The struggle of the Mundas against these imperialists is another significant landmark. Under the leadership of "Birsa Munda" the Munda tribals fought the British in 1900. On Jan 9th 1900, the British retaliated killing masses of people. But that did not deter them and history repeated itself.

This time the Munda's revolted against the Queen of Gangpur who was exploiting the people under the patronage of the British. Under the leadership of Nirmala Munda they fought the British m 1939 who in retaliation mercilessly shot down innocent lives at "AmekoSimako" near Raiboga, creating another black spot in the history of British in India The final of tribal struggle against British in pre-independent Orissa is that of the Koraput tribals under the leadership of Lakman Naik. The struggle was short and Lakman's life ended with martydom. He was hanged on March 29 1943 at the Berhampur jail.

In the hill tribal tracts of Andhra Pradesh a revolt broke out in August 1922 led by Allun Ramachandra Raju, (better known as Sitaram Raju), the Advisees of Andhra hills succeeded in drawing the British into a full-scale guerrilla war. Unable to cope the British-brought in the Malabar Special Force to crush it and only prevailed when Alluri Raju died.

As the freedom movement widened, it drew Advisees into all aspects of the struggle. Many landless and deeply oppressed Advisees joined in with upper-caste freedom fighters expecting that the defect of the British would usher in a new democratic era.

TRIBAL MOVEMENTS AFTER INDEPENDENCE

Unfortunately, even after fifty years of independence, tribals have benefited least from the advent-of freedom. Although independence has brought widespread gains for the vast majority of the Indian population, Dalits and Adivasis have often been left out and new problems have arisen for the tribal population. With the tripling of the population since 1947 pressures on land resources, especially demands on frosted have played have or on the lives of the tribals.

The basic issues behind the tribal movements in India after independence are and forest alienation training and job deprivation due to influx of the outsiders, cultural sub-mergence, and unbalanced development.

After independence, tribal movements may be classified into three groups (i) movement dueto exploitation of outsider's (ii) movements due to. Economic deprivation (like those of Gonds in Madhya Pradesh and the Mahars in Andhra Pradesh (iii) movements due to separatist tendencies (like those of the Nagas and Mizos).

The tribals movements may be classified on the basis of their orientation into four types:

- Forest-based movements,
- Socio-religious movements or social-culture movements
- Movements seeking political autonomy and formations of States (Nagas, Mizos, Jharkhand) and
- Agrarian movement, Naxalban movement-1967 and

Brisadal movement 1968-69. Reformative movement was found among the Mundas under powerful leadership of Dharli Aba, who preached Hindu ideals of ritual purity, asceticism and criticised the worship of priests.

The Naga revolution began in 1948 and continued upto 1972 when the new elected Government came to power and the Nag insurgency was controlled. The Mizo Government cam p formation of Meghalaya State in April 1970.

The Naxalite movement of the tribals in Bihar, West Bengal, Andhra Pradesh; the agrarian an movements of the Gonds and Bhils in Madhya Pradesh and the forest- based movements of Gonds were mainly launched for liberation from oppression and discrimination, backwardness and a Government which was callous to the tubal plight marked by poverty, hunger, unemployment and exploitation.

Jharkhand movement was started which demanded for the creation of new state due forest alienation, job deprivation, and influx of outsiders etc. The Jharkhand Party founded an Oxford educated Christian of the Munda tribe had demanded craving out of a new State, spreading from Palaman in Bihar to Keonjhar in Orissa and from Surguja in Madhya Pradesh to Manipur in West Bengal, of the Indian Union of which tribal people would be numerically dominant.

Ever since the entry of multinational companies for bauxite mining and processing in,993, the tribal people of Kashipur and Laxmipur blocks of Rayagada district Damantpur block of Koraput district and Thuamul Rampur of Kalahand, district of Orissa have been apprehensive of displacement and loss of livelihood.

Concerned over prospect of having to leave their hearth and home, people started organising themselves Road blockades, demonstrations were organised in front of Government offices at Kashipar and Rayagada. Survey areas of the companies were denied access to the area. The responses of tribal people were co-ordinated by organisations such the Prakrutik Sampada Surakya Parishad, the Baphilimali Surakya Samiti and Anchahk Surakhya Samiti. Every village now has a resistance body. Conflict over the mining of bauxite has taken a violent turn with killing of three innocent tribal people. Since 1993, the police have registered 80 criminal cases against the tribal people and activists. On several occasions, the police resorted to lathi charge. Activists were attacked and offices of the resistance movement were destroyed.

The resistances to the alumina project and the police firing have important implications. Successive Governments, various political parties that have been in power, local elites and local businessmen supported the alumina project. At the same time, the struggle of the people and their determination to make any sacrifice in order to protect their civil and political rights, right to livelihood and habitat clearly demonstrate that people at the grassroots are not going to tolerate the onslaught of market force.

Another movement has been started in Keonjhar district of Orissa against mining in the 90s for the displaced people, particularly tribals. In Keonjhar, the mining activities have led to heavy influx of workers from many parts of the country. The 90s decade saw an increase in migration due to geographical and socio-economic reasons, leading to a threat of cultural invasion. Violence of all type increased. Mining has led to indiscriminate deforestation and displacement of inhabitants.

The movement against mining is popular among the Advisees such as Bhuiyan, Juang, Munda, Santhal, and Kondh. The chief slogan of the movement against mining has been "Our lands,' our minerals and our rights". The villagers have been harassed by police and implicated in false cases for organising meetings, public rallies and hunger strikes. A number of villagers had been sent to jail in false cases between 1994 to 1999.

The villager and tribals of Rallagaruvu village in Vishakhapatnam district of Andhra Pradesh had put up a brave resistance against illegal mining by various companies in the last decades. Kondadora tribe is the biggest tribe in Northern Andhra Pradesh located in hilly terrains of the State Rallagaruvu is famous for its calcite, firestone and mica reserves and is one on the most sought after places for mining! There have been hundreds of attempts at illegal acquisition of tribal lands. Due to prolonged struggle of the tribals that much of the land still remains free from the clutches of the illegal mining.

Different tribal movement can be said to centre around the problem of their identity. Coming to the North-East, the Bodo and Naga movement are good examples of how ethnic identity takes up political route for raising their interests. In all these separatist movement, uneven development and modernisation, concentration of gains in some area and their non-dispersal to other, and urban-oriented models of growth are the chief causes.

Rise of tribal consciousness, tribal regionalism, frontier tribalism, etc. gained currency after the movements in North East Frontier areas. Tribal regionalism, political in nature, has been said to be a struggle for identity against alienation from basic sources, viz. land, forests and aspiration for preservation of traditional culture Of late the movement in Tripura led by TUJS and Bodoland in Assam. Gorkhaland movements have transcended that stage of aspiration limited in culture. The newly emerged elites in these regions prefer to have a share in the power structure.

The regional leaders who improvise or manipulate identity symbols to mobilise group sentiment, could rarely assess the likely responses of the political authorities and the dominant social groups. As the movement proceeds and identity assertions tend to transform the concerned ethic to a political conflict group, the leadership and the groups have to adopt modern skills and mobilise resources.

In the process, they become participants in modernization and get involved in the democratic power game. In both Gokhaland and Jharkhand, such democratization has been evident. The Gorkhaland agitation gained momentum on issues such as Indo-Nepal treaty, inclusion of Nepalese language in the Eighth Schedule of Indian Constitution and other sundry economic factors.

The main thrust was on assertion of Indian Nepalese identity through citizenship demand. In the Gorkhaland Accord (1988) enacting the establishment of Gorkha Hill Development Council, both the main issues remained untouched. The identity problem was said to have been solved by putting the word 'Gorkha' in the Council.

It remains to be seen if the grant of Statehood for Jharkhand and Chhattisgarh ameliorates the conditions for India's Advisees. However, it is imperative that all Advise districts receive special attention from the Central Government in terms of investment in schools, participatory forest management and preservation, non-polluting industries and opportunities for the Advise communities and preserve their rich heritage. Advises must have special access to educational, cultural and economic opportunities so as reverse the effects of colonialisation and earlier injustice experienced by the Advise communities.

At the same time, the country can learn much from the beauty of Advise social practices, their culture of sharing and respect for all their deep humility and love of nature and most of all their deep devotion to social equality and civic harmony.

AADIVASI MOVEMENTS FOR AUTONOMY

The world's largest democracy is suffering from various ailments in this representative system which is more suitable to 'democratic' 'symbolism' than providing solutions to issues of survival, identity and culture of the indigenous communities in India. That way, Indian democracy is largely inadequate and manipulative which has been coopted by various corporate interest groups who are fixing agenda for it through complete control over information technology and medium of communications.

The result of a corporate influenced democracy is the vast mass unrest which India is currently witnessing. While the media is enthusiastically reporting the anti-corruption movements yet it has little time to report the historical demands of the tribal and Dalits for their rights all over the country. The battle for the tribal culture and rights over resources in Chhattishgarh is not alone as Jharkhand, Odisha, Andhra Pradesh and Karnataka shamelessly looted tribal resources and handed over those regions to greedy miners and big corporates who sucked the natural resources, damaged the environment for their profit making ventures.

Though Indian parliament reserve seats for tribal representation, the fact is that this representation is more symbolic in nature and less representation of the community leadership. There are numerous tribal and Primitive Tribe Groups who remained unrepresented in Indian parliament. Is it not a paradox that a state like Chhattishgarh which was created on the issue of tribal identity does not have a tribal chief minister?

The region of Bastar which is the hotbed of Maoist insurgency at the moment has not seen a tribal leader at the moment. When democracy is manipulative and adjustment of a few votes here and there, the real representation of the communities will never happen. Unless there is a real representation of our representatives in

Parliament and assemblies, the issue of tribal would never get addressed properly.

Boxas, Kol, and Tharu are two very important tribal communities in Uttarakhand, Uttar-Pradesh and Bihar. They reside in the forest zones of foothills of Tarai and in Bundelkhand region. It does not look unprecedented that these communities virtually have no representation since independence neither in the assemblies nor in the Parliament. There might be some aberrations but yet the reality is hard. Indian democracy does not seem to have any concern on these issues and the result is that tribal have paid heavy price for this political brinkmanship of Indian political class. Kol resides in the Bundelkhand region which is partly in Madhya Pradesh and partly in Uttar-Pradesh. For them, there homeland is Bundelkhand as they don't care the new boundaries created by our state. Historical town of Chitrakoot is divided between Uttar-Pradesh and Madhya Pradesh and it is shameful how the politics have denied the tribal their due right. Kol are declared as scheduled tribe in Madhya Pradesh but scheduled caste in Uttar-Pradesh hence in Uttar-Pradesh the Kols cannot have the same right to the forest produce according to Forest Right Act as in Madhya Pradesh.

Similarly the condition of Boxas and Tharus is dismal in the Tarai region of Uttar-Pradesh and Uttarakhand. Their land has been illegally occupied by the migrant Sikhs who have misused the ignorance and naivity of the tribe communities for their own purposes. Today, right from Pilibhit to Rudrapur, Khatima and Nainital has become a new territory of the Sikh land lords who are selling their land in Punjab and buying huge plots of land here. There is another reality and dirty show. In the entire Tarai region, the sale-purchase of tribal land is prohibited under Indian law. Sale of land from tribal to non-tribal is now allowed yet it is happening fraudulently with active connivance of the authorities. Today, Tharus and Boxas have become bonded in their own lands. In the entire belt of Uttar-Pradesh, Uttarakhand as well as Bihar, there is just one Tharu MLA in Uttarakhand. This non-representation of the tribal population results in their alienation in public life and policy making

In the last 50 years over 90 lakh people have been displaced due to various projects in India and a huge majority of them belong to the tribal. The forest lands were out of reach for the government for years as they never ever thought of venturing into those regions. Hence there was no development in the region. It is not an irony that the state did nothing to the areas and people who should have been its first priority according to the directive principles of the constitution. Tragically, there are no hospitals where the people could go and get treatment. People are still dying of those diseases which have effective treatments such as Malaria, typhoid and brain fever. Ofcourse, in the absence of proper health care, cases of HIV AIDS have also been reported among many of the primitive tribe groups in Andhra Pradesh. The neglect of the state caused to education resulted in unemployment and more beliefs in supernatural powers. Today, the tribal zones have forest and water but no other facility. They live in dark as electricity is out of bound of them. In the name of development, new road networks are being developed in these locations where our planners never ever visited. The neglect resulted in these zones under the new regimes of the Maoists who redistributed some of the land and developed them as 'independent' Zone. It is not that the government is helpless in taking action against them but it is the government which has created them and both justify their positions.

If the Indian state is slaughtered one culture and community, it is the tribals as they are paying the price of our neglect to their welfare. Post 1990s when the big corporate started coming to India in search of their ventures.

Tribal population in India is 8.2 per cent of the total population which is 8,43,26,240 according to 2011 census. A majority of them are landless who live in difficult terrains and yet happier than others. The sex ratio among them was 978 as per 2001 census which was much above average to 'normal' Indian's 933 despite abysmally low literacy rate of 47 per cent. The tribal love their habitats which are now prized possession for the industries and for protecting that they have become victim of state highhandedness. According to an ILO report 85.39 lakh tribal have been displaced between 1947 and 2001 in various development projects in India. It is about 55.16 per cent of all the displaced population of India. More than 64.32 per cent of them are yet to be rehabilitated. Chhattishgarh government went much ahead when it created Salwajudam, an unaccountable brutal army of young Aadivasis to counter the Maoist insurgency in Bastar and other districts resulting in displacement of nearly four lakh people in over 644 villages. Over 40,000 people were living in relief camps and the situation was grim reminder of how state has thrown the people from their own land and converted them into strangers.

Article 244 of the Indian Constitution provide administrative control of the tribal in states other than Assam, Meghalaya, Tripura and Mizoram which falls under the Vth schedule of the Constitution in the hands of tribal community. This was extended in Panchayats also terming it as PESA (Panchayat Extension of Scheduled Areas Act) but it is deeply disgusting and shameful that Panahcyats have rarely been asked before launching a project in these regions. PESA came into force in 1996 which provided key provision of International laws into it particularly related to governance of natural resources in their region and protection of their culture. Over the years, the PESA has become a bone of contention for the Central and the state government as in their greed to handover the naturally rich resources to trans-national corporations, we have bypassed the tribal autonomy and Panchayat institutions. In fact in 1994, the Supreme Court gave the historic 'Samata' judgement delivered by Justice K.Ramaswamy who maintained that the government has no authority to bypass the Panchayat if they want to handover these places to big mining companies in India and abroad.

Today, the tribal question has jolted the people who have conscience. It needs a thoughtful and sensible understanding as why there is unrest in the entire tribal belt of Central India. Let us first have a look at the government records. According to Ministry of Rural Development,' 3.75 lakh cases of tribal land alienation were registered covering 8.55 lakhs acres of land. Out of the above, 1.62 lakh cases (43.2 per cent) were disposed of in favour of tribal covering a total of 4.47 (55. 28 per cent) lakh hectare of land.

1.55 lakh cases covering an area of 3.63 lakh acres were rejected by the courts on various grounds 57,521 cases involving.44 lakh acres of land are pending in various courts of the country. There are huge mining in these regions. Forests are out of bound for tribal now. The areas where they developed their culture and nurture India's huge forest are now under the government control. There was no attempt to bring them into national mainstream. Health, road network, schools, PDS, communications were out of bound for them. For years, tribal suffered in the abject and shameless neglect by the Indian state and hence different forces entered there to 'liberate' them. In the absence of credible leadership, tribal looked for messiah in different varieties of 'political' thoughts right from 'Marxism' to Maoism. The Christian missionaries also went to them but perhaps failed to reassure them of their future. The Hindu fundamentalists went there and only ensure that tribal become 'Hanuman' who can only ensure faith against all the odds and no questioning to the racist philosophy which isolated them. The fact is that tribal do not come to them because of their 'ideological' affinity to these people.

They come because it has become the issue of their survival. When the Hindutva fanatics rarely bothered about their cultural issues and never ever questioned the corporate take over the tribal habitat then why should they go to them? The Missionaries were pious enough to help them in education as well as provide them health facilities yet there was no answer to the growing annihilation of tribal home land and their culture.

Hence, when so called Maoists or armed struggle ventured into these forest zones, it gave them a new strength to fight back with keeping their head high to fight for their land and forests. They kept these forests intact and beautiful for generations and now government want to hand it over to companies for commercial greed without even talking to the community. The Maoist captured that vacuum left by democratic space. In the din of identity politics, nobody really cared for tribal questions. This is shameful that those who talk about dalit bahujan identities rarely thought beyond their own question and understood the tribal question.

Tribal questions cannot be spoken without understanding the issue of land, forest and water. For many of the Dalit Bahujan ideologues these are 'bogus' theories to keep us 'subjugated'. It is a dangerous connotation. The tribal community had a historic track record of fighting for their autonomy and we cannot ignore the historic and heroic struggle of Birsa Munda against the British colonialism. In the constituent Assembly, we had a historical representation from the tribal community of Jharkhand, Captain Jai Pal Singh who was also the captain of India's world cup winning Hockey team as well as Olympian with Gold medal. They all realized the tribal questions and its autonomy and that is why the constitution made specific provisions for maintaining them but our political class always tried to serve the bramanical interests and hence tribal were duped.

THE MOVEMENT FOR SELF-RESPECT AND SAVING THEIR RESOURCES

It is not that the tribal are just working under the leadership of non-tribal. The movement is strong and resistance is growing. In Jharkhand Dayamani Barla, indefatigable Aadivasi woman who has fought intensively for the rights of the tribal on their resources is behind the bar. She was arrested on a fake case filed by the state government several years ago when she organized the NREGS workers. In the Nagri village of Jharkhand, just about 25 kilometers from Ranchi, tribal residents are protesting against the government attempt to acquire over 200 acres of farmland for setting up a law university and a campus of the Indian Institute of Management.

Dayamani Barla has been in the jail since October 18, 2012 for a case dating back to 2006, where she was accused of leading a protest that caused a roadblock. Two days later, the land rights activist got bail in the case, but was immediately re-arrested and put back in jail in two other old cases where she is accused of disrupting law and order during a protest. It is tragic that the Jharkhand High Court too has rejected her bail petition. People have been protesting against her arrest which is absolutely unlawful and show how highhanded the governments have become when the question of tribal land is concern. Civil society organisations as well as tribal organisatons have been protesting against her arrest.

Jharkhand's state movement itself was the movement for tribal home land which was led by Shibu Soren who later became chief minister of the state. In fact, despite his weaknesses and media making him a villain on various issues, Soren, remains the tallest tribal leader of the community who organized his people against the regular onslaught of outsiders. It was not for easy reasons that the Bihar was ready to handover Jharkhand as a separate state but stiff tribal protest under the leadership of Jharkhand Mukti Morcha which was the sole tribal voice for the tribal home land.

In Odisha, the movements to save Niyamgiri hills have now reached internationally. The Vedanta after sucking the blood in

Chhattishgarh entered into a deal with Odisha government in 1997 for Boxite mining in these hills endangering the bio diversity as wel as the Kondhs tribals. People resisted and despite oppressive government machinery, they continue to fight against forcible land acquisition. Over 25 villages belonging to tribal with a population of 15,000 face complete destruction of their lives and they are resisting against the same. The anti Posco movement to save the tribal land is well known and building up. These movements may not be visible all over the country on our TV screens and newspapers but they exists everywhere. Tribal may not have credible face from their own community but there are many like Dayamani Barla working for their community at different places locally.

In Chhattishgarh, the tribal are resisting the mining being imposed on them. In the border areas with Andhra Pradesh the tribal are protesting against Polevaram Dam which will uproot over 3 lakh tribal from Odisha, Chhattishgarh and Andhra Pradesh.

The problem is that the tribal movement though growing in India is still fighting against forcible land acquisition and to save their culture. It is resisting land, forest and water in Chhattishgarh, Odisha, Andhra Pradesh, Bengal and Jharkhand irrespective of who is leading them. The reason for that is isolation of tribal from the beginning and their distinct cultural conditions which isolated them from rest of the country.

It has also to be noted that tribal movement in India for their life style and autonomy from the very beginning as the tribal would never allow their culture to be assimilated in the broader non-tribal culture. They may be simple yet would always resist any attempt to ruin their culture which is 'protection of forests, wild life and bio diversity. That way the unambiguous rejection of the forces of mining and 'development' by the tribal all over the country means that they are wary of the danger to their cultural value system and destruction of natural wealth in their region which they are not ready to do away with. They have lived with nature for centuries and have never termed those 'resources' in terms of material wealth and hence this resistance is a 'war of civilisation'.

There is a learning of lesson for the tribal today. They can learn a lot from Dalit movement and its success particularly in political spectrum. It may have weaknesses and we agree when the movement grows there are bound to have some weaknesses yet in terms of political representation and social movements, dalit succeeded in a much better way. The region is in their growth of leadership emerging from the communities and emancipation in Ambedkarism. While there is no denial that tribal should fight for their forest and water yet also important is to embrace modern values and democratic institutions. It is important that a credible tribal leadership is allowed to emerge from within those communities. What has happened that everybody else is ready to work for tribal as long as they are being made as leaders? Many of the people say that tribal could not have survived if Maoists were not there as there is a heavy onslaught by the government.

Unfortunately, this fact again ignore the historicity of tribal struggle in various parts of the country much before independence and even today without the Maoists being its leader. Yes, when the Maoist came, the issue of tribal question became important and that all the tribal who joined in their bandwagon may not know exactly what Maoism is and what Mao stood for as most of them are there to protect their land and resources. This has happened because the democratic forces failed there and did not even bother about their physical condition. It is surprising that despite so much of violence and displacement, we do not hear anything from Member of Parliament from Chhatishgarh and Jharkhand.

There is another danger which seems to be being played both by the government and the Maoists. By treating every tribal who is asking for his right as Maoist the government has conceded that the entire tribal zone has turned Maoist and idea that suits to the Maoists also who were feeling isolated for long and confined to a few zones of Chhattishgarh and Odisha. There are reports of rebellion in Jharkhand and Odisha against the upper caste imposed leadership from Andhra Pradesh. For government, this gives an excuse to enter the tribal zones with arms to vacate their land to handover to the powerful corporations who are eyeing these places. If the tribal were not projected as Maoists, the government of India would have been liable to answer to international community for the annihilation of tribal culture and people in the past sixty years but with branding all the tribal as Maoist they have escaped that and continue with their assault on tribal people without any shame. A credible tribal leadership must emerge from the communities and start open dialogue with the government as this is a historic moment to rise up and come out of the shadows of various 'isms' so that only issue to discuss and deal with remain the tribal identity and its protection.

TRIBAL SOLIDARITY MOVEMENTS IN INDIA

There have been a series of tribal rebellions during the early days of the British rule in the 18th and 19th centuries: Sardar Larai (1885) and Birsa movement (1895-1900) among the Munda: Ganganarain Hangama among the Bhumij;Kol rebellion (1832);Santhal rebellion(1857-58);Rebellion of the Kacha Nagas (1880s). Following these tribal rebellions there have been a series of reform movements emulating the cultural pattern of the higher Hindu castes: Bhagat movement among the Oraon, Vaishnavite reform movement among the Bhumij for Rajput recognition, Kerwar movement among the Santhal etc.

Emergence of inter-tribal political associations and movements for recognition as tribal states within Indian Union in the post Independence period: Jharkhand movement among the tribes of Chotanagpur and Orissa, Hill states movement in the Assam hills and Adisthan movement among the Bhil and so on.

Violent secessionist movements among the tribes located near the international frontier: Nagaland movement, Mizo National Front movement etc. Pockets of violent political movements in the tribal belt linked with the general problem of agrarian unrest and communist movement: Naxalbari movement (1967), Girijan rebellion at Srikakulam (1968-69) and Birsa Dal movement in Ranchi (1968-69).

The political solidarity situations and movements among the tribes of India may be arranged in a series of space from the least integrated to those who have merged with the general level of the regional Hindu peasantry.

The isolated tribes who accept their social, cultural and political independence as a matter of course and are therefore not involved in any self-conscious movements to assert solidarity, the tribes of Andaman and Nicobar Islands belong to this category. Many of the tribes of pre-independence North East Frontier Agency or of relatively remote regions of the Nagaland also belonged to this category.

Tribal blocks located near the international frontier self-consciously seeking political cessation from the Indian Union: Naga National Front movement, Mizo National Front movement etc.The self-conscious movements are led by an educated elite who are fully aware of the political entity of Indian Union.

Tribal blocks occurring as sizable encysted zones going in for demands for tribal state within the Indian Union: Jharkhand movement among Chotanagpur tribes, APHLC movement among the tribes of the Garo and Khasi hills.

Scattered isolated tribal pockets asserting rights as political interest groups as scheduled tribes: the Santhal and the Kora of West Bengal.

Tribes who are too far Hinduized to be effectively involved in solidarity movements in the company of non-Hinduized tribes: the Bhumij of Purulia and Singhbhum.

Bose characterizes the tribal political movements and emerging political associations as falling in the general category of sub nationalism along with political associations based on religion, language and caste. According to Bose sub nationalism is typically generated in economically backward communities of an emerging nation. The general assumption is that these movements are essentially based on the economic and political interest of the rising elite who wish to monopolize their dominance over a region and mobilize the relatively passive tribal and peasant masses to fulfill their limited class aspirations.

Roy Burman makes a distinction between two kinds of elite based movements among the tribes. In one kind infra nationalism the tribes are involved in a progressive movement in a phase of expansion from a primitive stage of tribalism towards nationalism. At this phase of infra-national agglomerates of tribes in search for identity at a higher level of integration than tribalism. In contrast to this sub nationalism is essentially a product of social disorganization where already acculturated elites of a tribe become involved in contra acculturative contraction of relationship. According to Roy Burman one can mark the interplay of these two analytically distinct series of phases in the actual solidarity situations of the different tribes.

According to Orans tribal groups concede rank to the dominant Hindus but resent their low position and desire to attain high position.

The pattern of socio-cultural activities for attaining higher rank is guided essentially by the broad nature of rank path. If the rank path is economic then the tribes particularly their upper strata move in the direction of emulation of the pattern of culture of the dominant Hindus. The more acculturated a tribal is the more severely he will feel the thrust of emulation-solidarity conflict.

Wallace in his concept of revitalization movement is concerned with the total reorganization of the cultural system of a group in an acculturative situation of extreme stress that threatens the entire cultural system.

A revitalization movement is defined as a deliberate organized conscious effort by members of a society to construct a more satisfying culture. The beginning of those movements may be traced to a threat to the sustenance of a cultural system by a group of people in a situation of cultural contact with a dominating group. After an initial period of increasing individual stress and cultural distortion it is followed by an active phase of revitalization. Wallace locates the origin of such movements in a threat to the total cultural system and not just to economic well-being; power and rank. He would also expect the primary goal of such a movement as a reformulation of the total cultural system to be initiated by a charismatic leader.

One of the major roots of tribal solidarity movements may be traced to their ecological –cultural isolation, economical backwardness and feeling of frustration about a lowly status vis a vis the advanced sections. Although it is true that a minority of emerging elite guides these movements it would be wrong to view the phenomenon exclusively from the perspective of sub-nationalism engineered by a few elites. There is progressive enlargement of socio-political and cultural phenomenon beyond the primitive tribal units and also a process of drawing solidarity boundaries around the expanded horizon vis a vis the Indian core.

JHARKHAND MOVEMENT AND THE LEFT

Attempts at carving out a separate Jharkhand state on the Indian map had started during the British regime itself. These still continue fifty years after independence. Jharkhand movement is no exceptional case for a separate state. In many other parts of the country, movements for separate states (within Indian Union) by various nationalities and regional forces have been going on for a long time. Even after the dissolution of the first State Reorganisation Commission not only did the formation of separate states continue, the proposals rejected by the Commission acquired depth and became more broadbased in the form of mass movements. Along with these movements the question of development of states has also come up. Jharkhand movement is one of them and the question of the attitude of the Left towards this movement is integrally linked with the outlook of the Left on the question of development of the Indian state.

The debate concerning the nationality is quite old among the Left but in the Indian context this has not taken a concrete form. Here the nationality question has been limited to some rhetorics and formalisms by the Left and this has pushed the Left out of the arena of struggle. One cannot deny the complexity involved in this question. It would be foolish to adopt only one criteria for looking at all nationalities in India because various nationalities are at different stages of their socio-economic development. But within the Indian political system the movements striving for autonomy are not only oppressed but they are also isolated from the rest of the country by creating suspicion and declaring them anti-national. The ruling class uses this instrument against all autonomy movements. A big section of the Left, instead of opposing it, gets entangled in this. The Left needs to take a look at its policies on the interrelation between national unity and autonomy for nationalities.

In its form and content the movement for a separate Jharkhand state is a struggle for autonomy of a backward nationality and it is trying to find a solution within the totality of the Indian state. The colonialism of the British period and the rulers of independent India in the age of neo-colonialism have given rise to old and new social tensions in Jharkhand. These tensions had dealt a blow to the stagnation of colonialism of the earlier period. Subsequently, the activism of the new class and sub-class social groupings is taking an effective role in the public arena. These are the new facets to the Jharkhand movement. The Left cannot confine them merely to the cultural context because these are coming up in the form of day-to-day political questions. The gravity of this question is increasing more due to the growing influence of reactionary forces. The truth is that the creative utilisation of these social tensions has not found a proper place in the agenda of the Left. Lamenting over opportunism of the parties calling themselves Jharkhandi or shedding tears over this will not solve the problem. The Left is facing lots of problems in powerfully mobilising Jharkhandi forces against this opportunism and then taking this mobilisation to the leading role. There is a need to make a threadbare analysis of this situation and remove the weaknesses.

After independence the period of industrialisation in Jharkhand began. To tackle the growing discontent in Jharkhand many developmental projects were started. Industrialisation and these development projects only added to the distorted and lopsided development of this region - these brought in new problems in a flood-like manner. In all, the result was that Jharkhand region was being pushed towards incurable backwardness. Jobs and resettlement were not made available but almost all of ancestral land slipped out of the fold of Jharkhandis. Forests were uprooted, traditional forms of production were destroyed, and in return, Jharkhandis were pushed into the army of unorganised labourers. The change in composition of the population due to urbanisation soon alienated Jharkhandis from their own land.

The worst victim of these changes was the Jharkhandi tribal life. The tribal identity of the adivasis - which is an important feature of Jharkhand - was attempted to be smothered under the facade of development and industrialisation. Surely, the ruling class was able to bring a small section of adivasis into its fold in this whole process. But the rest were left to suffer under this situation over which they had no control and which was forcibly thrust upon them from outside. The fallout of developmental projects and industrialisation also took the shape of sharp tendencies for regionalism. This provided strength to the unity of the tribal community and rationale to the cries of seperation from Bihar.

The question of unlimited plunder of resources from Jharkhand and spending virtually nothing in return gave birth to movemental forms like economic blockade. Independent mass movements on issues like resettlement, forest protection and environment came up. The issue of tribal self-rule is also giving rise to mass mobilisation. All these types of struggling tendencies have an integral connection with Jharkhand movement. The Left's attitude towards them is not yet clear even though they are very much the products of independent India. There can be many facets to the topic 'Jharkhand Movement and the Left'. But I will restrict my views to the above-mentioned context only. It could be that some aspects will be influenced by the limits of the topic. Secondly, there are many streams of left in India and I will mainly present my views on the basic assumptions and practices of CPI, CPI(M) and CPI(ML). Surely, the specific practice of Comrade AK Roy will also be discussed which is an important experience of the Left here.

The awakening against British imperialism provided the foundation for Indian nationalism. Now after independence when the British guns are not aimed at us, it is obvious that the nation had to be reorganised on the basis of democracy. Specially, the aspirations of the backward nationalities, minority nationalities and backward regional forces were to be respected in the formation of states. But with the transfer of power into the hands of comprador bourgeoisie and big landlords they gave protection to the fundamental neo-colonial feudal relations inside the country.

That is, there was a change from colonialism to semi-colonialism. To some extent the feudal special privileges still form the basis for the relations between the forward and backward nationalities and the redistribution of power between various nationalities. These special privileges are also operative in the relations between states and centre, in the relations between developed and backward regions within states etc. The communist principle is to abolish all these old kind of special privileges whether they are direct or indirect, even if the benefit of these special privileges is availed by the elites of backward nationalities along with the ruling class of the forward nationalities.

Regarding the emergence of Indian state contradictory ideas are present among a large section of communists even today. In the first place, the undivided communist party denied in toto the importance of independence and later making amends to this gave it a status of victory of national democratic movement. CPI(M) presents things in a slightly different way. According to CPI(M), democratic revolution is yet to take place but feudal-colonial relation is not the central target of this revolution. As a result democratic revolution is unable to break the limits of the rhetorics of the economic and cultural questions.

This means there is only a quantitaive difference between CPI and CPI(M) over the point that national unification is complete. In their eyes the problem of nationalities has almost been solved. And if at all it is strong anywhere it is because of the subversive forces acting from behind. Refusing to look for the roots of this problem in the Indian political arena, CPI and CPI(M) adopt the ruling classes' position of 'the external intervention'. In this way their nationalism is not much different from that of the ruling classes. These parties were never firm on the question of the right of nationalities to self-determination. And now they have deleted the word 'self-determination' from some of their recent documents.

Even though CPI(ML) is divided into many parts, we can consider two representative streams within it. The PWG overlooks the quantitative change in capitalism over the periods before and after independence. At the same time it belittles the importance of the Indian identity that was obtained with the struggle for independence. As a result, instead of viewing the nationality movement as part of the democratic movement it sees it as an important instrument to destroy state machinery and views the project of national unification as the union of independent and autonomous nationalities. This treats the movement of the Indian people against British imperialism as having gone waste. In this way, where CPI(M) raises the slogan of national chauvinism, PWG gets trapped in the advocacy of narrow nationalism.

The other view is that of CPI(ML) Liberation. It takes into account the development of Indian identity against British imperialism and also observes that the birth of multinational, multilingual state took place not only with semi-colonial distortions, but also the Indian unity and nationalism obtained during independence is under the burden of heavy bureaucratism and an overcentralised power. Because the imperialism stood as a real enemy before the people even after independence, the ruling class exploits the distorted nationalism. For Maley the movement of nationalities is an essential part of political agenda for the development of a true and composite nationalism. Autonomy for backward nationalities and national minorities are the preconditions for a federal and democratic India.

The violation of the right of backward nationalities in semi-colonial and semi-feudal Indian society means protecting the special privileges of the advanced nationalities. This rather provides labour for a pittance for imperialist economy and creates unlimited profits for it. Hence, communists are the staunch defenders of the autonomy for the backward nationalities so that the old type of special privileges can be done away with. At the same time real national unity can be strengthened from below. It is important to struggle against the discrimination of the nationalities to remove the distortions imposed by British imperialism or neo-imperialism. In this way we can say that the question of nationalism is not the residual question of 1947. On the one hand, the enthusiasm associated with the abolition of the jagirs, and on the other hand, partition on the basis of religious nationalism had for some time frozen this question and then later the formation of linguistic states had rendered it dormant. But fifty years later this question has acquired a new place and attained new importance.

On the nationalities question in Indian context the debates within the Left have not developed much. The main reason is that CPI and CPI(M), while mentioning the multinational character hesitate to pose this question as a fundamental problem of Indian politics. At the same time they were content with the initiatives taken by the Congress party and considered the Sixth Schedule as the maximum limit for autonomy. This looks more surprising in a situation when CPI(M) has been taking up seriously the demand for reorganisation of centre-state relations which is a justified demand. Let us look at CPI(M)'s outlook on the question of nationalities with the help of one of its documents: "During this period the movement for separate state/identity continued. Chiefly among them were the demands for Bodo adivasis in Assam and Jharkhand area in Bihar. The Fourteenth Congress had said that in these two regions the regional autonomous councils be established with adequate powers and if necessary the constitution could be amended for this." Similar recommendations have been given on other similar issues in this document.

Let us take an excerpt from CPI's document: "For our multilingual and multinational country the ethnic problem is a decisive problem. In spite of linguistic reorganisation even now many problems exist. Small tribes and adivasis are coming to new awareness. And they are struggling for the establishment of their languages, culture, political rights and identity.... The struggle of the adivasis for their identity and homeland has taken up a new dimension. Jharkhand, Bodoland and North Cachar Hills are involved in this. The movements have become mass movements. The centre has to begin talks to find a solution. There are going to be many such movements in many other states having a good percentage of tribal population." (Draft of the CPI's statement relating to its programme; 1-6 Jan. 1997). CPI mentions no reason for its sudden change in attitude because before this CPI had opposed movements for a separate state.

CPI(ML) Liberation views the question of nationality like this: "India is a land of various nationalities, ethnic and linguistic groups. Increasing economic and cultural homogeneity, anti-colonial freedom struggle and the decades old unity forged from anti-imperialist and democratic struggles have provided a unified Indian identity to our multi-national character. But the process of gradual development of this Indian identity has been a victim of big comprador and national chauvinistic distortions, economic and cultural discriminations and regional disparities on a large scale. Due to this various separatist tendencies have got a boost....We are for the construction of national unity from below where various nationality groups, national minorities will have a guarantee to the broadest possible autonomy. The unification of India on a democratic basis is an important part of democratic revolution".

Nationalities in India can be divided into three main categories. In the first category are developed nationalities like Tamils and Punjabis, in the second category are backward nationalities like Jharkhandis and in the third category are extremely backward nationalities like Nagas and Mizos. The attitude of the communists to different movements of the nationalities will be different. Where the ruling classes of developed nationalities want to strengthen their position in the Indian political structure through the movements of concerned nationalities, the people of the extremely backward nationalities express their resistance against the political constructions imposed on them through their nationality movements. There are two simultaneous trends in the movement of backward nationality like Jharkhand.

One is that of the emerging neo-rich sections of the concerned nationality who try to remove the outside rulers and take over their place and the other is that of the exploited people who along with their struggle against the outside rulers conduct struggle against the local neo-rich sections. In the movements of developed nationalities the communists can go to the maximum extent of extending negative support. The task of the communists in the movement of the backward nationality is to prepare the leadership of peasants and workers against the rich classes of the concerned nationality and to compete for the position of leadership in this movement and bring about a polarisation on the basis of classes. Communists are not only the staunch supporters of the movements of extremely backward nationalities but they also develop an appropriate structure for a progressive leadership. Let us look at the practice of these three streams of the Left in this light.

The CPI(M) wants to solve the problem of nationality through tribal autonomous councils even though in this very document it discusses the failure of Bodoland Council and says that adequate powers have not been given to it. The difficulty is that most of these movements have passed through the stage of autonomous councils. Even the movement of Gorkhaland, after having a taste of autonomous council, is coming up again while the government which is to devolve the powers to them is led by CPI(M). So what can we conclude from this: it is most likely that the CPI(M) would include this in "disruptionist activities".

There is one more possibility that CPI(M) opposes the movements of nationalities or regional forces so long as they are associated with real mass aspirations. But when the different strata of the movement get degenerated at the hands of the ruling class of the concerned nationality and lose their mass character, CPI(M) promptly establishes friendship with these degenerated leaderships. Perhaps, the change in CPI(M)'s relations with AGP and DMK suggests the same story.

In the past, CPI's attitude towards the nationality movement has not been different from this. The above-mentioned quotation from a CPI document doesn't present a self-criticism of its practice in the past. Even then the change that has taken place is positive and welcome. But if there is no holistic view about this then usually the change proves to be an opportunist exercise. Second thing is that the emphasis of CPI has been more for talks with the central government rather than on mass movements. It is doubtful whether this approach will inspire CPI to prepare for a real mass movement.

Maley (CPI(ML) Liberation) has adopted a critical view of the movements of advanced nationalities. For example, it adopted a negative position on the issue of Khalistan. At the same time not only did *Maley* support the movements in Uttarakhand and Jharkhand but it also actively intervened in them. Along with emerging as the strong supporter of the movements of extremely backward national minorities like Karbis and Misings, it has also built up organisations like ASDC, TPF etc., to provide these movements a leftward orientation. Practices like these enrich the experiences of the Left in the Indian context.

Lenin says that the overthrowing of the entire feudal crimes, entire oppression of nationalities and the special privileges of any one nationality or one language is the essential duty of the proletariat as a democratic force and this is certainly in the interest of the proletarian class struggle which is made hazy and hindered by the conflicts among the nationalities. (From *Critical Comments on the Nationality Question*). According to Lenin, the question of right to self-determination of the nationalities more than being a question of nationalism is a question of democracy and in this the communist principle is minimum nationalism and maximum democracy. This is the reason why the communists even while struggling against narrow nationalism on the question of nationality, in the relative sense are the staunchest supporters of maximum autonomy and their only aim is to direct the class struggle within the concerned nationality in favour of the people.

The modern composition of Jharkhand was developed in reaction against British colonialism despite the fact that conducive integrated economic structure based on geographic features, backward agriculture and forests, and integral cultural heritage, unique inter-tribal relations etc., were present for this. Tensions were sparked off in the society due to new polarisations caused by the growing pressures on land by the state at the time of colonial subjugation and the consequent transfer of the land constantly into the hands of usurers, as well as due to other external pressures. As a result, revolts in this region took the form of tradition and culture developed under resistance. In the initial period these revolts were of religious and retrograde form which is a special feature of peasant revolts. But progressively the development of these struggles took place in the form of looking for a new system against the raj, zamindari and usury.

The Munda resistance from 1789 to 1820, the Kol revolt of 1830-31, the Bhumij revolt of 1834, the Santhal revolt of 1855-56, the Sepoy Mutiny of 1856-57, the upsurge under the leadership of Birsa Munda during 1895-1901 etc., kept the entire region agitated with a series of revolts spanning over more than a century. If the people faced the repression together, they also enjoyed the fruits of victory together.

The laws that were made under compulsion were the achievements of these struggles. The Chotanagpur-Santhal Parganas Tenants Act (1872, 1886, 1903, 1908) that put a check on land sales in Chotanagpur and Santhal Parganas etc., were enacted under the pressure of these struggles.

The spontaneous struggles in Jharkhand have laid the foundation for a tradition of resistance. At the same time it also did the initial work of giving an identity to Jharkhand. There is no doubt that the hero of the above-mentioned struggles was the adivasi and he had the complete support of non-adivasi small peasant too. During this time, the growing activity of the missionaries and the efforts of the British government to coopt small groups of adivasis gave birth to a section of educated, Westward-looking adivasis. And in this process Chotanagpur Unnati Samaj, then Adivasi Mahasabha, and finally Jharkhand Party came into existence. Even before independence the demand for a separate state was proposed to the Simon Commission and the Cripps Commission.

The new leadership had no movemental programme and it lacked the energy for waging struggles. Its only asset was its allegiance to the ruling class and its party. At the centre of this leadership was the famous and brilliant Jaipal Singh Munda. In spite of a spectacular electoral victory of the Jharkhand Party, its entire leadership went over to Congress later. One reason could be that the State Reorganisation Commission (1955) had rejected the demand for a separate Jharkhand state. In spite of all weaknesses these happenings had two important contributions - first, this struggle for a separate Jharkhand state took a long-term character, and secondly, it pointed to the lack of unity between adivasis and non-adivasis as the weakness of the movement.

Four years after the demise of Jharkhand Party a momentary upsurge came in Jharkhand with Birsa Seva Dal. This was also a movement of educated adivasi youth but its character was just the opposite of Jharkhand Party. Organising peasants near towns and in farflung villages and bringing them in direct action against the oppressors was the main activity of Birsa Seva Dal. In spite of some remarkable initiatives this collapsed in the face of repression. This was the first movement in the history of Jharkhand which was influenced by the Left and its source of inspiration was Naxalbari. It is said that some leaders of the Birsa Seva Dal had relations with CPI(ML).

Then began the second phase of Jharkhand movement. This was the struggle for land seizure and against usury in North Chotanagpur and Santhal Parganas which in the beginning was an explosion of the adivasi peasant movement and later spread to wider areas in the countryside. Adivasi groups armed with bows and arrows along with non-adivasi small peasants would come and capture the land of usurers, harvest the fields and walk away with the crops. This struggle was actually a struggle between land grabbers and peasants. During this time with the efforts of Comrade AK Roy, this struggle was extended to the unorganised labourers in the coalbelt who were fed up with the Bihari mafias. The late Vinod Bihari Mahato was a militant leader of the Kurmis and he used to work through the Shivaji Samaj. Shibu Soren was leading the struggle against the usurers. With the merger of these three streams Jharkhand Mukti Morcha was constituted in 1973.

The speciality of this movement was the struggle of the poor peasants in the countryside, the anti-mafia struggle of unorganised labourers in the urban localities and the living unity of adivasis and the non-adivasis.

With the opposition to the mafia, the anti-Bihar tendency became prominent in the urban areas. The police and the administration used to look down upon the life style of the locals and this was also responsible for the anti-Bihari tendency. This phase of Jharkhand movement created a force of enlightened activists of the Jharkhand movement in all villages and localities.

It was in this phase of Jharkhand movement that Comrade AK Roy's formulation of 'Jharkhand and Lalkhand' came to the fore. Compared to all other phases in the past this phase was extremely broad-based, deep and all-pervasive. But with the waning of the first upsurge all the three streams again divided and Shibu Soren's opportunism came to the fore in the form of his agreement with Indira Gandhi. In spite of this, this struggling phase in the period of establishment of Jharkhand Mukti Morcha (JMM) took the Jharkhand movement to new heights and gave it a qualitative leap. The agreement with Congress not only made the leadership dubious but there was a degeneration in its pro-people direction. And the intrusion of anti-Jharkhand forces into JMM also took place.

The next upsurge in Jharkhand began in the eighties. This time the leadership was in the hands of the educated Jharkhandi youth and identity was the main issue. In this period the influence of the emerging petty-bourgeois elements on the movement was clear. Militant bandhs for two-three days and militant participation of the urban youth were a speciality of this movement. But All Jharkhand Students Union (AJSU) which was the convener of this movement soon got degenerated with a greed for power. During this time some well-known Jharkhandi intellectuals, some ML groups, Jharkhand Party and AJSU made efforts and formed the Jharkhand Coordination Committee (JCC). This also took up programmes like demonstrations and bandhs. But none of the constituents could emerge as a consensus centre. Even though it had some theoretical formulations it could not give birth to a movement that could generate theorisation.

From time to time there were talks with the centre and the state governments but these talks could not express the strength of the movement. The report of the expert committee on Jharkhand also ended up with a recommendation of a vaguely defined council. These talks were reduced down to a form of bargaining between the parties in power and the degenerated leadership. After each round of talks this leadership would return from Patna and Delhi, more inactive to take movemental initiatives and be more suspect in the eyes of the public. What a contradictory thing this is that such a broad-based movement could not exert appropriate influence over these talks. Once again, in the '90s, began the phase of joint activities with economic blockades and general strikes. These were militant and effective. This time JMM was with JD which was in power. As a result of this movement and various rounds of talks with state and central governments the present undemocratic and powerless JAAC was established which appears less as a product of a movement and more as a product of unholy bargains.

The criminalisaton of politics based on the development of mafiadom in Jharkhand area is a reflection of the lumpenisation of economy. Generally with the ongoing process of economic liberalisation and specifically with the intrusion of MNCs this lumpenisation of economy has gone from bad to worse. The result has been the consolidation of lumpen capital. On the one hand, this capital has developed such a network that it can absorb a section of Jharkhandi population, especially a section of the unemployed. On the other hand, this has been successful in establishing a unity of the neo-rich in rural Jharkhand and the kulaks. While this special phenomenon has on the one hand weakened the economic concept of 'locals vs. outsiders', on the other hand, it has strengthened the economic base of Jharkhandi type of regional parties (From the report of Jharkhand Regional Committee, CPI(ML)).

In this brief history of the Jharkhand movement the traditional Left could not take sides. The CPI and CPI(M) leaders say that "Jharkhand is no solution, class struggle is the solution". It is correct but the problem is that without solving the Jharkhand problem class struggle cannot be freed in this region. The second argument of CPI-CPI(M) leaders is that the leadership of the Jharkhand movement is in the hands of powerful sections of Jharkhand. There is truth in this too but this section also raises the slogan of freeing itself from the oppression of Bihari ruling class.

Does your silence not become a support to the Bihari ruling class in which bureaucrats, corrupt politicians and small and big mafia are present? Does this not mean that the fate of the people would be left in the hands of Jharkhandi exploiters? Does this not mean giving a consent to the special privileges of the Bihari nationality? Whatever be its meaning, the result was that the Left got removed from the social-political centre of Jharkhand and got reduced to some practices in the area of trade union and this provided arguments to the anti-Left forces within Jharkhand. Not only this, the Left could have established a bridge between the Jharkhandi peasants-workers and

Bihari peasants-workers. The Left could have enlightened the toiling masses of Bihar with this consciousness that without Jharkhand the process of democratisation of Bihar and the defeat of feudalism is not possible. But the Left could not take up this role. CPI, by taking the decision to participate in the Jharkhand movement has taken a welcome step but without its self-criticism this decision of their's could degenerate into opportunism.

From the very beginning *Maley* has supported the Jharkhand movement. This support gradually developed from active support to the policy of direct intervention. *Maley's* mass political organisation IPF started actively participating in the eighties. Its MLA vigorously raised the issue of Jharkhand in the assembly from time to time. As a constituent of the JCC, IPF took active part in its joint programmes. Later through the Jharkhand Mazdoor Kisan Samiti, Maley actively intervened in the Jharkhand movement. We shall discuss about this later. Finally, under the banner of Maley, programmes like Jharkhand bandh were successfully undertaken. At the same time, Maley also popularised the slogan "No Jharkhand, no democratic Bihar" among the toiling sections in Bihar. Even though Maley went into joint activities with the supporters of Jharkhand as well as with Jharkhandi parties both inside and outside the assembly, it also spoke against the vacillating attitude of these parties towards Congress and BJP and highlighted this as the main source of opportunism. *Maley* has always given a call for strengthening the leadership of workers-peasants in the Jharkhand movement on a class basis and stressed on the polarisation of anti-Congress forces in the Jharkhand movement. Due to Maley's tactics not only has it been accepted by the Jharkhandis but it has a special place in the movement for a separate Jharkhand state.

The different experiences of the Jharkhand movement has also given birth to many debates. Let us take a look.

26 Districts Vs. 18 Districts: With the formation of JAAC the debate related to the political, geographical boundaries of Jharkhand has come to a halt for the time being. At present 18 districts of south Bihar are popularly known as Jharkhand districts. It is claimed that Jharkhand comprises of 26 districts including the adjoining areas in West Bengal, Orissa and Madhya Pradesh. Socially and culturally these districts are similar to Jharkhand and in these regions Jharkhandi

sentiments are also present to some extent. Hence the proposal for a Jharkhand of 26 districts is not baseless. But the intensity of the movement is not the same in all the states and coordinating it outside Bihar is impractical and difficult. It is clear that the movement for greater Jharkhand can get its strength from the alienation of Jharkhand from Bihar and the process of state reorganisation once again. For the time being the actual force of the movement lies in the Bihar part of Jharkhand.

Internal Colonialism: This formulation in the context of Jharkhand was by Comrade AK Roy. According to this, backward nationalities are colonies of developed nationalities. This formulation of Comrade AK Roy was readily accepted by petty bourgeois intellectuals. The theory of internal colonialism changes the entire context of the Jharkhand movement. Instead of the Indian ruling classes or the oppressors of the developed nationalities, Bihari nationality becomes the target. Due to this, open or secret channels of bargaining are opened up with the ruling classes. At the same time this formulation is also favourable to the growing ruling class within Jharkhand. This formulation dilutes the class consciousness of Jharkhandi people and harms the unity of the toiling people of various nationalities.

Adivasi Autonomy: Industrialisation, urbanisation and the various legal webs have ended the control of adivasis over the material resources of adivasi life. At the same time the changes that came about after independence have dealt a blow to their social status. And as a result the traditions of adivasi community, their social institutions and culture have become insecure and their natural development has also been impeded. Today RSS on the one hand and the Christian missionaries on the other have started communalising the adivasi tradition. In reaction to this within the adivasi community itself retrograde conservatism is taking birth. At the same time the stagnant traditional institutions are being badly exploited by the oppressors and due to this stagnation the adivasi community has become the cheapest source of labour for imperialistic capitalism. Private capital like Tatas and state capital like HEC have converted the adivasis into insecure, contract labourers.

To break through this stagnation, it is needed today that the adivasis be provided with political autonomy so that they themselves can develop the administrative, social and cultural institutions. The need for adivasi autonomy will still be there in a separate Jharkhand state. Almost all the Left streams subscribe to this.

There have been some special experiments by the Left in the Jharkhand movement and this has enriched the experiences of the Left. These have been the experiment of Comrade AK Roy, the formation of Jharkhand Kranti Dal by CPI(ML) PCC and the experiment of JHAMKIS by CPI(ML) Liberation.

Comrade AK Roy has taken the Jharkhand movement as a part of the communist movement. He brought the theory of internal colonialism to the fore. He presented Jharkhand as the biggest internal colony within India. He called the adivasis communists by birth and the communitarianism of the adivasis as favourable to socialism. This is how his practice began. According to Comrade Roy, the liberation of Jharkhand would not only convert it into Lalkhand but will also inspire the communist movement all over India. In his scheme of things the next in line after Lenin and Birsa was Sibhu Soren. In this theorisation, communists had only to let themselves be simply swept away in the flow of JMM. Comrade Roy in his practice neglected some of the important historical experiences of the communist movement. First is that the communists can consciously provide direction to a spontaneous movement and convert them into a communist movement.

Or else these movements will in absolute terms become the victims of petty-bourgeois deviations. Second thing is that claiming adivasis to be communists by birth and comparing the consciousness of their communitarianism with socialist consciousness is not only based on a wrong understanding of communism or socialism but it also produces misunderstanding about their important role in the Jharkhand movement. Regarding the participation of communists in the flow of JMM, Comrade Roy himself had to take to the shores. From time to time Vinod Bihari Mahato also separated from JMM and Shibu Soren - on whom the responsibility of being the next link after Lenin and Birsa was bestowed - and went into the lap of Congress. In spite of the failures of Comrade AK Roy's practice, there appears the spark of a meeting point between the communist movement and the Jharkhand movement and it cannot be denied that this practice brought the movement as a broadbased front of workers and peasants, specially adivasis to the fore. Due to its weak ideological basis and the weak understanding of the class composition in Jharkhand, Comrade Roy's practice degenerated from a communist leadership to the development of the opportunist and petty bourgeois leadership of Jharkhand.

CPI(ML) PCC intervened in the Jharkhand movement under the banner of Jharkhand Kranti Dal. It developed a few pockets in Singhbhum and Gumla but this organisation had a non-political approach and was involved in grassrootist practice. As a result it got alienated from the politics of Jharkhand. It also participated in the JCC. Slowly this organisation declined and PCC withdrew from furthering this practice.

CPI(ML) Liberation intervened in the movement for a separate Jharkhand state under the banner of Jharkhand Mazdoor Kisan Samiti (JHAMKIS) in the beginning of 1990s. Its main slogan was *Separate Jharkhand state, Fight for forest, land and employment!* It displayed a militancy in its demonstrations and programmes, it tired to combine the economic struggles at the grassroots with the movement for a separate state. At the same time it also started developing relations with the movements based on the issues like displacement. But the tendency that differentiated it from other Jharkhandi organisations was its aggressive stance against Congress and BJP. After a long debate in the process of joint activities, it decided to come out of the JCC on the question of Congress. JMM was bringing in the Congress through all the doors into JCC and the stance of AJSU and JPP was also vacillatory. JHAMKIS was an organisation with a semi-political character and with the entry of *Maley* into the Jharkhand movement directly its role became that of mass organisation of workers and peasants.

From time to time the Left experiments provided strength to the Jharkhand movement on the one hand and on the other hand it also gave a direction to the class polarisation within Jharkhand. It is true that till now the work of understanding and formulating the experiences of these experiments in the correct context is still incomplete. But these experiments have proved that there lie hidden many favourable possibilities for the Left in the Jharkhand movement.

JAAC has made a mockery of the aspirations of Jharkhandis. Today Jharkhand movement is again facing a stagnation. The leadership of the traditional Jharkhandi parties are seen with suspicion by their own cadres and masses. They are declaring new programmes but these programmes are hardly producing any enthusiasm among the Jharkhandi people. The question now is probably not that of programmes. The question is of direction.

Only the Left, by polarising the Jharkhandi forces, can present the solution to this problem of direction at present. Jharkhand movement, in which along with the aspirations of nationalities class struggle is also present, awaits the arrival of new forces at this new juncture. BJP's Vananchal is a ploy to sabotage the possibility of class struggle here. It has been proved that the issue of Vananchal has gained ground due to the Jharkhandi opportunism. The unique peasant movement of which the struggle of the tribals is a part, and the anti-mafia struggle of the unorganised labourers within Jharkhand can be resolutely taken to their logical culmination only by the Left. The two real heroes of Jharkhand are these two forces and without bringing them to the centrestage, the struggle for a separate Jharkhand state cannot either be pro-people or be provided with a committed leadership. History is a witness to the fact that the coming together of Jharkhandi and Left forces has produced a stormy struggle for a separate state. But Left could not maintain its continuity. This has been its weakness. There could be many issues on which there are differences between Jharkhandi and Left forces. But we have to search for ways in which a principled cooperation could be developed between the two streams and all the efforts could be channelised towards breaking through this stagnation.

AUTONOMY MOVEMENT OF TIWA TRIBE OF ASSAM

The present study will highlight the factors of Tiwa autonomy movement and the activities of various Tiwa organizations for the cause of Tiwa autonomy. It is necessary to study the topic of Tiwa movement as it will bring to light the factors, organizations of the Tiwas and reaction of state government on the problem. In keeping with this purpose this chapter has been written so that people will know the Tiwa movement and impact in the socio political aspect of Assam. It will also help to know the socio political conditions of the Tiwa tribe. The ethnic movement launched by various organizations in Assam has created many complicated problems to the government and people of the state have to suffer a lot. An amicable solution of the problem is the need of the hour. For this purpose, it is very important to know the problem of Tiwas of Assam and an attempt has been made in this chapter to study the Tiwa autonomy movement in the region.

The Tiwas are one of the aboriginal tribes of North-East India. They are also known as the "Lalung", but they preferred to call themselves as the "Tiwa". They are one of the major ethnic tribes in Assam. The people of the Tiwa Community are mostly living in Asssam and Meghalaya, particularly in the Nagaon, Morigaon, KarbiAnglong, Dhemaji, Kamrup district of Assam and the Khasi and the Jayantia district of Meghalaya. The Tiwas of Assam have been enlisted as a scheduled tribes but a section of them resides in the hill areas also. They have their own language, culture and traditions distinct from other tribes of North-East India. But due to undue pressure of the non-tribals their culture and the identity of the community is now at stake. The Tiwas have remained backward in all spheres of social life.

During the time of the Ahoms there were several smaller independent kingdoms of indigenous people in the south bank of Brahmaputra. The smaller kingdoms like the Nelly, Gova, Topakuchi, Mayang, Dhing, Tetelia, Rani, Dimoria and Beltola etc., were independent. But the rulers of these states had to pay taxes to the Ahom king. Their relation among themselves was not cordial and to save themselves from the invasion of the Jayantia, the king of Dimoria and Kachari king made relation with Ahom king Pratap Singh by giving their daughters in marriage in 1627. The Lalung king of Gova though initially was under the dominion of the Jayantia king later shifted his allegiance to the Ahom kings.

Though the Tiwa people came under the control of the British power, but they acted against the British imperialism and prepared for the revolt against the British Government. They in 1861, revolted against the British imperialism which is popularly known as "PhulaguriDhawa". The Phulaguri Uprising of 1861 was the first agrarian revolt in Assam against the British Raj. In 1860 the British government banned the cultivation of opium. In Nagaon district rumours circulated that the government was planning to impose tax on their houses, barees (garden) and pan (betel leaf) cultivation. So, the Tiwas of Phulaguri protested through their melsagainst imposition of the new taxes. In September, 1861, some 1500 strong peasants marched to the district headquarter and demonstrated before the magistrate against the proposed new taxes. When the magistrate showed no sign of withdrawing the proposed taxes a Raj mel was held in October 1861 to discuss the matter. About this time the government introduced license tax.

This sharpened the belief of the villagers, particularly of the tribals of Phulaguri, on the impending taxes. Therefore, on 14th October, 1861, the ryots of Phulaguri revolted against the authority and in the ensuing clash with the police one English Officer, Lt. Singer, lost his life. This incident followed brutal suppression of the uprising by the military forces in which eight tribal leaders belonging to the Tiwa community were arrested and while some of them were sentenced to death.

In the freedom struggle against the British Government, the Tribal people of Assam played a significant role. The Tiwa people had joined the "Tribal League" which was formed in 1933 and actively participated in the freedom movement. The active participation of the Tiwa people of Assam in the freedom movement was seen in the Quit India Movement in 1942. The Tiwas of Raha, Bebejia, Barapujia, Kampur and Jamunamukh have participated in large numbers during the movement. Despite the police harassment they continued their struggle. Till September, 1942 four Tiwas died in the ensuing struggle: KulaiKach, HemoramPatar, GunabhiramBordoloi and Tilak Deka. On 25th August 1942, people of Kampur took out procession defying the prohibitory orders. The crowd attacked and damaged the local post office, the Circle Office and the Railway Station.

The furious people derailed a train at Kampur followed by military atrocities upon the village At Phulaguri the crowd damaged railway station. The people of Kathiatali destroyed an inspection bungalow. At Raha Government Circle Office was burnt down. In Jongalbalahugarh village, near Raha, people became panicky over a rumour that more police forces would be coming to Nagaon from Guwahati. A group of people, apprehending police raid, started to cut the approach road to a bridge, suddenly a military patrol party appeared from the eastern side and opened fire on them killing

HemoramPatar and GunabhiramBordoli belonging to Tiwa Community. On 28th August the police conducted raids upon Raha, Bebejia and Barapujia. Tilak Luka, who was a volunteer of the 'Santi Sena', was shot dead. Another Tiwa freedom fighter Kolai Koch (Originally Tiwa but converted to Koch) also sacrificed his life. The active participation of Tiwa people in the freedom movement led to the arrest of several people besides innumerable forms of police torture.

The development of social consciousness among the tribal people realized them about their self-identity in the society. The Tribal League in 1947 submitted a memorandum before the constituent Assembly demanding the creation of separate scheduled areas in the plains district of Assam under fifth schedule of Indian Constitution. When Mikir Hills and North Cachar Hills autonomous district was formed in 1951, there was a controversy about the Tiwa dominated areas of the hills whether it could be included with Mikir Hills or to remain with Jayantia Hills. In that tiem, Abra Malang of Ulukunchi demanded a separate autonomous district for the Tiwas of Assam for the first time.

Abra Malang organized a movement among the hills Tiwas with less followers. He can be say as the father of Tiwa movement for autonomy. Mr. LarshingKhyrim supported the demand of AbraMalong. But his movement was suppressed with cruelty and he was imprisoned for four year and the Government has also seized his property. Then Mr. BonnilyKhongman, the first M.P. from that ares, manipulating the population structure of Tiwa on chapter and showed less Tiwa population and more Karbi population by submitting bogus data to the Mikir Hills boundary Commission and accordingly the Commission recommended that they could be included with the Mikir Hills.

The language policy of the Assam Government which made Assamese compulsory brought the sense of feeling of insecurity among the tribal leaders in Assam. The Tiwa people of Assam also felt that their language and culture is in at stake. They wanted to preserve their own ethnic identity. During that time a dynamic youth Mr. IndrasingDeuri while he was in government job in Garo Hills left his job and came back to his native village and organized some educated Tiwas. A meeting of the Tiwa community was conveyed at

Umsuai of Mikir hills. Ananda Ram Deuri of Jagiroad and many others of Neilly delivered lecture in that meeting. They had spoken that the imprisonment of Abra Malang and confiscation of his property was the humiliation for entire Tiwa Community. The meeting took many resolutions and formed 'Lalung Darbar' as the political organization of the Tiwa people in 1967. Late Abra Malang was the first president of the 'Lalung Darbar' though he died soon. Regarding the death of Abvra Malan it is said that he was tortured physically in jail for which his health deteriorated later on. After his death Hemaram Bordoloi and Indrasing Deuri took the leadership of the organization.

The main aim of 'LalungDarbar' was to demand for the creation of 'Lalung Hill Autonomous District', taking the Tiwa dominated areas of Mikir Hills, Nagoan and Kamrup district of Assam and the Tiwa inhabited areas of Jayantia Hills. Since then, the 'LalungDarbar' had organised several public meetings among the Tiwa people. The "LalungDarbar" sent a telegram to the Home Minister of the Govt. of India on 8th July, 1967, demanding for the creation of Lalung Autonomous Hill Sub-division with separate council. But the government did not respond to this demand and on 19th May, 1968 a general meeting was held at Neilly under the president ship of Mr. GambhirBordoloiand adopted some resolutions. In the resolution No.5, it was stated that the Tiwa people supported the creation of Lalung Hill Autonomous Sub-Division and urged the central as well as the state government to take necessary step. When the government did not respond another telegram was sent to the Home Minister of India on 20th June, 1968 demanding to create an autonomous Hill Sub division.

Again on 24th July 1968, a public meeting was held at Chahari, Amsoi under the president ship of Madan Konwar and strengthened their demand for autonomous Hill Sub division. On 15th and 16th October 1969, the two days convention was held at Makangkuchi L.P. School, Jagiroad and was presided over by the Ex M.L.A. Baliram Das.

The convention took the resolution that the Tiwa people unanimously supported the "Lalung Autonomous Hill District" instead of "Hill Sub division" and urged the Central and State government to create Lalung Autonomous Hill District and to take necessary steps to implement the demand.

On 15th July, 1970, a delegation of Tiwa people consisting of 9 persons namely IndrasingDeuri, RaimanPatar, Bin Maloi, Narayan Kumar Kakoti, ThalAmsong, MinaramPatar, Butbarkharai, Madan Deka and Parshing Roma meet the then Governor of Assam, B.K. Nehru at Raj Bhawan, Shillong and submitted a memorandum to create " Lalung Autonomous Hill District" and urgerd to take necessary step for that. this delegation also met the chief minister of Meghalaya Mr. William Changma and the Health Minister of Assam Mr. ChatrashingTeron and requested them to create the Lalung Autonomous Hill District.

The Tiwa people became gradually conscious of their ethnic identity. They started articulating their identity to gain political power and overcome their socio-economic backwardness. After formation of LalungDarbar in 1967, the Tiwa people tried to organised themselves in different fronts. The Tiwa leaders realized that without co-operations of different sections of Tiwa people, it would not be possible to run their movement. But in 1971, a difference of opinion arose between the hills Tiwas and the plains Tiwas. In that time Mr. GiridharPatar, as young educated Tiwa with his friends MrBudhiramBordoloi and KhirodPatar organized a convention to form 'Tiwa (Lalung) YuvaChatraSanmilon'. After discussing the matter they convened a public meeting at Barapujia in 1971. In around 1971 the Tiwas were divided into two groups- Hills Tiwas and Plains Tiwas.

BudhiramBordoloi and GiridharPatar both president and Secretary of the Tiwa YuvaChatraSanmilon tried to bring unity among the Tiwa people of both hills and plains. They tried to make the people understand that the split between the hills Tiwas and plains Tiwas was only due to misunderstanding. So, for the unification of hills and plains Tiwa they convened a public meeting at Shahari village, Amsoi in 1977 in that meeting they changed the name of Tiwa YuvaChatraSanmilon and renamed as "All Assam Tiwa Sanmilan" with the Tiwas. This organization worked for the unification of all the Tiwa people and asked them to maintain their cultural identity. They wanted to revive the lost culture of the Tiwa people.

In 1977, the "LalungDarbar Youth Frony" was formed in a special convention which was held under the banner of LalungDarbar.

This LDYF was the youth wing of the LalungDarbar. The first president and Secretary of this organization was RabatsinghDeuri and MukundaBordoloi respectively. This youth front also demanded the creation of Lalung Hill Autonomous District. At the 9th general conferences of LalungDarbar held at Umsuai, 1978, there was great debate regarding the agitation programme. Majority members of the LalungDarbar did not agree for agitation but the youth wing was in favour of agitation to achieve its goal. Due to this controversy, it came out from the Darbar to establish its own identity. In 1980, it was re-organised and changed its name as "Lalung Youth Front".16TulsiBordoloi an educated Tiwa Youth of Jagiroad was elected as secretary respectively. Later on both the organisation united and on 24th June, 1983, the LalungDarbar and Lalung Youth Front jointly submitted a memorandum to the Prime Minister of India Mrs. Indira Gandhi for the creation of the Lalung Autonomous Hill District.

When the Assam movement was started in 1979, majority of the Tribal people participated in the movement against deporting the foreigners. The Tiwa people of Nagaon and Morigaon actively participated in the Assam movement. The Tiwa people of west part of Nagaon played active role in Neilly's violence. When the Assam Accord was signed in 1985 the Tiwa people were dis-satisfied over the article 10 of the Assam Accord which emphasised on the eviction of tribal people from forest land. From that time they became conscious for their self-determination.

On 30th October 1985, the Lalung Youth Front tried to co-ordinate all Tiwa people and all Tiwa organization into one common platform and held a public meeting at Jagiroad. In that meeting the Tiwa people formed the "Autonomous Lalung District Demand Committee" (ALDDC) as GiridharPatarand Narayan RaduKakat as president and secretary respectively. The main aim of this organization was to gain autonomy. The leaders of the organization decided that as majority of the Tiwa people are living in plains and so they would change their views and decided to demand the Autonomous Lalung District instead of Autonomous Lalung Hills District.17From that time the ALDDC has submitted several memoranda to the central and state government to formed Autonomous Lalung District. They demanded to include part of

KarbiAnglong, Nagaon and Kamrup district to the proposed Lalung Autonomous District. But significantly the ALDDC did not include any part of Khasi and Jayantia hills of Meghalaya which was formally demanded by the Darbar.

The Tiwa students and Lalung people realized that the main struggling fronts of the Tiwa people are becoming inactive. They failed to place the demand strongly in front of the central as well as state government. So, on 25th February 1989, the "All Tiwa Student Union" (ATSU) was formed with broad out look at the Tribal Rest House, Nagaon. The birth of ATSU was the result of the failure of ALDDC (Autonomous Lalung District Demand Committee) in fulfilling the aspirations of the Tiwa people. From its beginning this organization was very active and this organization succeeded in arousing the feelings of nationalism among the Tiwa people. The first conference of the ATSU was held on 16th and 17th March, 1990 at Raha.18 Madan Bordoloi and HemakantaDeuri was the first president and secretary of the student organisation. In the first conference the ATSU demanded the creation of an autonomous district to preserve the socio-economic and political rights of the Tiwas. The conference adopted a resolution to launched a mass of the constitution be upgraded granting more legislative, administrative and financial powers by the amendment of the constitution. They submitted a memorandum to the cultural and state government demanding the creation of a separate Tiwa autonomous district under the provision of the sixth schedule of Indian Constitution. But the Govt. did not respond to the call given by ATSU and so the ATSU launched several agitation programmes to strengthen their demand.

Though the Autonomous Lalung District Demand Committee, All Tiwa Student Union, All Tiwa Woman Association, the Lalung Youth Front (LYF), Tiwa Sanmilon had submitted several memorandums to the Central and State Government, but there was no reaction till July, 1992. On 13th September, 1992 the ATSU had organized a special convention at JagiroadCollege premises to discuss the autonomy problem. The convention resolved to continue the agitation until the autonomy demand was fulfilled. From that time the ATSU organized group meetings, Conventions and public meetings at different places of Morigaon, Nagaon and Sonapur area of Kamrup district on 11th March, 1993, the chief Minister of Assam

Mr. HiteswarSaikia announced in the public meeting at Lakwa of Dibrugarh district, that Government was considering to grant autonomy to the Mishings, Rabhas and Tiwas.19For that announcement the leaders of Autonomous Lalung District Demad Committee (ALDDC) became very happy and met the Chief Minister at Janata Bhavan on 10th May, 1993 and requested to create an autonomous Tiwa district. The delegation of ALDDC was led by GiridharPatar and Narayan RaduKakati both president and secretary respectively.

Gradually the ATSU had noticed that the leaders of the ALDDC were going away from the link of ATSU. The leaders of ATSU surprised that the Government had maintaining close contact with the leaders of ALDDC. So, on 30th August, 1993 the ATSU and ATWA convened a press meeting at ASEB Guest House, Jagiroad and chalked out new agitationalprogrammes. They protested the Government action for dividing the Tiwa people and asked the Government to grant autonomy to the Tiwa people immediately. They alleged that the Chief Minister was playing his own game in the name of autonomy among the different tribes of Assam. They demanded to stop the cavalier attitude of the Government towards the Tiwa people.

When the Tiwa movement was going on in full swing, the Government of Assam responded to the demand of the Tiwa community. Accordingly, the Govt. of Assam invited the leaders of ALDDC and ATSU to discuss the autonomy problem on 10th December, 1993. On that day the Govt. of Assam constituted an Autonomy Committee under the Chairmanship of MukutSarmah, the Revenue Minister of Assam. The other members were Mr. GomeswarPegu, Minister of State for Tribal Welfare and Backward classes, Mr. JatinHazarika, adviser to the Chief Minister, T.L. Baruah, the Commissioner of Home and Pollitical affairs and the special Secretary to the Chief Minister.20 On the other hand three different committees were also constituted for Mishing, Rabha and Tiwas on that same day.

The Government had also forwarded a draft proposal to all the autonomy demand committee regarding the problem of autonomy. Following this a meeting was held on 14th and 15th December, 1993 at Janata Bhavan, Dispur between Autonomy Committees and the

Govt. of Assam. They discussed regarding the modalities concerning the final draft. The Chief Minister was himself present on 15th December. The ATSU objected to some points of the Govt. draft proposal as there was no fix boundary where they would implement the powers of the council. The ATSU demanded greater autonomy and powers for the Tiwa autonomous council. But the ALDDC did not object and accepted the Government proposal.

Another round of discussion was held on 22nd December, 1993 at Janata Bhavan between five member delegation of ATSU headed by BhupenKholar and RimalAmsi and State Government represented by MukutSarma and GomeswarPegu. Govt. had assured to consider the demands of ATSU for greater autonomy.

On the other hand the ALDDC had submitted a 'Model' of autonomous council on 15th December with some modifications of their previous demands. Again discussion was held on 30th December, 1993 between autonomy Committee of the govt. and ALDDC and ATSU. On that day ATSU submitted a memorandum to the Chairman of autonomy Committee with a new type of proposal for granting autonomy. In that memorandum they clearly expressed their position and reached ot some consensus regarding the Govt. proposal. They demanded autonomy like the Bodoland type autonomous council. ATSU had completely rejected the Govt. draft proposal regarding the creation of Tiwa Autonomous Council.

On 4th March, 1994, another round of discussion was held between the Govt. of Assam and ATSU. But no solution was arrived regarding the final draft of the proposed Tiwa Autonomous Council. On the occasion of Independence Day on 15th August, 1994, after hoisting the National Flag at Judge Field, the Chief Minister Mr. HiteswarSaikia publicly announced that after discussing with the Central Govt. the State Govt. would grant autonomy to the Mishing, Rabhas and Tiwas according to the recommendation of the three man expert committee led by Bhupinder Singh. The ALDDC though submitted a memorandum for some modification of the Tiwa Autonomous Council but agreed to accept the Government proposal. The ATSU criticized the ALDDC for their division to accept the Govt. proposal without a fixed boundary. The Government was also interested with their supporting groups to grant autonomy in their hands.

The Government had signed the Rabha Accord on 16th March, 1995 and then invited the ALDDC to sign the Tiwa Accord. But interestingly ATSU was not invited. On 13th April at about 9.00 A.M. Mr. MukutSarmah, the Chairman of autonomy Committee called the AUST leaders over phone through Deputy Commissioner of Morigaon District. But ATSU did not accept such invitation. Because Govt. had no any clarification regarding the proposed autonomous council with fix boundary. So, they requested Mr. MukutSarmahtoposponed that day. But eht Government didi not give importance to the ATSU and on 13th April, 1995 the State Government had signed the Tiwa Accord with the leaders of ALDDC at about 1 P.M. From the Govt. side Mr. ArunodoyBhattacharjee, the Chief Secretary of Assam signed in presence of Chief Minister Mr. HiteswarSaikia and all the members of autonomy committee. From the ALDDC the Tiwa Accord was signed by SridamDeuri (President, ALDDC), Narayan RuduKakoti (Secretary, ALDDC), GiridharPata (Legal Adviser), MadiramDeuri and Kapana Patar.

In the accord signed on 14th April, 1995, the most important fact is that it did not mention the areas to be included in Tiwa Autonomous Council. According to the accord, there will be an Apex Council of the Tiwa Autonomous Council consisting of satellite areas of the village council called Lalung (Tiwa) Village Council (LVC). There will be no boundary of the proposed council. The Apex council will consist of 144 villages of Nagaon, Morigaon and Kamrup with 28 blocks. The ALDDC had demanded 174 villages. The Tiwa Autonomous Council (TAC) will consist of 30 elected members out of which 4 will be nominated by the Government to give representation to the people of other community. Out of these 30 seats, 15 will be reserved for the Tiwa Community and 3 seats will b reserved for women.

Each village council will consists of 10 elected members out of which 5 will be from Tiwa Community, out of 5 reserved seats one will be reserved constituency will be ex-officio members. There will be an elected president and a Vice – President. The term of office of Tiwa Autonomous Council and Village Council will be for 5 years. Moreover the signing of the Tiwa accord was strongly protested by the ATSU, ATWA and Lalung Youth Front. The general people also did not support the attitude of the ALDDC for signing an accord where there was no fix boundary of the Tiwa Autonomous Council. They alleged that the leaders of the ALDDC were more opportunists and as they had no mass support of the Tiwas, they had no right in signing the Tiwa Accord. The ATSU protested against the action of ALDDC and asked the Govt. of Assam to cancel the Tiwa Accord. When the leader of ALDDC arrived after signing the accord at Jagiroad, they were gheraud, humiliated with strong unbearable words and the mob insulted them.25 The mob threw stones and bricks at them. But the officer in charge of Jagiroad Police Station controlled the situation.

Already the interim council was formed by the Government of Assam on line of Rabhas and Mishings by an ordinance, namely, "Lalung (Tiwa) Autonomous Council", ordinance, 1995 effective from July27th m 1995 vide notification no. – AAD/ST/ 276/ 94- 95 and the Councils is expected to look after the additional duties of the village Councils till the same are constituted und eth aforesaid ordinance.

Accordingly, 28 members interim Tiwa Autonomous Council under the leadership of Mr. Narayan RaduKakoti was sworn in by the Upper Assam Commissioner Mr. BhaskarMushahari at a function at NelleyPujathali on 27th July, 1995.26The members of the TAC who took oath were Narayan RaduKakoti as Chief Executive Councilor, Kamal Patar, Basistha muni Rumdu and PanindraBordoloi as executive councilors. The other general members were MadiramDeuri, PuheswarBordoloi, Shashi Bordoloi, RuhitDeuri, BudheswarKonwar etc. The Chief Minister Mr. HiteswarSaikia, the Education Minister Mr. MukutSarmah, the Minister of Plain Tribes Mr. GomeswarPegu, the Chief Executive Member of Boroland Autonomous Council Mr. Premsingh Brahma, the Chief Executive Member of Rabha Autonomous Council Mr. SabyashashiRabha and the CEM of Mishing Autonomous Council Mr. Lakshmionath Panging were attended the oath ceremony.

Chapter 5

Tribal Development Strategies in India

The concept of *development* has different connotations in different contexts. In a narrow sense, 'it means, change, and progress, either whole or, partial'. There are people with difference of opinion regarding development. This is true since; the history of development has been shifted in thought, policy, and practice over time since the establishment of the BrettonWoods institutions after World War II. "It has constantly changed on an emphasis on infrastructure, industry, and agriculture in the 1950s and 1960s, to a "basic needs" focus on individuals and families in the 1970s, and followed by participation, sustainable development, and gender equity in the 1980s".

Fergusonhas written in the opening paragraph to his study of the development industry inLesothothat: "What is "development"? It is perhaps worth remembering just how recent a question this is. This question, which today is apt to strike us as so natural, so self-evidently necessary, would have made no sense even a century ago. It is a peculiarity of our historical era that the idea of "development" is central to so much of our thinking about so much of the world".

Later, the development paradigm shifts to economic liberalization, and civil society (Edwards 1994, Escobar 1995, Fisher 1998, Guhan 1988, Ruttan 1989, Sukhatme 1989). We can see a similar opinion in the words of the Swedish Nobel-laureate Gunnar Myrdal who once argued: "Development has implicitly been based on a series of modernization ideals or values". After the World War II, development is equated with modernization theory, and started to view states as, *developed*, less*developed* or, *developing*.

Despite numerous critiques of modernization perspectives (*e.g.*, from neo-Marxist and dependency theorists), modernization thinking remains strong in development thought and practice today. Contemporary development discourse continues to assign a central position to economic development (and the measurement of it) and is formally institutionalized in international bodies such as the World Bank, the International Monetary Fund, some organizations of the United Nations, various bilateral agencies, and in departments or ministries within each nation-state. Keeping these points and general perspectives of development, let us discuss what has, and had happened in the arena of development inIndia.

TRIBAL DEVELOPMENT – INDIAN SCENARIO

In India, the *development process* was started from the British Colonial rule. Most of those developments were designed, and implemented for easing their administration such as, construction of roads and bridges, and establishing institutions. Westernization followed later. In the post World War II-Postcolonial era, the governments of newly forming "underdeveloped" states, India and many other countries, saw modernization, particularly in terms of industrialization, as a means to economic growth. The Indian government, under the leadership of Pundit Jawaharlal Nehru, embarked upon a massive "planned development" strategy with considerable support from both within India as well as from international donors including the United States Agency for International Development (USAID) and the World Bank. Development at the time was built upon an ideal of economic progress, *i.e., greater production, economic growth, and industrialization.*

In the middle of 1960s, our development was mainly focused on industry towards issues of agricultural production due to drought and famine in eastern Indiaand a global food crisis. Thus Lipton and Toye (1990) have found that the total official aid allocated for agriculture rose from a mere 2 per cent to 30 per cent, while aid allocated for industrial development fell from 60 per cent to 30 per cent from the mid-1960s to the mid-1970s as a result, the Green Revolution technologies played an important role in development strategies from the mid-1960s, as India's planners sought to achieve self-sufficiency in food-grains. This period marked a shift in perspective amongst development planners away from 'macro level industrial growth strategies' to 'efforts focused on meeting the *basic needs of the poor'*. Thus, the government initiated programmes in the early and mid-1970s to improve food supply, nutrition, elementary education, rural health facilities, and basic infrastructure including water supply, roads, electrification, and housing.

This period was also notable for the planners and practitioners to refocus on the conditions of individuals rather than on the national economy at large, and was fueled by a pledge in 1973 by Robert McNamara, the then President of the World Bank, to allocate resources to improving productivity and welfare of the rural poor. In June of 1976, the International Labour Organization (ILO) organized a conference where it proposed a *Basic Needs Approach* to development 'aiming at the achievement of a certain specific minimum standard of living before the end of the century'. The increased attention to issues of *basic needs* was not, however, at odds with the perceived ideal of linear and ever-increasing economic growth. Advocates of a *basic needs approach* justified it in terms of relatively low-cost investments that would eventually lead to increased human and economic productivity.

Besides this, the government has taken efforts to *improve* the life of tribals. Then comes a rather relevant question, *why tribal development*? It is a social demand since, the tribals represent an early stage of socio-economic life. The progress is universal but, its pace has been differing at different times in different communities. Thus, there should be a need for a balance in progress among the three basic elements of development: organization, natural resources, and technology. It is also worth mentioning about the views of Roy Burman (1989a) on international convention on this, here before going to the details of tribal development in India: "In June 1957, an international convention (convention no 107) in respect of indigenous and other tribal and semi-tribal population was adopted by ILO. It was later ratified by a large number of countries includingIndia. The convention laid down that the member states should enable such populations to pursue their material well-being and spiritual development in conditions of freedom and dignity, of economic security and cultural specificities, which hinder them from benefiting fully from the rights and advantages engaged by other elements of the population and also help the process of integration of such populations into the national community".

HISTORY OF TRIBAL DEVELOPMENT IN INDIA

In 1951, the government of Indiahad started making efforts to raise the general standard of living of the weaker sections as well as tribal development in the form of *national extension schemes* (NES) with the objective to intensify the *block level development* activities. It was actually done to translate the spirit of the fundamental rights and Directive Principles of State Policy provided in Article 46: "the State shall promote with special care the educational and economic interests of the weaker sections of the people, and, in particular, of the Scheduled Castes and Scheduled Tribes, and shall protect them from social injustice and all forms of exploitation".

The NES was followed by the *Community Development Project* (CDP). In 1962, the block level programmes became found to be a blockade to the development of the weaker sections, and the *Tribal Development Block* (TDB) was introduced later. Since desired goals could not be realized through these programmes, the*Tribal Integrated Development Project* (ITDP) was started in 1972, and when it failed in practice another scheme, *Tribal Sub-plan Scheme for Tribal development*(SSTD), was introduced in 1972 without defining the coverage area, and plan objectives. *Integrated Tribal Development Projects* (ITDP), and *Integrated Area Development Programme* (IADP) were started functioning under this in almost all States.

Roy Burman had opined that: "there are four phases in the foci of tribal development planning in India. In the first phase, the emphasis was on providing immediate relief to the general mass of population, who were denied amenities of life during the colonial rule and at the same time to build up the productive infrastructure for the future growth. In the second phase, the emphasis was on resource mobilization and provision of social service infrastructure in the country side. In the third phase, the emphasis on educational level shifted to reduction of disparity and growth with justice. Simultaneously the commercialization of resources was stepped up. Fourth phase emphasizes programmes for meeting the basic needs of the population and poverty elevation had been stepped up. The

Advantage of the tribal development of the first phase was mainly taken by the non-tribals living in tribal areas who were having more contact with those who have administrative power" (1989b:5-6).

Different people have different views regarding tribal development. For instance, Sharma (1989:27-33) has argued that the question of tribal development has not yet received concentrated attention that it deserves, both in planning circles and in tribal studies. The real challenge of tribal development is to modernize the tribal economics and to integrate them with the larger national economy without at the same time disrupting their ecological existence, their socio-cultural systems and their traditions of socio-economic equity and innocence.

Slowly Non-Governments Organizations (NGOs) came into the development scene, during the late 1960s and 1970s in India. There are many examples but, some well established, and highly reputed NGOs are located in GujaratState. They are the *Aga Khan Rural Support Programme* (AKRSP), and the*Navinchandra Mafatlal Sadguru Water and Development Foundation* (Sadguru). Both NGOs are involved in planning and implementing village-level water resource projects, alternative biogas energy systems, and reforestation programmes, often involving citizen groups in planning, operating, building, and maintaining those activities. And, even the name of Sadguru's programme was Integrated into Rural Development (IRD), the same name used in the Government's Five Year Plan (Government of India 1978; Shri Sadguru Seva Sangh Trust 1978 and Ebrahim 2001:82).

The governmental way of development differs from the Sadguru kind of approaches, which had been more dynamic by more localized efforts, and was closer to the field reality. It has addressed accurate, specific local issues such as rural-urban migration caused by economic distress. It also sortout the needs directly from the village communities, and this was reflected in its decision to attempt lift-irrigation as an intervention.

Despite of these differences, the apolitical nature of the approach made it possible for Sadguru to work with government agencies, and to secure state support for its *service delivery* or, *welfare* activities. This approach was not adopted by all NGOs of that time. In the late 1960s and 1970s,India had witnessed a rise in NGO activities that were critical of state development approaches, and which, in some cases, were violently anti-state. During this period, state agencies continued to support such NGOs, especially those providing services and relief in flood-and drought-prone regions. Those who were linked to foreign funders, slowly involved in political activities because of their control over the people.

These new dimensions in development approaches pave the way to the idea of*participatory development* in the 1970s and 1980s. Then *participation* gets prominence in development, in terms of practice and policy. It had two reasons, first was that the benefits of centrally planned development strategies had failed to reach the poor. The emphasis of development programmes on large-scale, and heavy industry in the 1950s and early 1960s had little impact on the predominantly agricultural population, while green revolution technologies favoured regions with irrigation, and infrastructure (Bernstein 1992:56-57 and Ghosh and Bharadwaj 1992:155-156). It produced a class of rich modernized farmers, an increase in income disparities between regions, and people, and increased marginalization of the rural poor. This helped Indira Gandhi to return into power in 1971 with her campaign slogan *garibi hatao* (abolish poverty) that promised to help the poor more directly. A second reason for the attention to*participation* was that alternate *top-down* planning. It was also supported by the work, and writings of Freire in South America on *conscientization* (1973), and a set of methodologies known as *Participatory Action Research* (Ex. Fals-Borda and Rahman 1991 and Freire 1973). At the same time, however, more moderate social workers and organizations were promoting citizen involvement leading to more cost-effective economic change and service delivery. It also gave due consideration to gender equality in development, and a number of terms such as, *women in development* (WID), *women and development* (WAD), and*Gender and Development* (GAD), signifies a general transition from an emphasis on including women in development activity, to a focus on relations of power in society and seeing women as agents of political and social change (Moser 1989 and Rathgeber 1990).

We can understand from the foregone discussions that a new way of development, *participatory development* has already been initiated in our country a decade ago. Thus, we would like to illustrate our observations, and view points through two case studies from Tamil Nadu since, each of them has given us the current picture of tribal development, its effectiveness, and impact on the tribal life.

DEVELOPMENT OF LAND AND TRIBAL CULTURE

The first part of this chapter has looked at tribal impoverishment mainly through land loss. To the tribals land and forests are more than an economic commodity. They are the centre of their culture and of their very identity. They have built their economic, social and political systems around them and have developed sustainable management systems. Basic to their culture is equity *i.e.,* ensuring that every family gets enough for its needs. Secondly, the resources are treated as renewable *i.e.,* used according to need and preserved for posterity. Thirdly, as long as land and forests are community owned, the woman has some say in their management. All the tribes are patriarchal. So she is only has a higher social status than women do in other communities do but she is not equal to men. Her relatively high status depends on community ownership of their resources. These values are basic to tribal identity

All of them come under attack and a total crisis enters their life when the resource is taken away. Apart from being impoverished they also absorb a new culture. For example, once land alienation or deforestation causes a shortage of resources they fall in the hands of moneylenders. For sheer survival they begin to destroy forests and other resources that they had preserved till then for posterity. That causes more shortages and individualism enters their communities. Equity that is central to their culture gets weak. A few of them take over the livelihood of other tribals and impoverish them further. Class formation follows.

Because they destroy the resource for survival, the middle class that begins the vicious circle of their destruction for consumer goods, calls them enemies of nature. Poverty also forces many of them to fill the urban slums. Often they are evicted from there in order to keep the city beautiful. During 2006 evictions took place in Ahmedabad, Delhi, Mumbai and other cities. Most of its victims are Dalits who are 65 percent of the slum dwellers in the major cities. But today there are also many tribals whom deforestation and displacement have impoverished.

Together with equity and sustainable management of their resources also the relatively high women's status, the third base of their identity, gets weak. All the tribals and Dalits lose out but women and children suffer more than men do. The tribal woman's relatively high status as a productive member of the family depends on her work in the community owned land and forest and her role as the main decision-maker in the family. The man was in charge of society. Once these resources are lost, she ceases to be an economic asset. If jobs and land are given, they are in the name of men. So power passes from her to the man and to his son. She is reduced to being only a housewife. With it also her social status suffers. One of the tribal reactions is to internalize the male culture of the dominant society according to which her place is in the kitchen and she is not intelligent enough to take up other work. Children too suffer. Child labour increases among them. For example, because of impoverishment 56 percent of the families studied in Assam and 49 percent in West Bengal pulled their children out of school to turn them into child labourers.

TRIBAL REACTION

Many tribes have reacted to their exploitation, some of them peacefully and others violently. Violent reaction began with Nagaland demanding sovereignty already before 1947. Mahatma Gandhi seems to have been sympathetic to their demands of self-rule but other national leaders did not understand the aspirations of Northeast India where most tribes belong to the Mongoloid stock. So the Naga leaders declared independence on 14th August 1947, a day before Indian independence.

The nationalist struggle that began with it continues to this day. An agreement was reached in 1963 to create the State of Nagaland and recognise their customary law. Not much has happened after it. A ceasefire is in place for a decade but negotiations do not seem to make progress. The positions have remained almost unchanged for sixty years. Neither the Naga leaders nor the Indian State seem to be ready for a compromise. The struggle has spread from them to some other tribes of the Northeast. The Mizo who made the same demand in the 1960s gained a State of their own and recognition of their customary law.

Those who demand sovereignty have not defined it till today. The State and those opposed to it interpret "sovereignty" and "self-determination" as independence and secession. That is the main reason why India has not signed Convention 169 of the International Labour Organisation that speaks of the sovereignty and self-determination of "indigenous peoples". The State is not even ready to discuss the indigenous status. Most tribal leaders are aware that acceptance of this status can protect their land and culture but have not come out with a viable definition either to it or to sovereignty and self-determination. Hence the stalemate continues. Some tribes of Middle India who demand sovereignty interpret it as control over their economy and administration because their struggles are by and large for the protection of their land and forests. The struggle around the Narmada dam in Gujarat in western India is known internationally. Such struggles exist all over tribal India. For example, the tribals of Jharkhand in Eastern India succeeded in stopping the Koel-Karo dam and the Netarhat test firing range. Others have been less successful. For example, many tribals who have been opposing their land acquisition for copper mining at Kashipur in Orissa have been jailed. Some have been killed in police firing. Also the tribes who demanded a better deal when 6,500 hectares were acquired at Kalinga Nagar in Orissa were suppressed.

Twelve of them died when the armed police opened fire on them on 2nd January 2006. On the other side, the Fifth Schedule area won a major victory in 1996 by getting the federal parliament to enact a law on their self-rule at the village level. This law respects their traditional political systems and stipulates that the villagers be consulted before land acquisition. It is a beginning and much more has to be done.

One can probably end by quoting the Austrian anthropologist Haimendorf who did a study of the tribals in the 1940s. After a second study of the same tribes in the 1970s he asked "How do you explain the fact that their communities that were self-reliant thirty years ago today need State subsidies? Their women had a high status three decades ago. How have they lost it today?" The question is not about development but about its type. One should ask whether the colonial system continues in a new form by impoverishing the tribals to the benefit of another class. The Indian and foreign private sector that wants more of their land do not question that pattern of development. But those interested in the their progress have to search for the type that combines economic growth with the development of every human community.

TRIBAL DEVELOPMENT IN TAMILNADU

Out of the 36 Scheduled Tribes living in Tamil Nadu, The Toda, theKota, the Panniyan, the Irula, the Kurumba, and the Kattunayakan, who are residing in Nilgiris are only considered as primitive tribal groups (PTG). A bulk of the Government's funds earmarked for tribal development is directed towards the developmental activities of PTGs. Thus, tribals who are residing in other areas are receiving less attention by the Government whereas; the NGOs are helping the tribals all over Tamil Nadu. This is illustrated through our case studies.

The Irulas of Vandavasi, Thiruvannamalai District

The Irulas, a primitive tribe of Tamil Nadu, occupies second position in the State among the tribes as far as numerical strength is concerned. We can see them residing in deep forest, its finch, and in plains.

Traditionally, they are food gatherers and hunters but, later turned as cultivators and labourers. The Irulas of Vandavasi is not an exception to this. Most of them are eking out their livelihood on farm and its related activities. As the land comes under the control of private individual and as State property, the communities depending on such occupation for their basic livelihood left with no options. The process of development has not provided an alternative to these communities and left them behind without any property of their own.

Madhura Sathya Nagar settlement of the Irulas is located in Vandavasi Taluk of Thiruvanamalai District of Tamil Nadu. The nearest town, Vandavasi is at a distance of six km, and the Akilandeswari Women'sArtsCollege, Vandavasi, is the nearest land mark.

We can see the Kannimara Koil at the north, and a water tank at the western side of the settlement. A Balavadi is functioning, and a Community Hall in the middle of the settlement.

Table. Type of Houses

Sl. No.	House Type	No. of Households	%
1.	Thatched	25	55.55
1.	Tiled	02	04.44
1.	RCC	18	40.11
Total		45	100

The settlement is comprised of 45 houses, which includes 25 thatched houses, 18 Reinforced Concrete Cement (RCC) houses, and two tiled houses. The RCC houses were built by the government. Drinking water is provided with pipe-line, and the settlement is electrified. Since their hygienic consciousness is low, only one house had toilet facility. The Irulas population in the settlement is estimated as 184, of whom 86 are males and 98 are females.

Table. Gender and Population of the Irulas

Gender	Population	%
Male	86	46.7
Female	98	53.3
Total	184	100

They neither own homestead land nor cultivable lands of their own. The only option was to take up available jobs and work as daily *coolies*. They are residing in plains and closely associated with, and depending on the mainstream population for their basic livelihood. The major occupation in which they are involved presently is as agricultural coolie, working in Brick Kline and in Rice Mills. These occupations have been considered as unskilled labour and their wages are not structured. Most of them work for the same employers without any periodical change in their work as well as monetary changes.

Education is a dark area of Irulas life. It is estimated that 63 per cent of them were illiterates. Recently, one boy has managed to pass the SSLC. They openly express their negative attitude towards formal education. Illiterate Irulas are being exploited by the non-tribals residing in that area. The Irulas work in non-tribal farms and firms over several years and in the process they are indebted to their masters. Their Ration Cards and Voter Identity Cards are kept by their masters. Groceries are procured by the master through the servants' ration cards and supplied to them at a higher rate.

For instance, a person is working as labourer in the teak forest for more than six year along with his wife and a five year old son. They hardly come out of the forest for any thing. The family solely depends on 'Thalaivar', the owner of the form for their basic survival. He says; "I have not seen my Ration Card or my Voter Identity Card. It is always with my master and he sends *arisi* (rice) and dal to me through some one and says the prices of all groceries have steeply raised". In Tamil Nadu rice is sold at Rs.1/- per Kg in all the ration shops. He further says; "I do not have home and land. I am not educated and do not have any alternative occupation than this. My father and mother lead the same life in another place and now I am here and so far I never even thought about putting my son in school, because I could not see any opportunity for it. I do not think about things which are beyond my reach". His son shyly looked at us and went inside the 4×4 sq.ft single bricked, not cemented shelter and smiled at us with some hope. Basing on our experience with this tribe, we feel that the development activities have not reached them till date. Thus, we suggest that first, houses and farm land should be provided to the Irulas so that they can come out of the clutches of exploitation by the non-tribals over years. Once, they are settled at one place, they should be provided with educational and health facilities. Slowly, other developmental activities should be initiated by taking into consideration their specific needs.

The Sholagas of Gedhesal, Erode District

Gadhesal is one of the Sholaga settlements in Tamil Nadu, which is found in theDhimbumForestRangein Sathyamangalam Taluk, Erode District. Mountains, and reserve forest all around bound the settlement, which is situated approximately about 3300 fts above sea level. The geography, and the presence of wild animals in the reserve forest kept the place to remain isolated. They migrated to Gadhesal during the British period to assist the British in hunting, and other activities, and also to collect the forest produce.

Table. Population of *Sholagas* in Gadhesal

Gender	Population	%
Male	194	52.4
Female	176	47.6
Total	370	100

The population in the Gadhesal is estimated as 370, living in 99 houses. Out of these, 91 are thatched huts, and the remaining eight are small concrete houses constructed by the Forest Department. Those who live in the thatched huts still stare on these concrete houses, and are waiting for their turn for getting their own houses. Women are viewed as hard-working. Their economy is a kind of mixed one, usually shown in their life with material simplicity. They live on small-scale cultivation, animal husbandry, and collection of minor forest produce in seasons. Including the staple food Ragi, most of their products are meant for family consumption only, except beans, which they sell in the market.

The 'development' among the Sholagas is distinguishable. Some were governmental, and non-governmental, which include land and other amenities present in the settlement.

The relative isolation in terms of geography and other problems confront on the effectiveness of the developmental activities. The inhabitants need to go to distant places even for obtaining their every day needs. The absence of essential basic amenities in-and-around the settlement set unresolved challenge to the Sholagas, and their development.

The settlement comes under the control of the State Forest Department, which posses all the land but, the forest dwellers, Sholagas, now leading a settled life even though, they do not have a piece of their own land! They told us that they were very eager to cultivate ragi, beans, and a few other vegetables, and greens but, the problem was that they did not have sufficient land for excess cultivation rather than their domestic use.

Indeed, the wild animals such as, boar, and elephant also caused problems whenever, they went for cultivation. The Forest Department Officials always watch every action in the settlement and ask them to get prior permission for every innovation. The absence of implements, both mechanized and other, for cultivation too causes dilemma since, they are skilled to perform only small-scale cultivation.

Hence, they usually pray for the mercy of nature for a better yield. Yet, the Forest Department vested land keeps them out from enjoying the developmental schemes implemented by various Government Departments.

Table. Availability of the Basic Amenities in and around in Gadhesal

Amenities	Location	Distance from the settlement (in Kms)
Agricultural Office	Hassanur	15
Bank	Arepalayam	10
Bus Stop	Gadhesal	In Settlement
Drinking Water	Gadhesal	In Settlement
Electricity	Gadhesal	In Settlement
Forest Office	Hassanur	15
Higher Secondary School	Hassanur	15
Milk Society	Arepalayam	10
Panchayat Office	Arepalayam	10
Police Station	Hassanur	15
Post Office	Arepalayam	10
Primary Health Centre	Germalam	10
Primary School	Gadhesal	In Settlement
Provision Store	Arepalayam	10
Public T.V.	Gadhesal	In Settlement
Ration Shop	Arepalayam	10
Revenue Office	Talavadi	40

Some of the other issues related to the amenities are the absence of Health Centre, Ration Shop, Milk Society, andHigherSecondary School. The people feel very bad in respect of medical aid since, they are suffering from malnutrition, skin-disease, and other ailments. The designated health caretaker expresses all her helplessness in attending the Gadhesal settlement because, she is also given in-charge of neighbouring settlements. In off-seasons, the Sholagas find it difficult to run the family.

Relatives are ever ready to extend help by providing ragi, and other essentials when in excess but, such an act will not be possible in all times. They are literally immobile during the rainy season when the mud, and cow dung made the streets impossible to walk. All these lead to two demands, first, a road with proper drainage that eases their movement and also the animals, and second, establishment of a permanent ration shop in the settlement. Most of the households are having milch-animals but, a single family alone is selling the milk daily, even by travelling a distance of 10 kms. They opine that if a society is functioning within the settlement, the others can also sell milk, and it would also help to increase the number of animal stock. Thus, the settlement badly needs a milk society.

Table. Educational Status of the *Sholagas* of Gadhesal

Age group	Sex	Educational Status Not schooling	Lower Primary (Std. 1-5)	Upper Primary (Std. 6-8)	Secondary (Std. 9-12)	Graduation	Illiterate	Total
0-6	M	18	08	—	—	—	—	26
yrs	F	19	06	—	—	—	—	25
7-12	M	—	10	06	—	—		16
yrs	F	—	11	05	—	—		16
13-19	M	—	05	15	04	—	01	25
yrs	F	—	07	04	05	—	02	18
20-39	M	—	39	17	03	01	19	79
yrs	F	—	26	04	01	—	42	73
40-59	M	—	14	05	02	—	14	35
yrs	F	—	04	—	—	—	29	33
60 &	M	—	01	—	—	—	12	13
above	F	—	—	—	—	—	11	11
Total		37	131	56	15	01	130	370

The Sholagas hardly gave due importance to formal education. Our investigation reveals the reality that out of 370-total population, 130 (35.14 per cent) persons are illiterate. The illiterate women (84, *i.e.,* 22.7 per cent) are almost double in number of men (46, *i.e.,* 12.43 per cent). However, 54.86 per cent (203 out of 370) are managed to be literate but, the fact is that 187 (50.54 per cent) of them could not go beyond the level of primary education. This is only due to the presence of theTribalSchoolin the settlement. Informants told us that the majority among the upper primary level achievers done their schooling in theTribalSchoolitself since, it has been upgraded to a secondary school. We observed only 16 (15+1 graduate) of them, 4.32 per cent of the total population that was able to climb up to the secondary level because, there was no facility either inside the settlement or, the nearby area for getting higher education. They have to go to distant places for getting higher education. Thus, only one individual had managed to climb up to the graduation level, so far! Our observation coincides with that of Thaware (2004): "Educationally, tribals are still backward and this contributes to their backwardness further".

A well-equipped tribal residential school of the government, functioning in the settlement, offers formal education up to 8th

Standard. This school was started in 1969, and offered education up to 5th standard. Latter on, it was upgraded in 1998 as a secondary school, equipped with facilities for schooling up to 8th standard. Since it is a residential school, the students are served with breakfast, lunch, and supper. Consequently, all the children are sent to the school, not for getting educated but, for the sake of food. It also provides uniform, books, etc.

Now, there is no stagnation, and dropout until 8th standard, when all of them get free pass to the next standard, irrespective of their standard. We observed that it made a 'double impact' over the Sholagas. First, they could get educated up to 8th Standard. Second, it puts a permanent end to their studies after 8th standard, a *forced dropout*!

Above and beyond, the difficulty in getting Community Certificate from the Revenue Officials brings about another huge hurdle in the realm of development. Thus, the Sholagas are not capable to have the benefit of many constitutional privileges like reservation in education, employment, and so on. We found a couple of them, who are seeking admission to higher courses, patiently waiting for the mercy of authorities, only because of this reason. We also informed by our informants that, because of the same reason, a few of them had been forced to stop their education, forever. Do not think that the snags of development come to an end here but, the list would be getting larger and larger every day. Any one can easily identify that these are a few issues in the sphere of tribal development in general, and the Sholagas in particular. Nobody disagrees that they make plain about the inadequacy of our adopted policies, and approaches. Sadly, in practical life, we don't have much time to attest, and address these burning issues of the tribals since, we are dreaming about many things such as, 123 Nuclear Deal Agreements, Agni and Prithvi Missiles, Rocket Launchers and Chandra Yan, Information Technology (IT) Corridors, and Special Economic Zones (SEZ). As a result, the problems remain, and get enlarged.

The resolution of these issues starts with the identification of problems, which failed many times in the development arena. The immediate remedy is nothing but, *putting the people first* who told us that the problems they were facing in their day-to-day lives. The land problem can be solved even in a day or, a week or, it might take a few months by issuing *patta* to the real inhabitants. Since, the tribals are much concerned about the Nature, and its preservation than a government officials, the issuance of *patta* provides two benefits, in one way by solving a major problem of land ownership, and the other by 'appointing' ever-permanent guards of Nature.

Starting a ration shop and health care center is also easy. But the problem actually lies in the attitude of the officials and administrators, who never paid any attention on the real essentialities. The Sholagas themselves can take effort to establish a milk society either by them or, by seeking help from some government or, other organizations. The health, and hygienic conditions can be improved either through awareness campaigns or, by constructing appropriate drainages, and latrines. Providing school bus from the settlement will discard one of the hazards that are de-motivating the pupils to go for higher studies. The young ones of the Sholagas are deficient in developing their career. Thus, the schools must have an *employment-cum-career guidance officer*, who can give proper direction to the students to think about their career. The awareness campaigns, and timely interventions of the officials have to play an equally important role in bringing the people come closer to the higher levels of education.

Chapter 6

Tribal Law, Society and Culture in India

LAND RELATIONS, CUSTOMARY LAWS AND TRIBAL CULTURE

Apart from their legal status and the presence or absence of protective mechanisms, the general state of the tribal customary laws varies according to the nature and extent of their application and the manner in which they are invoked and adhered to. Besides, changes introduced in the colonial age and continued after 1947 have modified their customary law and traditions, and have, by implication, changed many values governing their culture. Among the first to change are land relations because except in the Sixth Schedule areas, the formal law recognises only individual ownership while central to the culture of most tribes is community control over the common property resources (CPR). Since the culture of equity and the relatively high status of women depend on the CPRs, changes in the management have implications for these values.

Despite the commonality of a community ethos, the land tenure system is not uniform all over the region. Some tribes have complete community-based ownership and others combine individual with clan ownership. Among the former are the Aka who lacked the very concept of individual ownership till recently and only had usufructuary rights. Each family cultivated as much land as it needed in the *jhum* season after which it reverted to the community. However, a family could use wetlands on the banks of the river for settled agriculture but it continued to belong to the village. Among the latter are the Angami of Nagaland and the Dimasa of Assam who combine community with individual ownership. The Garo of Meghalaya made a distinction between the regular residents of a village and strangers. The former could cultivate as much land as they needed but the latter required the *nokma's* (chief heiress) permission and had to pay a tax. In theory land remained with the owner-lineage but was in practice with an individual family as long as it cultivated it. Traditionally the Karbi villages did not have a fixed boundary or name since they kept shifting. Communal ownership was the norm among them. The Boro followed the Ahom custom of allotting 3 *purahs* (about an acre) of land to each family in return for free labour for about a third of the year.

Community ownership was basic to intra and inter-generational equity as well as the relatively high status of women. When a community controls the resource, every family is able to use it according to its need since it cultivates land according to the number of mouths to feed. Community ethos ensured inter-generational equity because they treated even individually owned land as their community livelihood coming down from the ancestors that they could use to meet their needs but had to preserve for posterity according to ecological imperatives.

Studies show that tribal natural resource management was by and large geared to this need. For example traditionally *jhumia* tribes cultivated only up to 20-degree slopes and planted root crops before the rains to ensure soil protection. Then followed other crops harvested in different months in order to ensure food supply for most of the year till fruits, edible leaves and roots became available. Most tribes left the plot fallow for 18 years after cultivating it for 3 years in order to let forests regenerate.

Only the Tripura and some other tribes in the predominantly bamboo growing regions followed a five-year cycle suited to that crop (Banerjee, Das Gupta and Roy 1986: 26-27). Some tribes in Mainland India practised also bush-fallow *jhum.* They left the plot fallow for 5-6 years for bushes, not forests, to grow. One is not aware of this system anywhere in the Northeast. *Jhum* is considered environmentally healthy for the hilly terrain.

Before the *jhum* season, the village council made up of men alone decided which area was to be cultivated that year, which family was to get how much land according to the number of mouths to feed, which family with excess labour would help which one with very few adults and the day before which cultivation would not begin. After it the man of the house chose the plot and performed the worship to mark the beginning of cultivation. At this stage the woman took charge of production and organised work. As a result, gender-based division of work was more gender friendly among the *jhum* cultivators than in settled cultivation-based communities (Fernandes and Menon 1987: 68-70). In settled agriculture, the man does what is considered difficult work such as ploughing and digging. Back breaking work like transplantation and harvesting that involves long hours of standing in wet fields is left to women. In *jhum,* on the contrary, hoeing, digging and other difficult work is shared by men and women. Even keeping watch at night that is considered dangerous work is shared in the sense that the whole family shifts to the *jhum* field at that time.

Differences did exist so did inequalities. For example, the tribal woman's status was higher than in caste societies but she was not equal to men. That too had exceptions. For example, despite their CPR based *jhum* economy, traditionally Aka women's status was low. So one cannot make a statement about all the tribes with no exception. One can only say that if resources like land, forests and water bodies are community owned women have a say in their management. The relatively high status it confers on them is based on their role as economic assets in the family, not in their society. Most tribal traditions kept a clear separation between the family and society. Women were in charge of the family production and economy while men controlled social power. Even the matrilineal tribes like the Khasi, Garo and Jaintia of Meghalaya are patriarchal. Descent and inheritance are through women, they are uxorilocal but social power is with men. They control the village council and other decision-making bodies and also take decisions concerning land alienation.

CONSTITUTIONALIZATION OF CUSTOMARY LAWS AS CULTURAL RIGHTS

The Constitution of India has given a mandate to the cultural rights of the Scheduled Tribes under Article 13 for the customary law at par with the other branches of the civil law. Article 13(2) has the provision that the State shall not make any law, which takes away or abridges the rights conferred by this part and any law made in contravention of this clause shall, to the extent of contravention be void. In this context Article 13(3)(a) defines "law" as any ordinance, order, bye-law, rule, regulations, notification, custom or usage. The customary rights have the force of law and can be taken as judicial notice by the courts under section 57 of Indian Evidence Act, 1872. This legitimization of the customary laws only reinforces the cultural rights of the indigenous peoples in India.

The Bhuria Committee in 1995, under the chairmanship of Dileep Singh Bhuria, in view of guaranteeing tribal autonomy, recommended firstly, a democratic decentralization in the tribal areas taking cognizance of the indigenous institutions, leadership, and ethos; secondly, recognition, continuation and validity of usages of customary laws and traditional tribal conventions and an attempt at their harmonization with the modern system; and thirdly, participatory and effective implementation of the Panchayati Raj institutions in the tribal areas in view of meeting the socio-economic goals for addressing the problem of illiteracy and ill health (Menon and Sinha, 2003: 78-80). Some of the recommendations of the Bhuria Committee were adopted in the Provisions of the Panchayats (Extension to the Scheduled Areas) Act, 1996, popularly known as the PESA Act. These provisions have been specially framed for Scheduled Tribes of the Schedule V and Scheduled VI Areas.

The PESA 1996 provides for safeguarding the social, economic, political and cultural rights of the tribals through provisions, such as (1) a State legislation on the Panchayats in consonance with the customary law, social and religious practices and traditional management practices of the community resources; (2) a competent Gram Sabha for safeguarding and preserving the traditions and customs of the people, their cultural identity, community resources and the customary mode of dispute resolution; (3) consultation with the Gram Sabha before starting any welfare related activities in the village, namely, acquisition of any land, grant of mining lease, identification and selection of beneficiaries for poverty alleviation programmes and other schemes, management of the water bodies, etc.; and (4) State legislature following the pattern of the Sixth

Schedule while designing the administrative arrangements in the Panchayats at the district level in the Scheduled Areas, implying the establishment of the Autonomous districts and Autonomous Regions and District Councils and Regional Councils in the Scheduled Areas..

Thus, the Indian state in fact gives legitimacy to the cultural identity and rights of the tribals, which is the basis of their assertion for political rights, especially, in the context of the parliamentary democracy.

INTERNATIONAL SUPPORT FOR CULTURAL RIGHTS

Apart from the legitimacy to the cultural rights, several international conventions have supported the customary laws of the indigenous people. For instance, the Convention on the Biological Diversity (CBA) adopted at the Earth Summit (1992) brought conservation of biodiversity into focus. The convention, which has been ratified by India, envisages that nations respect, preserve and maintain knowledge, innovation and practices of the local communities relevant for conservation and sustainable use of bio-diversity (Krishnan, 2000). Rio Declaration on Environment and Development Agenda 21 and Forestry principle also encourage the promotion of customary practices conducive to conservation (ibid.).

The International Labour Organization (ILO) Convention 107 pertaining to the protection and integration of indigenous and other tribal and semi-tribal population in independent countries emphasizes on protection of the social, political and cultural rights of the indigenous people. In a similar fashion the ILO 169 Convention, too, has special provision for safeguarding the social, cultural, religious and linguistic identities of the tribal people. The Convention extends its support to these people to have control over their institutions, ways of life and economic development.

The ILO and UNO have been trying to protect and integrate the indigenous and the tribal people into their respective national communities and improve their living and working conditions.

The General Assembly, before the end of the sixty-first session, adopted the United Nations Declaration on the Rights of Indigenous Peoples. The General Assembly affirmed the equality of indigenous peoples with all other peoples and the right of all peoples to be different, and to be respected as such. There was recognition for the urgent need to respect and promote the inherent rights of indigenous peoples which derive from their political, economic and social structures and from their cultures, spiritual traditions, histories and philosophies, especially, their rights to their lands, territories and resources (UN 2008).

It was reiterated that control by indigenous peoples over developments affecting them and their lands, territories and resources would enable them to maintain and strengthen their institutions, cultures and traditions, and to promote their development in accordance with their aspirations and needs. The General Assembly 2007 also recognized respect for indigenous knowledge, cultures and traditional practices contributes to sustainable and equitable development and proper management of the environment.

Social, civil and political rights of the indigenous peoples are adversely impacted by the dominant societies. At the international arena the United Nations' reinforcement of the cultural rights of the indigenous populations emerged powerfully as human rights.

CULTURAL RIGHTS AS HUMAN RIGHTS

Indigenous peoples have, according to Article 1, "all human rights and fundamental freedoms" as enshrined in the Charter of the United Nations, the Universal Declaration of Human Rights and international human rights law (UN Declaration 2007. Article 4 has special measures for safeguarding persons, institutions, labour and environment of the indigenous people. The human rights promoted by the UND 2007, enshrines the cultural rights of indigenous peoples in terms of the following rights as well-(a) social and civil rights; (b) right to indigenous institutions; (c) right to belong to a community/ nation; (d) right to preservation, protection and promotion of culture; (e) right to spiritual relationships; (f) right to free, prior and informed consent; (g) right against forced assimilation; (h) right to self-determination; and (i) right to cultural practices and repatriation. These can be briefly discussed here.

First, the social and civil rights include the right to freedom from discrimination. Article 2 provides freedom and equality to indigenous peoples from "any kind of discrimination", particularly "based on their indigenous origin or identity".

Second, indigenous institutions are important components of the indigenous communities. These show their historical and collective consciousness. In conformity with the indigenous collective ethos Article 5 provides "the right to maintain and strengthen their distinct political, legal, economic, social and cultural institutions". It also gives them right to participate in the "political, economic, social and cultural life" of the State. The Declaration maintains that the social, cultural, religious and spiritual values and practices of these people need to be recognized and protected.

Third, it is the right of the indigenous peoples to belong to a community or nation "in accordance with the traditions and customs of the community or nation concerned".

Fourth, preservation, protection and promotion of culture are the human rights issues enshrined in the UN Declaration. Article 11(1), for instance, makes provision for indigenous people's right to "practise and revitalize their cultural traditions and customs including their right to "maintain, protect and develop the past, present and future manifestations of their cultures, such as archaeological and historical sites, artefacts, designs, ceremonies, technologies and visual and performing arts and literature". This cultural right is very significant in view of preservation, protection and promotion of the culture of indigenous groups across the world. Article 13(1) provides indigenous people the right to "revitalize, use, develop and transmit to future generations their histories, languages, oral traditions, philosophies, writing systems and literatures, and to designate and retain their own names for communities, places and persons".

Fifth, it is the cultural right of the indigenous peoples to spiritual relationships. They have the right to "maintain and strengthen their distinctive spiritual relationship with their traditionally owned or otherwise occupied and used lands, territories, waters and coastal seas and other resources and to uphold their responsibilities to future generations in this regard". According to Article 31(1), indigenous peoples have the right to maintain, control, protect and develop their cultural heritage, traditional knowledge and traditional cultural expressions, as well as the manifestations of their sciences, technologies and cultures, including human and genetic resources, seeds, medicines, knowledge of the properties of fauna and flora, oral traditions, literatures, designs, sports and traditional games and visual and performing arts. They also have the right to maintain, control, protect and develop their intellectual property over such cultural heritage, traditional knowledge, and traditional cultural expressions.

Sixth, free, prior and informed consent is the prerequisite of the collective rights of the indigenous communities. Article 10 provides that the indigenous peoples cannot be "forcibly removed from their lands or territories". They cannot even be relocated without their "free, prior and informed consent". Moreover, if there is an agreement between the two parties, there should be a "just and fair compensation" and where possible, there should be the option of their return to the original place. This right is very significant in the light of rampant displacement within the framework of economic liberalization in India accelerated by the process of globalization.

Again, Article 19 seeks consultation and cooperation of the State in good faith with the indigenous peoples concerning their "free, prior and informed consent" before adopting and implementing legislative or administrative measures that may affect them. Article 32(1) insists indigenous people's right to determine and develop priorities and strategies for the development or use of their lands or territories and other resources.

According to Article 32(2), the State should consult and cooperate in good faith with the indigenous peoples concerned through their own representative institutions in order to obtain their free and informed consent prior to the approval of any project affecting their lands or territories and other resources, particularly, in connection with the development, utilization or exploitation of mineral, water or other resources. No. 3 of the same Article also provides "effective mechanisms for just and fair redress for any such activities and appropriate measures shall be taken to mitigate adverse environmental, economic, social, cultural or spiritual impact".

Seventh, forced assimilation of indigenous populations into the dominant society has been a problem. However, Article 8(1) provides indigenous peoples the right "not to be subjected to forced assimilation or destruction of their culture". According to Article 8(2) these people shall retain their own customs and institutions where these are incompatible with fundamental rights defined by national legal system and internationally recognized human rights.

Eighth, right to self-determination is the fundamental right of every indigenous community. Article 3 makes a provision for indigenous people's "right to self-determination" by virtue of which they can "freely determine their political status and freely pursue their economic, social and cultural development". Oftentimes the right to self-determination is misinterpreted as secessionism or separatism from the State. The United Nation's mind in this regard is very clear. The right to self-determination does not encourage indigenous peoples and groups to demand separate status outside the State. The United Nations envisages transparency in the perusal of indigenous people's political assertion within the framework of the State and also in their economic, social and cultural progress according to their own traditional genius, rather than any imposition from outside.

Ninth, cultural practices and repatriation are the basic rights of the indigenous communities. Article 12(1) provides indigenous peoples with the right to "manifest, practise, develop and teach their spiritual and religious traditions, customs and ceremonies". Moreover, it also gives them the right to "maintain, protect, and have access in privacy to their religious and cultural sites". Indigenous peoples also have "the right to the use and control of their ceremonial objects; and the right to the repatriation of their human remains". Article 11(2) also seeks "the access and/or repatriation of ceremonial objects and human remains in their possession through fair, transparent and effective mechanisms".

THE GROUND REALITY OF CULTURAL RIGHTS

It has been the experience of the indigenous peoples in the world at large with a few exceptions that in general there is a resistance to giving rights to the indigenous populations. The resistance comes from the dominant countries at the international arena and from the dominant societies in the national scenario. These are the pressure groups that try to block any legislations and conventions trying to make provisions for the indigenous populations. In such circumstances negotiations take place and whichever party is able to lobby and put more pressure, gets a bigger share of the cake. In the international forum as well as in domestic front we have some clear examples of the compulsions of stakeholders in not supporting the rights of indigenous peoples.

In spite of mandate at international and national levels for protection of the rights of the indigenous people, there has been rampant infringement of those rights by government machinery and private agencies. The forces of modernization and modern development pose threat to the survival of customary rights, social fabric and natural biological resources of the indigenous people.

It took more than 20 years for the United Nations Human Rights Council to adopt the U.N. Draft Declaration on the Rights of Indigenous Peoples on June 29, 2006. The Declaration emphasized the right of indigenous peoples "to maintain and strengthen their own institutions, cultures and traditions and to pursue their development in accordance with their aspirations and needs" (http://www.globalissues.org/article/ 693/rights-of indigenous-people). This declaration is not legally binding on the nation states. However, the indigenous peoples across the globe have been pressing for it "against discrimination, racism, oppression, marginalization and exploitation". There were major hurdles created by some countries primarily due to the core provision being "the right to self-determination of indigenous peoples and the control over natural resources" on their lands. These rights would imply the injustice done to the indigenous communities in the past and make a case for restoration of their lost land. Australia, Canada, New Zealand and United States argued against the declaration stating that the "notion of creating different classes of citizens" was not agreeable to them.

The 'Survival International' (2005) was critical of Britain, France and the United States for their opposition to some of the aspects of the indigenous people's rights, such as collective rights. Britain and France formerly commanded vast empires and colonies and subjected native peoples to cruel denial of rights and oppression. One of the main reasons as to why these countries seem to be opposing the collective rights is that the collective rights could threaten access to valuable land and natural resources for exploitation.

The history of Independent India is a silent witness that it is never enough to have the law for the well-being of the tribal community and promotion of their culture. The main rationale for customary laws is the long established customs of certain communities reflected in the cultural ethos and traditions of the indigenous people. They enable them to live their lives in conformity with the established customs of their community. Customary laws safeguard the social, political, economic and cultural rights of the indigenous people. They provide a sense of well-being and autonomy of the community. The customary laws protect and preserve the values of indigenous communities, such as collective consciousness, harmony, reconciliation, collaboration, etc. despite all odds. Customary laws facilitate the tribals' contribution towards preserving environment and bio-diversity.

The customary laws came into existence when certain customary norms and practices from long usage obtained the force of law. Oral traditions were the foundation of the customary laws in the context of the tribals. Ancient customs were generally the base of many laws in many systems of jurisprudence. In Indian jurisprudence, immemorial custom is not merely adjunct of the ordinary law but a constituent part of it. The Indian courts, according to B. J. Krishan, regard a custom valid on two criteria-firstly, its reasonableness; and secondly, its long usage. The customary laws have to be reasonable and the courts do not regard a custom as valid unless the custom has been in usage for a long time in its extent and mode of operation. The customary laws are neither codified nor are the customs listed out separately by legislation of India. It may be recalled that the customary rights were recognized as early as 1872, when Indian Evidence Act was enacted. Section 13 of the Act deals with the facts relevant for the proof of the customary laws. The Indian Forest Act, 1927, under section 12 to 16 recognizes the right to pasture and forest produce at the stage of settling rights before a given area of the forest is classified as the reserve forest. These rights are no doubt customary rights.

Despite the Constitutional legitimacy to the customary laws there has been sometimes silent and often hostile reaction to the existing cultural rights. The example of the hostile distortion of the PESA Act is quite glaring.

PESA Act in Jharkhand

Although the State legislation on the Panchayati Raj in India needs to be in conformity with the PESA 1996, many States have not been serious and sincere in its implementation for protecting the autonomy of the tribals and safeguarding their social, political, economic and cultural rights. The State Panchayati Raj Acts of Jharkhand, Andhra Pradesh, Orissa, Gujarat and Madhya Pradesh, for instance, made some crucial omissions in delegating power to the Gram Sabha. Such enactments are contravenous to the customary laws of the indigenous people. The record of the Jharkhand Government in this regard has been extremely poor. The Jharkhand Panchayati Raj Act, 2001, does not delegate powers to the Gram Sabha in matters related to the acquisition of land, ownership of minor forest produce, power to grant licence for mining and management of the water bodies.

In the Jharkhand Panchayati Raj Act, Gram Sabha as a unit of self-governance does not have any safeguard to prevent the transgression of its powers by the higher tiers of Panchayati Raj structure. Such grave omissions in the Act leave Gram Sabha at the mercy of Zilla Parisad and the State Government. It reveals a serious flaw in the entire process of legislation for self-rule in Jharkhand and lack of conceptual clarity about self-governance among the bureaucracy and the politicians. Nearly all the provisions of the Jharkhand Panchayati Raj Act, 2001, are contravenous to the Extension Act, 1996, which makes the Act not only antithetical to the customary laws but also anti-people in nature.

Tribals have a right to self-rule in the Scheduled Areas. However, there are rampant violations of the PESA Act, 1996, in mining and land acquisition in the Scheduled States of Chhattisgarh, Jharkhand and Orissa. Clause 4.e.(1) of the Panchayats (Extension to the Scheduled Areas) Act, 1996, provides that "every Gram Sabha shall approve the plans, programmes and projects for social and economic development before such plans, programmes and projects are taken up for implementation...".

Again, clause 4.(i) provides that "the Gram Sabha or the Panchayat at the appropriate level shall be consulted before making the acquisition of land in the Scheduled Areas for development projects and before re-settling or rehabilitating persons affected by such projects in the Scheduled Areas; the actual planning and implementation of the projects in the Scheduled Areas shall be coordinated at the State level." According to clause 4(k), "the recommendations of the Gram Sabha or the Panchayats at the appropriate level shall be made mandatory prior to grant of prospecting licence for minor minerals in the Scheduled Areas." Clause 4.m(III) endows Gram Sabha "the power to prevent land alienation of land in the Scheduled Areas and to take appropriate action to restore any unlawful alienated land of a Scheduled Tribe".

Despite the above provisions for the rights of the tribals, the Panchayati Raj elections in Jharkhand are yet to take place. In general. in most of the Scheduled Areas across the country no Gram Sabhas have been constituted in line with the PESA Act, clause 4(c). The Gram Sabha is not being convened. The Gram Sabhas are not even consulted for approval of plans, programmes and projects for social and economic development, leave alone taking their consent. If at all they are consulted on matters of land acquisition, there are rampant manipulations and terrorization. The recommendations of Gram Sabha are not made mandatory prior to granting prospecting licence or mining lease in many cases.

For instance, in Chhattisgarh in a short span of time 112 MOUs are signed only in Jashpur district earmarking 6,022 sq. km. land out of 6,093 sq. km. to be acquired for mining and industries. The Gram Sabha is not at all taken into confidence in the negotiations in the Scheduled Areas. Further, in Bastar district of Chhattisgarh 644 villages are cleared due to the Salva Judum-Maoist conflict and since the Gram Sabha does not exist there due to the conflict, there is a forced evacuation and displacement of the people of these villages. In Jharkhand about 71 MOUs are signed in the recent past for acquiring 98,547 acre of land. The Gram Sabha is non- existent because there have been no Panchayati Raj elections there. In Orissa, too, the story is no different. In Orissa at least about 33,268 acres of land is to be acquired at present by the corporate sector completely ignoring the role of the Gram Sabha in the matter.

Setback of the PESA Act

The efforts of some non-tribal groups for de-reserving the post of the vice-presidents for the Scheduled Tribes at the levels of up-mukhia, up-pramukh, and up-adhyaksha zilla parishad, have made a breakthrough.

According to the PESA 4(g), the reservation of seats in the Scheduled Areas at every Panchayat shall be in proportion to the population of the communities in that Panchayat for whom reservation is sought to be given under Part IX of the Constitution: Provided that the reservation for the Scheduled Tribes shall not be less than one-half of the total number of seats; provided further that all seats of Chairpersons of Panchayats at all levels shall be reserved for the Scheduled Tribes (Appeal against Amendment of JPRA 2010.

To give effect to the provisions of PESA the state legislative assembly of Jharkhand passed the Jharkhand Panchayati Act 2001 (JPRA) which included the following provisions: Firstly, the JPRA 21 (B) Reservation of Posts of mukhia and up-mukhia in Gram Panchayat (In Scheduled Areas), according to which the post of mukhia and up-mukhia of the Gram Panchayats in the scheduled areas shall be reserved for the Scheduled Tribes. The Act also provided that the Gram Panchayats, in the Scheduled Areas, where there is no population of Scheduled Tribes, the allotment of reserved posts of mukhia and up-mukhia for Scheduled Tribes shall be excluded in a prescribed manner.

Secondly, the JPRA 40 (B) provided the Reservation of Posts of Pramukh and up-Pramukh in Panchayat Samiti (in the Scheduled Areas) for the members belonging to the Scheduled Tribes. Thirdly, the JPRA 55 (B) Reservation of Posts of Adhyaksha and Upadhyaksha in Zila Parishad in Scheduled Areas shall be reserved for the members of the Scheduled Tribes. Cases were filed against the above provision in the Supreme Court.

On January 12, 2010 the Supreme Court of India gave judgement on PESA (civil appeal number 484-491 of 2006 Union of India vs Rakesh and others).

This verdict included section 44 (of the Judgement) the proviso of 4 (g) of PESA and 21 (b), 40 (b) and 55 (b) of JPRA 2001 were held to be constitutionally valid. However, an ordinance was brought by the Governor of Jharkhand, as the house was not in the session. The ordinance had to be passed by the House within six months of its notification. In the meantime the State Assembly was suspended and the state was under President Rule until the Arjun Munda Government was sworn-in on September 11, 2010.

The Ordinance proposed amendments which could bring negatively dangerous effects to the socio-cultural and political rights of the tribals in terms of their disempowerment in the local self-governance of Scheduled Areas.

Those amendments are as follows: first, the JPRA Ordinance 01 of 2010- 2(I) the word "and up-mukhiya" shall be deleted from the phrase "mukhiya and up-mukhiya" in section 21 (A), 21 (B) of JPRA 2001; second, the JPRA Ordinance 01 of 2010- 4 (V) post of up-pramukh shall be kept unreserved or shall be dealt with in accordance with the provision made by the state government; third, the JPRA Ordinance 01 of 2010- 5 (I) (last para) provided further that if the total number of Chairpersons belonging to Scheduled Tribe in the Scheduled Areas is beyond the proportion of their population in the state, further reservation shall not be provided (for the post of Chairperson of Zilla Parishad in Non-Scheduled Areas); and fourth, the JPRA Ordinance 01 of 2010-5 (V) post of Deputy Chair parsons of Zilla Parishad shall be kept unreserved or shall be dealt with in accordance with the provisions made by the state government (Appeal 2010). This amendment to de-reserve the post of up-mukhiya, up-pramukh and up-adhayaksh in the Scheduled Areas was thought to be a clear violation of Section 4 (g) of PESA according to the members of the Scheduled Tribes in Jharkhand. This amendment was tabled and introduced in Lok Sabha on 12 August 2010 and passed on August 17 after discussion and debate. This Bill was also presented in Rajya Sabha and passed.

This clearly shows that there are forces working against the assertion of the cultural and political rights of the tribals which the Constitution has guaranteed through its 73rd amendment.

TRIBAL SOCIETY IN INDIA AND ITS FEATURES

India is known to be a vast country with scanty population in the prehistoric age. During this period there were small groups of people scattered throughout the country in different spots having a characteristic look and life style.

A tribe is a group of people, usually staying in jungle areas, in a small locality, absolutely illiterate poor, hardly clad in clothes, usually dark and frail, fully living within their own community whose marriage always takes place among themselves, engaged in hunting and searching for roots, shoots and fruits as their veg food and roasted animals as non-veg food, completely oblivious of the country's political and economic condition, resisting all efforts of development and have a strong dislike for strangers and educated modern community. The number of such tribal community is very large *e.g.* Santhals, Kora people, Kol, etc. most of whom fall under scheduled caste, scheduled tribe and other backward classes. Most of the projects and efforts for uplifting their health, education and economic condition have failed both for their own unwillingness for change and absolute non-cooperation as well as lethargy, dishonesty and corruption of the intermediaries.

STRUCTURE AND FEATURES OF A TRIBAL SOCIETY

1. *History:* A tribal society is a primitive society which lived in early period of human history but can be found in large number of groups in all countries including India. There has not been any change of tribes in their belief, life style and religion which prevent them from mixing with any outsider or educated community whom they greatly dislike.
2. *Economic structure:* Tribal people live within nature and absolutely clean environment and this determines their economic activity which consists of hunting small animals and look for food like roots and wild fruits.

   They have their own social functions and festivals where they sing and dance in characteristic body movements in the same dress by girls, the males playing on musical gadget like drums, metallic gongs, flutes etc.

   They hardly have any transaction because nobody has any currency or coins and do not have any knowledge and experience of organizing market.
3. *Social Life:* The life style of tribal society is primitive, and depends entirely on their characteristic ways of non-monetary transacted life. The families live within themselves, without knowing about their neighbours in the country who are educated, developed, move in cars, have modern dress etc whom they hate and consider them enemy. The domestic division of labour depends only on age and sex.

CHARACTERISTICS OF TRIBAL SOCIETY

The tribe inhabits and remains within definite and common topography.The members of a tribe possess a consciousness of mutual unity. The members of a tribe speak a common language. The members generally marry into their own group but now due to increased contact with outsiders there are instances of tribal marring outside as well. The tribes believe in ties of blood relationship between its members. They have faith in their having descended from a common, real or mythical, ancestor and hence believe in blood relationships with other members.

Tribes follow their own political organization which maintains harmony.Religion is of great importance in the tribe. The tribal political and social organization is based on religion because they are granted religious sanctity and recognition.

INDIAN TRIBAL SOCIETY

Ralph Linton the legendary and respected anthropologist of mid-20th century has given a definition of the term 'Tribe'. According to him a 'tribe is group of bands occupying a contiguous territory or territories having a feeling of unity deriving from numerous similarities in culture, frequent contacts and a certain community of interests'. Others refer to the tribal society of India as an imperfect segment of the Hindus. Indian tribal society can be underlined as a social group with strict territorial affiliation, possessing characteristics of endogamy, with no specialisation of functions ruled by tribal officers hereditary or otherwise, united in language or dialect recognising social distance with other tribes.

HISTORY OF INDIAN TRIBAL SOCIETY

India is not only a multilingual and multiracial country, but is also multi-cultural. Peaceful coexistence of fundamentally varied culture typos and styles of living has always been a characteristic feature of the Indian stage which has often seen the arrival of new immigrants with paradigm shifts. However, their life style hardly caused the disappearance of earlier and materially less advanced ethnic groups.

The old and the new co-existed. This does not mean, however, that none of the tribes ever became incorporated in the systems of hierarchically ranked castes. As economic requirement or encroachment of their habitant by progressive communities led to systematic inter-action between tribes and Hindus, cultural distinctions were blurred, and what had once been self-contained and more or less independent tribes eventually acquired the status of castes. This influx prevailed as long as interaction thrived to be of a plain and casual temperament. Though looked upon as strange and dangerous by the tinted Eurocentric vision, they were taken for granted as part of the world of hills and forests, and a more or less frictionless co-existence was possible, owing to the lack of population pressure, or the imposing acts of the cultured civilization to incorporate the tribes to the mainstream.

Even Muslim era noticed the similar condition. Military campaign extending for a sudden exploration into the wilderness of tribal sectors would account the inhabitants temporarily to the detection of princes and chroniclers, but that was all. However, British Imperialism that confiscated the Indian empire penned down a different fate for these tribes. The extension of a centralized administration over areas, which were outside the borders previously now were, included thus leading to the deprivation of many aboriginal tribes of their autonomy. The colonial lords hardly nourished any desire to interfere with tribesmen's rights and traditional manner of living, the very process of establishment of law and order in outlying areas exposed the tribes to the pressure of more advanced populations.

EDUCATION IN INDIAN TRIBAL SOCIETY

When it comes to India, mainstream tribes live under poverty line. Their inherent occupation consists of civilization's archetypal occupations such as hunting, gathering, and agriculture without the hope of any surplus or agrarian profit. Hence their per capita income is meagre as compared to the so called cultured. Often amidst uncountable debt in the hands of local moneylenders and Zamindars, poverty is their only companion. In order to repay the debt they often mortgage or sell their land to the moneylenders. Indebtedness is almost inevitable since heavy interest is to be paid to these moneylenders.

Educationally the tribal population is next to illiterate and more often thus a prey to the cunning snares of the capitalistic money lenders. This permanent settlement has witnessed some reformatory changes owing to the steps taken by the government, as for example the reservation policy. Religious bigotries and grey horizon of orthodox mythical faiths has been a barricading fence to their quest for education. Formal education is rarely considered to discharge their social obligations. Moreover it is the evil of poverty that makes them include their off springs in their struggle for existence as helping hands. Again, most of the tribes are located in interior and remote areas where teachers would not like to go from outside.

OCCUPATION OF INDIAN TRIBES

An enormous section of Indian tribal societal population depends on agriculture as their sole way for survival. Some of the agricultural tribes are: Oraons, Mundas, Bhil tribe,Santhal tribe, Baigas, and Hos. The Toda tribe serve as a fabulous illustration of pastoral economy whose social and economic organisation almost always revolves around buffaloes. They obtain their living through exchange or barter system. In some parts of India tribal people are engaged in shifting cultivation. It is known by different names, like, Nagas refer to it as Jhum, Bhuiyas call it Dahi and Koman, Maria of Bastar refer to it as Penda, Khond refer to it as Podu and Saiga call it Bewar. Many auxiliary occupations, like handicrafts are undertaken in various tribal societies of India. These include basket-making, spinning and weaving. For example, the Tharu tribedepends upon furniture making, manufacturing musical instruments, weapons, ropes and mats. The Korw and Agaria tribes are well known iron-smelters producing tools for local use.

Indian tribal society possesses their own set of languages, which are unwritten. Hence the degree of communication both in time and space is predictably narrow. At the same time tribal societies demonstrate an outstanding economy of design and have a compactness and self-sufficiency surprisingly lacking in modern city society. Members of a tribe possess an awareness of mutual unity speaking a common language.

The continual amalgamation with other tribes, the tribal culture is undergoing a revolutionary change. Influence of the Christian missionaries has administered the growing problem of bilingualism which has developed progressively leading to indifference towards tribal language. The tribal people are imitating western culture in different aspects of their social life and leaving their own culture. It has led to degeneration of tribal life and tribal arts such as dance, music and different types of craft. According to Indian aboriginal traditions, the tribal societies inhabit and remain within a definitive and common topography.

These members generally marry within their own group, but now due to heightened contact with outsiders there are instances of tribal tying the knot outside as well. A typical Indian tribal societal group believe in ties of blood relationship amongst its members. They have faith in their having descended from a common, real or mythical, forerunner and thus believe in blood relationships with other members. Tribes follow their own political organisation which preserves eternal harmony. Religion is of supreme importance in an Indian tribal society. A tribal political and social organisation is always based upon religion, because they are granted religious sanctity and appreciation. When speaking of Indian tribal society, their variety and usage of novelty in every dance they perform is absolutely one of ecstasy, one of bliss.

TRADITIONAL VIEWS OF TRIBAL SOCIETY

In general usage, the word "tribe" is taken to denote a primary aggregate of peoples living in a primitive or barbarous condition under a headman or chief. The unnecessary moralistic overtones that this usage implies can be avoided or minimized by the use of the expression "tribal society," which is to be preferred to such synonyms as "primitive society" or "preliterate society." At the same time, the word "tribe" need not be discarded. Indeed, it has become a technical term denoting a territorially defined political unit, a usage that recalls the original Latin use of the word for the political divisions or patrician orders of the Roman state.

Traditional views. Evolutionary writers of the last century attempted to distinguish between tribal and modern society in terms of imputed differences in their legal and political institutions. Morgan (1877) saw tribal society as having social, but not political organization, a judgement echoed by Sidgwick (1891) and some later authorities on politics. Both Morgan and Maine (1861) contrasted the territorial foundations of the modern state with what they considered to be the kinship basis of tribal societies. Maine regarded tribal emphasis on the status structure (ascribed through birth) to be dominant over relations of voluntary contract that could be achieved by skill or effort. This assessment, of course, formed the basis for the great legal historian's famous aphorism expressing the transition from tribal to modern institutions in terms of the "movement of the progressive societies" from status to contract.

The remarkable advances that have been achieved in the empirical study of tribal societies in recent years make these judgements in many respects untenable. It is true that no one seriously questions the importance of kinship organization in most tribal societies, but the conclusion that this implies the exclusion of territorial ties can no longer be maintained. Almost all sedentary tribal societies have well-defined groupings based on common occupation of territory, and even where these are lacking, kinship is not coterminous with the political cohesion of a tribe. On the other hand, Maine's emphasis on the paucity of contractual relations in tribal society has been widely sustained, particularly by such anthropologists as Gluckman and Schapera (1938), who have made fundamental contributions to the study of tribal legal institutions.

Yet here much naturally turns on what is meant by "contract." Davy (1922), who seriously attacked the question, regarded status and contractual relations as inseparably intertwined in tribal society and saw what Maine took to be the complete replacement of the first by the second as a gradual process of separation and specialization. Evidence supporting this position may be cited from the pastoral Somali nomads of the Horn of Africa, where contract is explicitly employed as a political device for the purpose of supplementing, curtailing, or defining the range of blood solidarity. Even in the Lozi kingdom of central Africa, contractual relations of a kind can be discerned, cloaked though they may be in the idiom of kinship.

It is evident, therefore, even from this brief discussion, that neither contract nor territoriality provide in themselves adequate criteria for distinguishing between tribal and modern society. Nor, indeed, is it easy to find any other acceptable criteria of this order. What is necessary is an entirely different approach, for it is not the presence or absence of particular principles of social grouping that is significant here, but the form, shape, and design of society itself.

Characteristics of tribal society. While taking account of the implications of such homely synonyms as "simple society," "preindustrial society," or "folk society," a satisfactory characterization of tribal society must therefore concentrate upon criteria of form rather than of content. Here the most useful general criterion is that of "scale".

Ideally, tribal societies are small in scale, are restricted in the spatial and temporal range of their social, legal, and political relations, and possess a morality, religion, and world view of corresponding dimensions. Characteristically, too, tribal languages are unwritten, and hence, the extent of communication both in time and space is inevitably narrow. At the same time, tribal societies exhibit a remarkable economy of design and have a compactness and self-sufficiency lacking in modern society. This is achieved by the close, and sometimes unilateral, connections that exist between tribal institutions or principles of social organization, and by the concentration of a multiplicity of social roles in the same social persons or offices. There is a corresponding unity and coherence in tribal values that are intimately related to social institutions and are endowed with an intensity characteristic of all "closed" systems of thought. Tribal societies are supremely ethnocentric.

Economic relations are usually of the subsistence type, although trade and barter often extend outside the community. At the same time, economic differentiation and specialization are not developed, and by modern standards technological knowledge and environmental control remain restricted. Ideally, indeed, a position of socioeconomic equilibrium has been attained in relation to environmental conditions. In these circumstances social change tends to be on a limited scale, reproducing rather than drastically altering the existing order, and innovations are profoundly affected by the established institutions of society.

Yet the isolation and unchangingness of tribal communities must not be exaggerated; above all, it must be remembered that knowledge of tribal life derives mainly from studies made at a particular point in time. Even where the history of a tribal society is not known with any certainty, the ebb and flow of contact and influence between cultures is too widespread a phenomenon to be denied on the basis of negative evidence alone. As Forde very properly emphasized, the diffusion of technical, moral, and aesthetic ideas is something that all societies have experienced to some degree. Indeed, contact by either peaceful penetration or conquest, has, in many cases, wrought far-reaching, and often radical, changes in material techniques, values, and social institutions. Hence, if tribal societies are to be regarded as having achieved a state of balance with their physical and social surroundings, they must be understood to be in dynamic rather than static equilibrium. Only when these qualifications are accepted is "tribal society" a useful working concept that applies to a wide range of actual communities, existing as they do in reality in both time and space.

The concept applies best to such small, relatively isolated and self-contained societies as the Tro-briand Islanders of Melanesia, the Tikopia, and many peoples of the hinterlands of America and Africa, as for example, the Tallensi of Ghana. Many other traditional societies generally regarded as tribal conform less closely to the ideal type. There is, for instance, what might be described as a middle range of large centralized states, such as the east African Baganda, whose population numbers well over a million; the central African state of Ruanda, with nearly two million people; the west African state of Nupe, with a population of almost half a million; and in southern Africa, the Zulu state, which in 1870 was similar in strength to Nupe. The famous *League of the Iroquois* presents another example of this type.

In the degree and range of internal differentiation, especially in their political and legal institutions, these examples do not conform fully to the ideal conception of a tribal society. It is clear that the issue is not merely one of the degree of political and administrative centralization achieved, for there are many other tribal societies that lack these features and yet in terms of sheer numerical size assume the proportions of small nations. For example, both the Galla and the Somali of northeast Africa have a population of about three million, and the Yoruba, Hausa, and Ibo of west Africa are probably even more numerous.

Other exceptions are encountered when one deals with much smaller, but equally uncentralized, tribal peoples who live in Arabia and in north, northeast, and west Africa. Through trade, the Muslim religion, and the partial use of the Arabic language, these communities participate in the world culture of Islam. In Asia, the Hindu world provides parallel instances of small societies which are culturally and linguistically distinct, but which participate through religion and the caste system in the macroculture and society of Hinduism. Although it is common practice to regard these communities as laterally organized tribal units in the vertical world of Hindu caste, here the closed horizons of tribal societies in the strict sense are patently absent. Similar reservations have to be made in the case of rural Chinese communities, although these share many tribal principles of organization.

In these latter cases we are concerned with communities that belong emphatically to two worlds, where the category of tribal society overlaps with that of peasant society and, according to Redfield (1956), the "little tradition" in many respects partakes of the more inclusive "big tradition" in which it participates.

The chief difficulty here is that of determining where the tribal community begins and ends. With the spread of modern values, of industrialization, and of urbanization, this problem of course is becoming almost universal, and in its urban aspects gives rise to the so-called phenomenon of "detribal-ization" discussed below. In the typically isolated and self-contained tribal society, however, there is a common awareness of social and cultural identity —a common set of values—and no dispute about the social frontiers of the community. But in the fluid conditions just described, this no longer applies. Instead, there is a lack of generally accepted, precisely defined limits to consciously recognized social and cultural identity. In these cases, the frontiers of cultural and social interaction are ill-defined, shifting, and inconsistent.

The concept "tribal society," therefore, although having general utility as an idealized type of society, is in no sense an absolute category. Some societies are merely more or less tribal than others. In the classification of societies according to their scale, "tribal society" can be regarded at most as a loosely bounded area at the opposite end of the continuum to that of "modern society."

Typologies of tribal society. Various criteria have been adopted by different schools of anthropologists in the classification of tribal societies. For the purpose of reconstructing historical connections, German and Austrian workers such as Schmidt and Koppers and their followers have classified societies according to the particular configuration of institutions, or *Kulturkreise,* which they incorporate. The theoretical premise is that peoples sharing the same cluster of institutions have a common origin, an assumption that has proved better founded when the cultural traits shared have belonged to the material rather than to the social sphere of organization.

Attempts to correlate social and political institutions with types of tribal economy, usually in order to construct evolutionary scales of progress, have fared little better. Certain crude correlations undoubtedly exist between the extent of environmental control and scope of economic exploitation on the one hand, and the complexity and scale of juridical and political organization on the other. This has been elegantly demonstrated by Hobhouse, Wheeler, and Ginsberg (1915). But, in spite of this, there is no necessary and inevitable connection between particular social and political institutions, or clusters of them, and modes of livelihood and economy. Recent research in cultural and structural anthropology has consequently abandoned the holistic search for origins and has applied the comparative method to the functional analysis of institutions.

The British school and its adherents, stimulated by the pioneering work of Fortes and Evans-Pritchard (1940), have devoted much attention to problems of political organization. These studies have shown equally how the same institutions may in one tribal society provide a basis for a complex administrative and governmental structure, while in another they are invested with different functions and provide only for ephemeral political cohesion without any formal positions of leadership or authority.

More generally, this work has demonstrated how as political units increase in size (but not necessarily in population density) their internal organization inevitably becomes more complex. Among the politically diffuse Nuer of the Sudan, or among the equally equalitarian Somali nomads of northeast Africa, quite large communities may for short periods act as political entities. However, stable and concerted political unity requires a degree of centralized government and administrative specialization that these peoples traditionally lack. Here, moreover, there is often a separation between morality, or the system of values, and political cohesion. In the Somali case, for instance, the boundaries of traditional political unity stop short at the clan, although all clans share common value and moral systems and recognize the same code of indemnification for wrongs.

This concentration on the comparative functions of political institutions has greatly advanced the study of tribal societies and has led to a deepened understanding of the various institutional principles by which tribal cohesion is maintained. It is now clear, for example, that in many politically inchoate societies the threat of vengeance, rather than its execution, serves to maintain social order. In this manner the potential for violence activates the network of personal allegiances founded on residence and kinship, and thus affords a system of social control in the absence of government and courts of law. These enquiries have emphasized the significance of the counterbalancing forces in the elastic fabric of social relations, which in certain areas of all societies contribute to social stability and integration. Stripped of their particular cultural idiom, similar social processes can be seen to be at work in all human societies. One of the principal values of tribal studies is that in these alien, small-scale, and closely knit communities it is easier to perceive the mechanisms of cultural dynamics.

"Tribe" as a technical term. The increasingly detailed functional analysis of tribal institutions has naturally entailed a reformulation of concepts. In English anthropology, although not always in America or on the Continent, the term "tribe" has acquired a restricted technical meaning. Usually the term now refers to the widest territorially defined, politically independent unit in a tribal society. It no longer refers to the culturally and ethnically distinct tribal society as a whole except where, as in such tribal states as Baganda or Ruanda, tribe and society coincide. Some tribal societies, therefore, consist of several tribes; others comprise a single tribe. But in both cases the emphasis of the definition is on territorially based political unity, an emphasis that reflects tribal realities. In truly nomadic societies, of course, where there are no proprietorial rights asserted over definite areas of land, tribes in this strict sense do not exist.

Thus the introduction of the word "tribe" as a technical term makes possible a fuller and more accurate description of the nature of political cohesion within the tribe and facilitates the distinction between purely territorial loyalties and those founded on such other principles of association as kinship, clanship, or age-grouping. But, while it is always easy to describe the tribe in its territorial aspects, its political qualities are not always easily defined, especially in tribes without chiefs or other formally installed rulers. Thus, in dealing with the Nuer of the Sudan, Evans-Pritchard (1940) found it necessary to define the tribe as the largest territorial unit within which the members of the tribe would unite against external aggression and settle their internal differences by arbitration.

Tribalism and "detribalization." When tribesmen move out of their native society to join, however peripherally, a larger multitribal or plural society, the tribal identity that they carry with them is that of their tribal society as a whole, irrespective of whether or not it originally represented a single political unit. An interesting example is provided by the Luapula kingdom of Kazembe in central Africa studied by Cunnison (1960). Here peoples of various tribal origin have settled and owe common allegiance to the Lunda King Kazembe and yet also retain their external ties with their tribal homelands. There is a single multitribal Luapula political unit under Kazembe, a tribe; yet cultural, social, and political ties extend outside the kingdom from among its heterogeneous subjects. What is significant is the retention of original tribal links and their use as a principle of association within the kingdom as well as outside it, a situation that implies something more than dual citizenship.

This purely tribal phenomenon, which is not restricted to central Africa, is analogous to the common situation today caused by the spread of urbanization and industry throughout the world and the increasing involvement of tribesmen in the new plural societies that result.

Contrary to the deep-seated traditional view, many tribal societies do not disintegrate or lose their identity in these situations of contact or acculturation between widely diverse cultures. Indeed, as long as the traditional economy is not radically changed and the weight of foreign influence is not overwhelming, much of the traditional tribal culture and values persists and shows remarkable resilience in adapting to the new conditions.

Tribal cohesion has, moreover, in most cases shown itself to be capable of surviving and even profiting from quite radical changes in political organization under colonial rule. Frequently indeed, and especially where the policy of indirect rule has been followed, colonial administration has buttressed and strengthened rather than weakened tribal identity.

When tribal identity and cohesion persist outside towns, those tribesmen who move into the industrial areas in search of work do not necessarily become "detribalized." Recent studies, such as those of Mitchell and of Southall (1961) in Africa, reveal how inadequate this traditional evaluation has become. Especially where urban conditions are insecure, the tribal townsman maintains a foot in both town and country and is not unequivocally committed to urban society.

Social, political, and property interests (particularly where land or livestock are involved) tie the townsman to his rural kinsmen, whom he helps to support with his new earnings. In turn, the effective maintenance of these ties with his rural kin guarantees that the townsman's place in his tribal social structure will be kept open for him. Thus, between tribal area and urban conglomeration a kind of social continuum is established. In the multitribal or plural society of the town itself, tribal identity is now enlarged to the limits of the individual's tribal society as a whole. It becomes a category of social interaction competing for the townsman's allegiance with other social categories, such as residential ties, class, and modern nationalism.

Hence, what is carried forward into the mixed and often polyglot urban community with all its new values is not tribal allegiance at the level of "tribe" in the strict sense, but tribal institutions and patriotism on the wider scale. For the townsman, and also to an increasing extent for the tribesman who remains at home, the tribal way of life and system of values are now one institution among several that are variously opposed and conflicting.

With these developments, the gap between the real situation and the ideal concept of tribal society grows even wider. But the concept will remain useful, not only for understanding the way in which tribal societies have changed and are changing in the modern world, but also as a theoretical construct in the comparative study of social systems and institutions. Even when all truly tribal communities have disappeared, the fact that under certain conditions certain combinations of institutions have provided the basis for a viable social system at some point in man's history is of the utmost significance to the student of society. No empirically sound general theory of society can be elaborated unless account is taken of every known form of man's existence in society.

IMPACT OF THE INTERFACE ON TRIBAL CULTURE

The interface of the customary law with the formal systems has to be situated in the context of an egalitarian society that also had seeds of inequality. Some inequalities such as women's subordinate status have been modernised. Among the forces influencing these changes are the individual-based formal laws, administrative systems, education and religion. Most changes began in the colonial age. For example the office of the village leader or *gaonburah* created two centres of power since he is rarely the same as the traditional chief. Its other examples are colonisation and appropriation of their common lands and forests through military campaigns or legal fictions, and their eviction from their territories. These changes are at times accelerated by the rapid integration of their economies with the national and global markets especially today in the age of globalisation. This rapid integration continues to expose them to economic exploitation because they are either excluded from the processes of trade and governance or are marginal actors in them. This section will study some of their implications for land relations, equity and women's status.

INDIVIDUAL OWNERSHIP AND EQUITY

New land relations are not only an economic measure but also the beginning of new power equations in the tribe. The first is class formation in their egalitarian societies and the second is strengthening of patriarchy because it usually transfers power over land from the community to a few men, usually from the elite. The first steps towards it were taken in the colonial age with the enactment of individual ownership based land laws that turned the CPRs into State property.

Their basis is the colonial principle of the eminent domain. Its first facet is that land without an individual *patta* is State property. The second is that the State alone has the right to define a public purpose and deprive even individual owners of their assets. In this view land is a commodity for construction and cultivation while in the tribal worldview it belongs to an ecosystem with the local community at its centre. The formal law ignores this view and imposes its own outlook on them with no understanding of their customary law. This view prevailed because the objective of colonialism was to turn the colony into a supplier of capital and raw material for the British Indus-trial Revolution and a captive market for its finished products. With that in view the colonial regime enacted in the 19th century land laws in order to exploit the resources to suit the need of changing its economy to achieve monopoly over land for schemes such as coalmines, coffee and tea plantations, railways and roads. The process of turning land into a commodity in order to transfer it for colonial purposes began with the *Permanent Settlement 1793* and culminated in the *Land Acquisition Act 1894* that remains in force today.

However, the colonialist left the hill areas of the region more or less untouched since he needed them more for their taxes and handicrafts than for land. For example, after the conquest of Manipur in 1891 he kept its hill areas directly under the British Crown and entrusted village administration to the chieftain. The *Manipuri (Meitei) Maharaja* claimed absolute ownership of all land in the Valley. The regime recognised him as the ruler but exercised much control over land in the Valley (Guite 2000). Similarly, the colonialist who needed land in Assam for tea gardens at first and petroleum later enacted the *Assam Waste Land Settlement Rules 1838* to make its acquisition at a low price easy. That resulted in massive land alienation among the Ahom and ethnic Assamese as well as the Boro and other Kachari tribes.

Then *The Assam Land and Revenue Regulations 1886* (AL&RR) that superseded the Settlement Rules of 1870 and 1883 made tribal land alienation easy. AL&RR became the basis for other States where the need to occupy tribal land arose mainly after 1947. So it was promulgated in Manipur and Tripura as the *Manipur Land Revenue and Land Reform Act, 1960* and the *Tripura Land Reform and Land Revenue Act, 1960* without changing its basic structure. Other areas have measures such as the Sixth Schedule and recognition of the customary laws that can protect land if implemented properly.

EXTERNAL ALIENATION

The AL&RR facilitated tribal land alienation both to the State in the name of development projects. to the immigrants and to the settlers. For example in Tripura most tribal land is CPRs but it is considered State property according to the individual-based law. As a result, by the late 1960s its indigenous tribes had lost over 60 percent of their land to Hindu Bengali migrants from Bangladesh who encroached on their CPRs. Because of it the tribal proportion in Tripura has declined from 58 percent in 1951 to 31 percent in 2001. Amid such encroachment and conflicts with the settlers that followed, in the mid-1970s, the State announced the Gumti dam that submerged 46.34 sq. km of their land. They opposed it but were forced out of their land. By official count it displaced 2,558 families with *pattas*. Another 5,500 to 6,500 CPR dependent families were not counted. The insurgency in Tripura that continues till today is attributed to such land alienation.

Immigration is an issue in Assam too. The 2001 census shows 40 lakh persons in the State over and above the natural growth compared to 1971. Some 18 lakhs of them (45 per cent) are Bengali speaking Muslims presumably of Bangladeshi origin and 22 lakhs (55 per cent) Nepali and Bihari Hindus. What matters in this analysis is not the religion and origin of the immigrants but the legal status of land that makes encroachment easy. Much of it is tribal CPR that are considered State property except in the Sixth Schedule areas. Immigrants can occupy it with impunity. (Fernandes and Pereira 2005: 141-142). Since there have been similar attacks on tribal land in most States, the people of the region view the growing number of immigrants as a threat to their economy.

Development projects too have a similar impact as the example of the Dumbur dam shows. A recent study on development-induced displacement in Assam 1947-2000 showed that by official count water resources, refugee rehabilitation, environment protection, defence, transport, industries and other projects used 3,91,772.9 acres 1947-2000. The reality, as brought out by the study is not less than 14,01,184.8 acres. More than 10 lakh acres are not counted because they are CPRs that have been the sustenance of the tribes and others for centuries. By official count alienation of this land affected 3,43,262 persons. The study showed that their number is not less than 19,09,368. The 15.5 lakh persons who have not been counted in the official files inhabited the 10 lakh acres of CPRs. It was their sustenance before the law turned them into encroachers in their own habitat.

A result of such land alienation to outsiders is shortages and impoverishment that change their culture of sustainable use of the natural resources. Because of the shortages caused by land alienation, communities that had hitherto used the resources according to human needs and environmental imperatives, begin to overuse them by cutting trees for firewood or timber, often under timber smugglers and contractors. With competition beginning for the limited resources, the culture of sharing and of using them according to each one's need is weakened. Each family has to look after itself. The woman was an economic asset because she worked on the land and in the forests lost to the projects. That was also the basis of her relatively high status. With its loss she loses both her economic utility and social status.

Another result is ethnic conflicts, most of which arise from the shortages caused by land loss to the immigrants and development projects. Because of the close link with land, many tribes of the region view the shortages as attacks on their culture and identity and interpret conflicts as modes of protecting them. In order to protect their livelihood, they rewrite their history to show that they themselves are the original inhabitants of a given area. Based on this history they lay exclusive claims to its resources. For example, both the Dimasa and the Naga claim Dimapur as a land they once ruled. Some Boro leaders claim that since they are the Boro Kachari are the first inhabitants of Assam, they alone have rights in that State. Alienation of land, culture and identity and the resultant indigenous claims are the bases of the Naga-Kuki conflict in Manipur (Fernandes and Bharali 2002: 52-55), the Bodo-Santhal and Dimasa-Hmar tension in Assam (*The Telegraph,* 23rd April 2003) and the Tripura tribal demand for a homeland.

In other words, conflicts result because the local people try to defend their livelihood by reacting at first to outsiders who, they feel, prosper at their cost and then by competing among themselves for the scarce resources. Exclusive claims existed in the past too because a tribe is essentially territory related and tries to defend that territory against others. That culture of self-defence has been modernised by re-writing their history and laying exclusive claims over all the resources, not for the survival of the tribe but in order to gain access to modern benefits.

INTERNAL ALIENATION AND INDIVIDUAL OWNERSHIP

Given above are some implications of land loss to outsiders. The process continues also within the community. The very act of a few members of their elite monopolising community land is a major change in their culture of equity. This change occurs among them in spite of their customary law being in vogue because only recognition by law does not ensure protection of their livelihood. The elite among them that takes control of all decision-making interprets the customary law to its own benefit. The change takes different forms in the region.

The Boro are a tribe with a CPR tradition and their customary law has not been recognised. Among them change caused by this interface has taken the form of internalisation. Though the individual-based formal law is in vogue among them for a century, even today a large number of them continue to live on the CPRs. Most of them call themselves encroachers, not CPR dependants (Fernandes and Pereira 2005: 52).

A few individuals among them make use of this contradiction to appropriate more than their due share of that land. Some Aka individuals have started moving away from their community tradition by appropriating wetlands on the riverbanks and treating them as individual property without a *patta,* thus denying access to others who need it (Fernandes, Pereira and Khatso 2005: 7). Similar processes are visible among the Dimasa whose elite are moving towards individual *pattas*. One of their leaders has appropriated 200 acres by depriving others of their due.

Among the forces facilitating this change is the mode of implementing the Sixth Schedule. The administration uses its individual-based culture in these areas too. For example, by treating the *gaonburah* as the owner of all land though he only represents the village. Besides, decisions on land have been transferred from the village council to the DAC. Both the DAC and one person, the *gaonburah* can be influenced to give *pattas* to individuals as one sees in the N.C. Hills and Garo Hills. The individual-centred approach of different State bodies is another step in the culture of *pattas* entering their tribes. In the N. C. Hills the Coffee Board gives subsidies and loans only to individuals. However, a voluntary agency has introduced oranges on a commercial basis in some of their villages without changing the ownership pattern. Some families in these villages accept individual ownership and also confer inheritance rights on women. Thus the trend towards individual *pattas* goes hand in hand with new land use without changing the ownership pattern drastically.

In the East Garo Hills, in the 1990s the Rubber Board, the administration and the financial institutions gave subsidies and loans to individual owners and "heads of families" by which they meant men in this matrilineal tribe. To study its impact two decades later we compared some families in East Garo Hills with others in West Garo Hills. Around a third in the former are landless and income disparities are high among them.

The demand for male inheritance that began in the 1980s is growing more in East than West Garo Hills. The families in West Garo Hills that live according to their tradition have not emulated the villages in the N. C. Hills that have combined commercial crops with their traditional ownership pattern.

Some of these processes also result in a shorter *jhum* cycle and the consequent shortages. In most of Mainland India, the cycle has come down to six years. The cycle is getting shorter in many part of the Northeast but not as much as in Mainland India. A bigger population, land alienation and reservation of forests are among its causes in Tripura and Karbi Anglong. Other processes cause it in other States.

CHANGE IN THE CULTURE OF EQUITY

The first result of the changeover without adequate preparation of the community is a transition from their culture of equity to class formation. Individual *pattas* are a tool in it. In other words, what changes their culture is not individual ownership in itself but imposition of the formal law without adequate preparation. The failure to prepare them for this interface results in class formation in their egalitarian societies. It also shows that only legal recognition through the Sixth Schedule does not ensure protection of their livelihood. Through defective implementation, for example by giving loans and subsidies only to individual owners, the Boards take the Sixth Schedule away from its objective of protecting their community assets. The tribal elite too accept individual-based modernisation unquestioningly in order to get these benefits. But the masses by and large lose their traditional rights without any other gain.

On the other side, the effort of a voluntary agency in encouraging some Dimasa villages to grow oranges without changing their land ownership pattern shows the possibility of modernising their tradition. The basic issue in it is not individual or community ownership in its pristine form but equity. It can be maintained even with individual ownership if a community ethos is retained. For example, in the Dimasa tradition, an individual family is allowed to use a plot of land on which it plants trees, as long as the trees survive. By planting oranges some families have thus appropriated that land as long as those trees last. However, they took this decision as a community and are planting oranges under its control unlike the individuals among their elite who monopolise the CPRs by depriving others of access to them.

Besides, the law is not the only component in the process of class formation. Also other factors such as education contribute to it. Their approach is by and large individual-oriented. That is not a negative value in itself. It is acceptance of this value without linking it to their community ethos that results in class formation. The legal changes bring all these components into one whole. Besides, the customary law is basic to tribal identity. As a result, changes in it are an attack on their culture and identity. Hence one has to find ways of allowing the law to change within their culture of equity, not necessarily by preventing individual ownership.

IMPACT ON WOMEN'S STATUS

Since, as stated above individual ownership also reduces the little power women have in their tradition over their CPRs, gender relations become an area of concern around modernisation. For example, before the Rubber Board began to provide subsidies and loans only to individual owners and heads of families understood as men, the *Nokma* or chief heiress used to take decisions on land though men played an important role in them. With the State dealing with men alone in decisions on land transfer, the *Nokma's* husband has become the main decision-maker especially in the distribution of individual *pattas*. The tribal leaders, especially the elite, consolidate such change triggered by external inputs like the formal law and education, by internalising the dominant ideology. More than in the past, men interpret the customary law in their own favour. For example, during the Naga Nationalist Struggle, most Angami Naga men who led it went underground. Women took charge both of the family and of their society.

They also gained access to schools that were built in their area in the 1970s. As a result two thirds of the graduates among them are women. However, men continue to demand adherence to their customary law according to which the husband has to be better educated than the wife. Since there are relatively few educated young men among them, a large number of women remain unmarried. The State too seems to take the man as the breadwinner though two thirds of their graduates are women. 75 percent of the persons having a salaried job in the administration are men.

Another example of modernising the tradition and consolidating social power is elections to the legislature. For over a decade after its formation, Meghalaya did not have a single woman legislator though all three of its major tribes are matrilineal. At present it has 3 or 4 in a total of 60. But for one Rajya Sabha member Ms Rano Shaiza in the 1970s, Nagaland has not had a single member of Parliament or of the State legislature. Some women wanted to contest the parliamentary elections in 2004 but they were dissuaded from doing so in the name of their customary law that confers all political power on men. Even the DACs have not had any women members. A few who contested the Karbi DAC but could not win.

Religious conversion can add to men's power but it remains ambiguous. Both Hinduism to which sections of tribes like the Boro and Adivasi have converted and Christianity that many tribal groups have embraced in recent decades are male dominated. There is, however, a difference between the two. Being a religious body with an organised structure, Christian churches have gone beyond religion to education.

Access to schools depends on the situation of each tribe. As stated above, Angami women gained access to them because in the 1970s when many schools entered their area, a large number of men had gone underground. Since Hinduism lacks such structures and investment on education has been low, relatively few schools were opened among them and women's access to education was limited.

Despite religious change, Garo access to schools is less than that of the Angami. It is true particularly of women. Where there was access to education, for example among the Angami, women have gained greater awareness of their rights but men continue to interpret the customary law in their own favour. Thus, it is not religious change as such but the access they gained to education after it, that has made some change possible. Because of this divide between the religious and secular spheres women gain access to education without necessarily becoming equal in the Churches.

TRIBAL CULTURE

"Tribal" is the word used in India to refer to inhabitants known elsewhere as "indigenous". British ethnographers classified tribals as "animists". As per the National Census, they are classified as "aboriginals" and listed according to the tribe. The Hindi word for tribal is adivasi, meaning "ancient inhabitants."

Tribals are not Hindus, though they have imbibed many features of Hindu culture. The chief of the tribe, the Sarpanch, acts as the main advisor and mediator in disputes, a role in which he is assisted by a team of 5 advisors, each called panch. The sarpanch and 5 panchs are an integral and highly respected part of the village community and live in pretty much the same manner as the rest of the tribe.

There are many types of tribals in India, and Chhattisgarh is home to many of them. In fact, the state has India's oldest tribal communities, and it is safe to assume that the earliest tribals have been living in Bastar for over 10,000 years, since the time the Aryans occupied the Indian mainland and the rich plains became

- War-infested and
- De-forested for agriculture.

The main tribes in Chhattisgarh are:

- Bastar - Gond, Abujmaria, Bisonhorn Maria, Muria, Halba, Bhatra,
- Parja, Dhurvaa
- Dantewara - Muriya, Dandami Mariya or Gond, Dorla, Halba
- Koriya - Kol, Gond, Bhunjia
- Korba - Korwa, Gond, Rajgond, Kawar, Bhaiyana, Binjwar, Dhanwar

- Bilaspur and Raipur - Parghi, Savra, Manji, Bhayna
- Gariabandh, Mainpur, Dhura, Dhamtari - Kamar

Surguja and Jashpur - Munda

Each of these has its own rich (and distinctive) history and culture of music, dance, dress and food. What's common to all is a simple, basic, in-tune-with-nature way of life that has changed little over centuries because it works so well. Marriages tend to take place within the tribe. Both burial and cremation are used for the dead, but since cremation involves multi-day rituals, which are expensive, it is not so common. Important elders, though, are always cremated.

TRIBAL VILLAGES

A visit to a tribal village for a taste of life as it once was, is a must - an overnight stay can be arranged on special request. These villages are immaculately clean, and have winding mud roads running through them. Typically, tribal houses are made entirely of mud with thatched or red tiled roofs. Each village tends to specialise in a particular kind of handicraft - pottery, bell-metal work, iron work. It is useful to take a guide who knows and respects the tribes. Just avoid going when there is a haat on nearby, as the village empties out on those days.

The tribals are a bit shy, but friendly - they are as curious about you as you are about them! They will welcome your interest, so long as you do not treat them as exotic. So, smiling, asking questions about local customs, appreciating their crafts and culture is perfectly acceptable, gawping, clicking pictures without permission and doling out money is not

HAAT BAZAARS

Haat is the weekly market in rural areas. It's colourful, friendly and fun! Villagers gather her to socialize over a cup of *landa* (rice beer), *salphi* (the sap of fish-leaf sago-palm) or *mahua (the local brew, very heady);* sell their (agricultural or forest) produce, from salt to tribal jewellery to live red ants; and buy supplies for the week ahead. Visiting a *haat* is highly recommended, for a memorable peek into tribal life and a glimpse of commerce at its most primary stage (you can see barter deals taking place). It might interest you to know that the raw material for many fancy products come from here (for example, Bastar *sal butter* is an ingredient in many international chocolate brands).

TRIBAL DANCES

Dances are the chief amusement of the tribals. Like all folk dances, they are community affairs, characterized by robustness and earthiness. All the dances are group dances involving complex footwork, and they are wonderful to watch! The dancers are usually in a line, gyrating in a circle, always in the anti-clock direction.

The most spectacular dances are those of the Maria tribes. The men lace a strip of cloth round their torso, wear head-dresses of peacock and cock feathers, and tie bells around their wrists and ankles. Some also wear stag and bison horns on the head.

In the case of the Bison-horn Marias, the boys and girls dance in separate sub-groups, with the steps of the girls being simpler. Drum-beats are central to the dance.

In the case of the Hill-Marias, the group is often mixed, with a girl between two boys. The men wear heavy buttock-bells. Singing is important in these dances.

Saila Dance

Only males participate in this group dance, performed during public functions, national festivals, and political rallies, and in January after cutting the crop. All the dancers hold two hard bamboo sticks and strike the sticks of their neighbour in unison.

Suwa Dance

This is a dance by which a young girl lets a young boy know she is interested in him. When a marriageable young boy listens this song and sees the girl dancing, he sends a marriage proposal to her parents. It is also danced to please the goddess of wealth.

Karma Dance

"Karam" is a tree worshipped by the locals. According to legend, in an ancient war, only a young couple that hid in the hollow trunk of this tree was left alive, and ever since then this tree has been regarded as sacred. The karma dance is peformed according to caste, but holds the same significance across all castes. Male and female dancers are chained together to form a circle. A branch of the karam tree is passed among the dancers as they sing and dance in praise of the karam tree. This branch should not touch the earth. At the end of the dance, it is washed with milk and rice beer and later it is planted in the middle of the dancing arena. Also worth watching is the stilt dance.

TRIBAL JEWELLERY

Both men and women wear ornaments - in fact, at celebrations, it is the men who are more gaily bedecked! Most of the ornaments are made of beads (made from bones, seeds, wood) worn as laces, ropes, fillets and collars. Earlier, iron, brass and copper wires were into armlets; today, silver and gold are used. Gold is worn mainly on the ear, nose and neck (men wear gold collars to indicate their standing in the village), not on the hands and legs. Silver is worn on the neck (as a hoop); on the wrist (as a loose, hollow, twisted tubular bracelet); on the legs (as a solid, square-bar anklet, arched below the ankle-bones). Conical twin-tops are common in the nostrils and ear lobes. Rings are worn on the helix of the ear.

Precious stones are not very popular, but when used, red and green stones are preferred, mainly because of their bright colours.

Tassels of red wool are still worn by both men and women of the Hill-Maria tribe.

You can buy tribal ornaments and combs from any of the major haat bazars as well as in the jewelry showrooms in the towns of Jagdalpur, Kanker and Kondagaon.

COCKFIGHTS

Bastar is home to the aseel cock, noted for its pugnacity, high stamina, majestic gait and dogged fighting qualities. Cockfights are a favorite sport of the tribals here. If you have the stomach for these, they are held throughout the region, on Sundays, in shady areas under the trees. They draw a large crowd, all of it male.

PRESERVATION OF TRIBAL CULTURE

For the sake of simplicity and to do justice to the given topic, let us adopt the simple definition of culture as the way of life of a people which includes their material things, their political and social institutions, and their habits, customs and ideas.

We need to take actions to preserve our culture for the following reasons:

- Culture is an identity and it distinguishes one human group from others. And it also distinguishes humans from animals; so we need culture for our own identification;
- It is the most important concept in the study of aspects of human life; it acts like a measuring stick to our life and development;
- It is the most important concept in the study of aspects of human life; it acts like a measuring stick to our life and development;
- Culture is like a living organism, if looked after properly, it can grow, multiply and spread; if not, we become responsible for its eternal destruction. We must look after it and make it grow, or else we shall have to lose our value when it loses its vitality.
- Culture can be alive, culture can be dead or extinct. There are various aspects of our culture, which we can perhaps claim to be neither alive; nor dead. An inert, dormant culture does us no good.

We know that culture mainly has two forms material culture and non-material culture. Material culture includes material benefits and advancements such as development in the fields of communication, households, etc., non-material culture on the other hand, includes folklore, beliefs, tendencies etc. In our society, the material culture changes earlier and moves faster than the non-material culture; and in the process the latter is left behind. This lagging of a culture (behind the other) is called 'Cultural lag'. This cultural lag has become more and more pronounced in our society and it causes confusion. To minimize the degree of confusion, we need to speed up our cultural activities to cope up with the velocity of material culture.

INSTITUTIONALIZATION

An institute in the given context may mean any organization, group, or any building or place wherein and under which the teachers and the taught shall come and interact with one another and, teach and learn the art. Some institute can be run centrally, say, at Agartala, while others may have to be run at a village to be supervised by the

Community or the Village Council, any interested NGO, registered or non-registered organization, whichever the government may deem fit and proper to do the job.

Recognition of Artists: Recognition of the artists may be ensured. There are unsung artist who could never come up to the limelight due to want of recognition, and their artistic know-how will also die along with them.

This recognition will encourage the new learners and people of the new generation to learn, uphold and practice their culture with pride and confidence. Awareness Programme: Awareness Programme among the communities may be effective to encourage the people to learn their culture and to practice them.

In the past our forefathers lived in a monoculture society and cultural practices were instinctively inherited. In the multi-cultural world, the center of attention is obscure and confusing. Now, it is a time for paradigm shift to ensure surer protection of one's culture, the sole identity of a people.

Popularizing the Art

To popularize the arts, programmes such as cultural exchange, cultural exhibition may be frequently organized through which the people will uphold and spread their culture and they will also learn about other's culture and the spirit of mutual appreciation will develop.

DOCUMENTATION OF CULTURAL ART FORMS

The tribal people of Tripura, who live in hilly, forested and scenic habitat of rivers and valleys, reflect high accomplishment in the fields of culture, especially in art and crafts with all its variety and uniqueness. But the modern civilization, coupled with industrialization and urbanization, has cast its influence in such way that some traditional cultural art forms are either on the verge of extinction or under the spell of sea-change improvisation. Now, it is crying need of the hour that all these artistic expressions and creations of tribal people, be it material or non-material culture, need immediate attention, preservation, documentation and encouragement by the concerned people before they are completely lost in oblivion.

The cultural art forms of Tripura can be classified into two groups:

Table. Cultural art Forms.

Material	Non-material
Weaving and textiles	Music
Wood work Basketry and cane	Dance
works	Folk
Pottery and terracotta	stories Beliefs Rituals (religion)
Metal works and ornamentation	Oral Literature
House-type and decoration	Festival and Deities
Productive activities	Games and Sports

The documentation of cultural art forms of tribal people of the State may be of four types.

They are:

1. *Written Documentation:* By undertaking research work, publishing monographs etc.
2. *Photographic Documentation:* By photography and microfilming.
3. *Computerized Documentation:* By data storing, CDs etc.
4. *Human Documentation:* By conducting training programme involving traditional scholars and by institutionalizing the traditional learning.

TRIBAL CULTURE OF ODISHA

Odisha occupies an unique position in the ethnographic map of India for having the largest variety of tribal communities.Although they are found in all the districts of the State, yet more than half of their total strength are found in the districts of Koraput, Rayagada, Naurangpur, Malkangiri, Kalahandi, Nauapara, Kandhamal, Baudh, Keonjhar, Sundargarh and Mayurbhanj.

The tribes of Odisha are at various stages of socio-economic development. At one extreme are the group which lead a relatively secluded and archaic mode of life keeping their core culture intact, while at the other extreme there are communities which are indistinguishable from the general agricultural communities.

Any society - tribal or otherwise, comprises of organised groups of people who have learnt to live and work together interacting in the pursuit of common goals. Each society has its own rules of business and tricks of trade which helps its people to define their relationship with one another and live and work together. Therefore a society is a going concern and functions and perpetuates itself on the basis of the rules for living together.

The tribal people express their cultural identity and distinctiveness in their social organisation, language, rituals and festivals and also in their dress, ornament, art and craft. They have retained their own way of managing internal affairs of the village mainly through two institutions namely, the village council and the youth dormitory. The dormitory is the core of tribal culture and it reinforces the age-old traditions. In Odisha this institution occurs among many tribal communities in some form or other. The Juangs call it Majang and Darbar, the Kondhs call it Dindaghar, the Bhuyans call it Dhangarabasa and among the Bondos it goes by the name Ingersin. Of all the tribes the dormitory system is well organized among the Juang. Conspicuous in the village, the Mandaghar is the largest hut. It has wall on three sides and is open in front. The wooden parts and side walls are carried with decorative symbols depicting animals. The boys hang their changu, a flat tambourine like drum which is used at the time of dancing. In front of the Mandaghar is the small open space where dance takes place almost every night after the day's work is over. The dormitory is so to say a school of dancing and expression of the communal art of the people. The elders of the village assemble at the dormitory house every day for every important event in their corporate life. Here they discuss matters concerning the welfare of the village, settle the distribution of swidden and fix date and time for celebration of the village festivals, etc. In these respects the dormitory may be considered as the centre of social, economic and religious life of the village.

The amazing conglomeration of traditions, beliefs, sorrows and philosophies that together constitute and vitalise the rituals and festivals of the tribes, has descended from antiquity and has been preserved unimpaired to the present day. Every facet of their life covering round-the-year activities is intimately connected with religious beliefs and ritual practices. It is these aspects of their culture that give meaning and depth to their lives, and solidarity to their social structure.

The tribes believe that their life and work are controlled by supernatural beings whose abode is around them in hills, forests, rivers and houses. It is very difficult to standardize the Gods and spirits as their composition continually changes when old ones are forgotten with the introduction of new ones. Their Gods differ from one another in composition, function, character and nature. Some are benevolent; some are neutral and some are malevolent. The malevolent spirits and Gods are cared more than their benevolent counter parts as they can bring misery.

Manipulation of environment being the main concern of the tribals, all the ritual acts are directed towards stimulating natural processes. Illness or misfortune is attributed to displeasure and malicious act of the Gods or ancestors. The sacrifice of different kinds of livestock accompanied by all the rites and ceremonials of fetishism is considered appropriate appeasement. Moreover, their extremely superstitious nature prohibits the undertaking of any enterprise unless the Gods are first appeased and the omens, after being carefully considered, are adjudged to be propitious.

Among the tribes there are religious functionaries who cater to their spiritual needs. For example, the hierarchy of priests among the Saoras may be divided into three categories. The Buyya is a priest who presides at agricultural festivals and offers sacrifices that especially characterize these occasions. The Kudan is a shaman who combines the functions of priest, prophet and medicine-man. The sacerdotal head among the Juang is called Nagam or Buita, Pujari or Sisa among the Bondos and Jani among the Kondhs. The post of these officials are mostly ascribed but not achieved.

The ceremonies and festivals of the tribes can be classified into two groups, that is, those that relate to the individual families and those that relate to the village as a whole. The ceremonies and rites relating to birth of a child, marriage, death are observed family-wise whereas those relating to various agricultural cycle, eating of new fruits, hunting, etc. are observed by the village community.

Some of the important festivals observed by the tribal communities of Odisha include Guar ceremony of the Saora, Gotar of the Gadaba, Push Punei of the Juang, Kedu of the Kondh, Karam festival of the Oraon, Chait Parab of the Bondo and Magha Parab of the Santal.

With the advent of time, traces of borrowing from Hindu Pantheon and religious ceremonies are noticed among the tribes of

Odisha. They have started worshipping Siva, Parbati and Lord Jagannath. Hindu festivals like Raja, Laxmipuja, Dasahara and Gamha are also becoming popular among them day by day.

The tribes of Odisha, despite their poverty and their pre-occupation with the continual battle for survival, have retained the rich and varied heritage of colourful dance and music forming integral part of their festivals and rituals. Among them, the dance and music is developed and maintained by themselves in a tradition without aid and intervention of any professional dancer or teacher. It is mainly through the songs and dances the tribes seek to satisfy their inner urge for revealing their soul. The performance of these only give expression to their inner feelings, their joys and sorrows, their natural affections and passion and their appreciation of beauty in nature and in man.

Although the pattern of dance and music prevalent among them vary from tribe to tribe yet there are certain features common to all. Tribal dances have some accompaniments by means of which the rhythm is maintained. This consists of clapping of hands or beating of drums or an orchestra of different instruments. Every dance is accompanied by a song which is sung by the performers. Both men and women, young and old dance and invariably sing but the accompanying orchestra or music is usually provided by the male members. Tribal dance is characterized not only by its originality and spontaneity but also for its wide range of movements. Many parts of the body such as head, back, arms, feet. finger, etc. are brought into play. Some of the tribal groups put on colourful dancing costume during their performance.

Like dance, the songs sung by different tribal groups differ from one tribe to the other. Among the tribes everyone is a musician and poet. When happily inspired, they can coin a song then and there and sing it. Like any others, when they see things of beauty and meet pleasantly, they exhibit this pleasure and happiness by composing songs. One finds in these songs humours, jokes, romance, satires, criticisms, acquisitions and anger. Though there is no modernity and fineness, their ideas being natural, the compositions are good, inspiring and melodious. On the occasion of performing Pujas and observance of festivals the songs sung are different. Such songs are adopted from the past so many years. These songs describe the history of gods, the process of creation and some epic stories. The joy of free life find expression in tribal art and craft. It is through this endeavour their cultural self-image and aesthetic sensibility are visualized. The artistic skill of the tribal people is not only manifested in their dance and music but also in their dress and ornaments, wall-paintings, wood carvings and decorations, etc. The beautiful wall-paintings and floral designs of the Santals and the ikons of the Saoras which depict geometric designs and stylistic figures of plants and animals are the best example of tribal art. The multicoloured designs and relief figures of animals and human beings which decorate the walls of Mandaghar in Juang society are indeed works of very high order. Similar wall-paintings and decorations as observed among the Mundari group of tribals are also very attractive.

Some of the tribal communities like the Bondo and the Gadaba have their own looms by which they weave clothes for their own use. These hand spun textiles of coloured yarn are examples of best artistic skill of these people. So also among the Dongaria Kondhs the ladies are very much skilled in making beautiful embroidery work in their scarf. The tribal women in general and the Bondo, the Gadaba and the Dongaria Kondh women in particular are very fond of using ornaments. The Bondo women who are considered most primitive, look majestic when they wear headbands made of grass, necklaces of coloured beads and girdles made of brass on their bodies. All these are expressions of their artistic quality and aesthetic sense. The tribal people turn out excellent handicrafts for their own use. The wood carving of the Kondhs, metal works by lost wax process among the Bathudis, cane and bamboo basketry works among the Juangs and Bhuyans, are all symbolic of artistic creation.

Some of the famous tribal dances of Odisha are mentioned in the description that follows:

- *Juang:* The Juang dance which goes by the popular name of "Changu dance" is performed by both men and women. Besides, they perform other types of dances such as deer dance, elephant dance, bow dance, pigeon dance, bear dance, koel dance and peacock dance. They dance and sing when they are in happy mood. The dance also forms an integral part of their social and ritual festivals. The Juang do not have any special dress for dancing. While dancing the girls stand in a straight line in front of the boys. While the dance goes on, the line becomes semicircular. The girls hold each other's wrist or hand-in-hand and move forward and backward in bending posture. The boys stand in a straight line which becomes a curve during dance. The musical instruments which are used during their dance are Badakatha (Drum), Dhola (Small drum), Madala and Changu (Tambourine).

- *Saora:* The Saoras do not dance frequently as the Juangs and the Gadabas do. The Saora dance is very simple and lack all the artistic exuberances. Generally the Saoras dance during ceremonies and festivals, marriages, and when some important person visits their village. In their dance, group of men and women jumble up together and while dancing the drummers and the dancers advance towards each other alternatively with the rhythm of the music. Colourful costumes are worn during the dance. Other decorations include feathers of white fowl and peacock plumes. Besides, old coloured cloths of cotton and silk are tied as turbans by men and wrapped around their chest by women. While dancing they carry swords, sticks, umbrellas and other implements and blow whistles and make peculiar sounds. The musical instruments used at the time of dance consist of drums of various sizes, brass cymbals, brass-gongs and hide-gongs.
- *Gond:* Among the Gonds of Koraput, dance is performed throughout the year. Besides this, dances are performed on special communal occasions like marriage. The boys dress themselves with colourful aprons and turbans during the dance. The turbans are adorned with "cowrie" shells and the apron is adorned with small pieces of mirror. The girls are dressed in hand-woven sarees and silver ornaments. A dancing group is ordinarily formed with 20 to 30 persons of both sexes. Only unmarried boys and girls participate in the dance. The musical instruments are played by boys. Two boys lead the dance with wooden drums. The girls dance in circles with simple steps of one and two, very often bending their bodies forward. The steps of the boys are more varied and subtle.

- *Koya:* Dance among the Koyas is richly varied and sophisticated. The most important occasion for dancing is the worship of the mother goddess in the month of Chaitra (April-May). Ordinarily both boys and girls participate in dancing but the girls are more conspicuous. However, in the festival only girls participate. During the dance, the girls keep rhythm by beating sticks on the ground which are fitted with small bells. Dance groups are formed by about 30 to 40 persons. The most conspicuous movement about Koya dance is the complicated winding and unwinding of circles formed by girls.
- *Gadaba:* Gadaba dance is performed by women who wear the famous "Keranga" sarees and have their distinctive hair style. The men play the musical instruments. Chaitra and Pausa are the dancing seasons. The Gadaba women dance in semi-circles with steps of three and four which they gradually change to eight. The body is often bent forward. Very skillful moves are made on the heels.
- *Kondh:* Kondh dance is mostly confined to unmarried boys and girls and free mixing of the sexes is allowed during dancing. The dances are performed especially when the boys or girls of one village visit another village. The dance forms an item in the daily routine of the Kondh, when the boys and girls in their dormitories meet after the day's toil. No instrument accompanies the dance of the Kondhs of Koraput. The girls dance in lines and the boys dance behind and in front of them. The dance of the Phulbani Kondh is more colourful. The girls wear sarees in two pieces and bangles on their ankles. They dance in rows, facing rows of boys who sing songs and play on hand drums. Songs play a very important part in the dance. Special dances are performed during buffalo sacrifice, called the Kedu festival.
- *Oraons:* The dance of the Oraons of Sundargarh and Bolangir districts is performed in front of the village dormitories. The boys and girls participate in the dance. The line of dancers go round and round headed by the leading dancers.
- *Paraja:* The Parajas dance during the Chaitra parba, the dance often lasting from dusk to dawn. The girls wear colourful

handwoven sarees; silver and brass jewellery; and hold a bunch of peacock feathers in their hands. The movements are extremely graceful and the music is provided by the drum, flute and the "Dudunga" - a country-made string instrument.

TRIBAL CULTURES AND PEOPLE OF INDIA

India has traditionally been the home of different cultures and people. Unity in diversity is one of the most prominent features in the people of India. Among the diversified population a significant portion is comprised of the tribal people, the original inhabitants of the land. The tribal culture of India and their traditions and practices pervade almost all of the aspects of Indian culture and civilization.

In India one can find almost a new dialect, culture, and different people after moving 50 kms in any direction. Like wise the tribal population is also very much varied and diversified. The tribes each one of them is a distinctive community either migrated from another place or the original inhabitants of the land. These different tribes still inhibits the different parts especially the seven states of the North Eastern part, and almost each and every corner of the land. The distinctiveness of the tribes lies their rituals, cultures, beliefs and above all the harmony in which they survive in unison with nature. Their living perfectly depicts a well balanced give and take procedure that in no way disrupts the ecological balance.

Tribals constitute 8.14 per cent of the total population of the country, numbering 84.51 million (2001 Census) and cover about 15 per cent of the countrys area. The fact that tribal people need special attention can be observed from their low social, economic and participatory indicators.

Whether it is maternal and child mortality, size of agricultural holdings or access to drinking water and electricity, tribal communities lag far behind the general population. 52 per cent of Tribal population is Below Poverty Line and what is staggering is that 54 per cent tribals have no access to economic assets such as communication and transport.

These indicators underline the importance of the need of livelihood generating activities based on locally available resources so that gainful employment opportunities could be created at the doorstep of tribal people. Recognizing this need for initiating such livelihood generating activities in a sustained and focused manner, the Ministry of Welfare (now Ministry of Tribal Affairs) established an organization to take up marketing development activities for Non-Timber forest produce (NTFP) on which a tribal spends most of his time and derives a major portion of his/her income.

In 1987, the Tribal Cooperative Marketing Development Federation of India Limited (TRIFED) was set up with an aim to serve the interest of the tribal community and work for their socio-economic development by conducting its affairs in a professional, democratic and autonomous manner for undertaking marketing of tribal products.

Chapter 7

Tribal Education in India

People should develop along the lines of their genius and should avoid imposing anything on them. We should try to encourage in every way their own traditional arts and culture...We should try to train and build up a team of their own people to do the work of administration and development. Some technical personnel from outside will no doubt be needed, especially in the beginning. But we should avoid introducing too many outsiders into tribal territory...We should judge results, not by statistics or the amount of money spent, but by the quality of human character that is evolved.

JAWAHARLAL NEHRU, 1958

The aboriginal tribes of India are the oldest inhabitants of the country. For millennia, tribal societies have been subjugated by more recently arrived groups; their land was taken away, they were pushed further into the hilly gorges and wilds, and they were forced to work for their oppressors often without payment. Today tribal groups, which number more than 40 million, require special attention from the government even though they live largely isolated from the national culture.

In the past, many tribal groups were forced to assimilate into the dominant culture of the country. But some groups, such as the Bhils, Gonds, Santals, Oraons, Mundas, Khonds, Mizos, Nagas, and Khasis resisted change and assimilation to maintain their cultural identities and languages. According to many Indians, their continued isolation poses problems to national integration. Under the banner of national unity, the government is now bringing these minority groups into the national mainstream. The main question is whether tribal societies can enter the national mainstream while preserving their distinct social, cultural and political beliefs.

TRIBAL EDUCATION SYSTEM

Government planners see education as indispensable for helping tribal peoples cope with national integration. Education will also determine their prosperity, success and security in life. The tribes which remain either deprived of or negligent towards education will suffer the consequence.

Compared with the literacy rates of 29.34 per cent for the general population, literacy among tribal peoples in India is at most 6 per cent. The Union and the state governments have spent considerable sums of money for tribal youths' education, but the results are meagre. The Commissioner for Scheduled Castes and Scheduled Tribes asserts that unless exploitation among the tribels is combatted and eliminated through education, no improvement in tribal welfare will occur. Within tribal areas, education can be the basis for integrated development.

Government reports indicate that there is no scarcity of schools, other facilities or scholarships for the implementation of tribal education schemes. Most tribal youth find these incentives unattractive, however. Consequently, the government's dream to assimilate the tribes remains unfulfilled and raises basic questions about the implementation of such policies and strategies.

TRIBAL FESTIVALS, FREEDOM AND YOUTH VS. EDUCATION

The educational schedule - the school year, daily classes and holidays - is organized with little understanding of tribal cultures. Tribal festivals and celebrations and the seasonal pursuit of agriculture and gathering are not taken into consideration in planning educational timetables. All too often teachers hold classes as they would in cities or towns, ignoring the daily or seasonal habits of tribal pupils.

EDUCATIONAL INSTITUTIONS

The schools and their surroundings shape the minds of the children who frequent them. Most tribal schools do not blend well into the tribal environment. They are alien and often ugly structures in tribal villages. Shortly after schools are opened, they acquire the look of neglected and dilapidated buildings. Even after tribal youths' educations are completed and they find employment, negative attitudes fostered in the classroom remain a real social hurdle. They do not belong in their tribal culture, nor in the national culture.

THE MEDIUM OF INSTRUCTION

Some tribes still speak their language. While adult males are often bilingual, the women and children speak tribal dialects almost exclusively. Yet, a tribal child, on entering school, is suddenly expected to understand the state language. Children cannot understand the teacher, let alone answer questions. Many teachers assume that tribal students are slow; even if the teachers are sympathetic, overcoming this language barrier requires a great deal of effort. It would help considerably if tribal pupils were taught, during their first years in school, in their tribal language. They could then be gradually encouraged to learn the regional language.

The Constitution of India, under Article 350A, affirms that every state must provide adequate facilities for instruction of pupils in their mother tongues. Decades have passed and state governments have ignored this prescription for tribal people. Since initial instruction to the tribals is given in a foreign language, they understand and assimilate very little. Consequently, their response to education is poor. Had the instruction at the primary stage been in their own tongue, the progress of tribal students would have been better, and today there would be awareness of the importance of literacy among the tribal populations. Some attempts are being made to educate Gonds, Bhils, Santals, and other groups in their own tongues. According to recent reports, tribal children are responding well to such programmes.

CONTENT AND METHOD OF TRIBAL EDUCATION

The content and the method of tribal education must be objectively evaluated. Tribal youth have unique historical and social backgrounds but need special attention and orientation in their attempts to bridge two cultures. Many school and college curricula which tribal youths encounter are either irrelevant to them and/or offer only negative views of tribal societies. While national and state governments, in theory, offer many benefits, concessions and facilities to tribal students, few of them reach the intended recipients.

INTEGRATION OF TRIBAL YOUTH IN THEIR OWN CULTURE

- Tribal youth, even while they Study at the secondary and college levels, should, be encouraged not to jettison their own cultures and to remain integrated in their own societies. Once they become culturally and socially alienated, it is impossible for them to protect and lead their own societies and maintain traditions that may be essential to the viability of tribal cultures. Furthermore, tribal leaders often begin to imitate non-tribal peoples' exploitive tactics, even looking down on their own people. In some cases they treat tribal populations worse than non-tribal populations. Development in tribal societies should focus on educational programmes that encourage keeping tribal youth genuinely integrated in their own culture.

EDUCATION OF TRIBAL LEADERS

Tribal leadership has been subverted by outside influences and agencies such as the police, the courts and political parties. In the case of political parties, tribal leaders are often manipulated for the block of votes they can deliver rather than encouraged to take the initiative of leading their people to find locally derived solutions to local problems. As a result, village autonomy was destroyed, law and order has deteriorated, and respect for authority was lost. Tribal leaders began to exploit their own people politically, socially and economically.

Tribal students, even while they are receiving their education, must be trained to be dedicated to the service of their own people. They must help to develop their people's inner resolve to resist exploitation and to safeguard their own rights.

SOCIAL INCLUSION AND EXCLUSION OF INDIAN TRIBES

The term 'social exclusion' and 'social inclusion' are two terms most widely used in recent years by politicians,

Social scientists and the public as well. The term social inclusion originated in French social policy in the 1970s. It came into play in the 1980s economic crisis when state sponsored republican tradition of solidarity was in vogue. By the year 1990 the term was theorized by scholars like Bourdieu and Luhmann. The latter clarified the concept in the following terms: The concept of inclusion means the encompassing of the entire population in the performances of the individual function systems. On the one hand, this concerns access to these benefits and, on the other, dependence of individual modes of living on them. To the extent that inclusion is achieved, groups disappear that do not or only marginally participate in social living. With this adoption, social exclusion moved on to the political agenda in Europe in the 1990s. The conceptual development of social exclusion draws from two leading social policy traditions: that of social democracy, in terms of concerns surrounding inequality and equal opportunities, and that of the social catholic concern for social ties in the community and within the family. The term 'social exclusion' is ambiguous and contested. Definitions range from little more than a re-naming of poverty to broader based concepts based on a lack of, or inability to participate in society. Rodgers (1995: 46-7) visualized exclusions which include, 'exclusion from goods and services', 'labour market exclusions', 'exclusions from land' and 'exclusion from security'.

Discussion of social inclusion and exclusion also relates to citizenship debates, particularly in terms of the dichotomy between individualism and collectivism. Atkinson and Davoudi (2000: 434), for example, refer to the differentiation between: the European social model [which] places considerable emphasis on maintaining social solidarity and ensuring that all individuals are integrated into, and participate in, a national social and moral order' and 'the concept of poverty which lies within the Anglo-Saxon tradition, where a liberal model dominates [and] is based on the idea that society is fragmented and composed of individuals who are in constant competition with one another.

Silver (1994) distinguished three paradigms of social exclusion, depending in particular on the ways social integration has been conceptualized, and associated with 'theoretical and ideological baggage'. In the 'paradigm' dominant in France, exclusion is the of the social bond between the individual and society cultural and moral. The poor, unemployed and ethnic minorities are defined as outsiders. National solidarity implies political right and duties.

A 'specialization paradigm', dominant in the US, and contested in UK is determined by individual liberalism.

According to liberal individualistic theories, individuals are able to move across boundaries of social differentiation and economic divisions of labour, and emphasize the contractual exchange of rights and obligations. In this paradigm, exclusion reflects discrimination, the drawing of group distinctions that denies individuals' full access to or participation in exchange or interaction. A 'monopoly paradigm' is influential in Britain and many Northern European countries, and views the social order as coercive, imposed through hierarchical power relation. Exclusion is defined as a consequence of the formation of group monopolies. The term 'disadvantage' has been widely used for conceptualization of 'social exclusion.' Hence, disadvantage refers to circumscribe the opportunities and life chances of individuals and groups in a given society. Now, poverty is recognized to be a multi-dimensional phenomenon, encompassing income, assets, education, health, dignity, and voice. But, still poverty continued to be understood as a single phenomenon that is the root of social exclusion in economic terms. Sociologists, on the other hand, have paid greater attention to identity-based forms of disadvantage. Such disadvantage reflects the cultural devaluation of groups and categories of people in a society.

The identity in question may relate to a distinct and bounded group of people who are defined by their distinct cultural practices and shared way of life Caste, ethnicity and religion are examples of such group identities.

In practice, the dominant sections of society construct and re-construct the members of these groups or categories as persons of lesser worth through beliefs, values, attitudes and behavior which disparage, stigmatize, stereotype and discriminate. Group based disadvantages give rise to 'horizontal' model of inequality where the inequalities in question cut across economically defined strata and differentiate the ability of different groups and categories within society to access valued resources and opportunities. The two paradigms, thus, focus on a quite distinct understanding of disadvantage: one relating to lack of resources and the other to identity based discrimination.

Another dimension, the spatial disadvantage may lie in the remoteness and isolation of a location which makes it physically difficult for its inhabitants to participate in broader socio-economic processes or it may operate through the segregation or urban environments and the 'sub-cultures' of violence, criminality, drug dependence which often characterize the territory excluded. Social exclusion has to be seen as an institutionalized form of inequality, the failure of a society to extend to all sections of its population, the economic resources and social recognition which they need in order to participate fully in the collective life of the community. Social exclusion is a kind of mechanism by which 'access' and recognition is granted or denied. Economic theory suggests the distinction between 'open' and 'closed' groups as one way of understanding access and exclusion. Open groups are those which achieve their objectives by expanding their membership because the benefits they seek increase with the increased membership and outweigh the bringing new members. Closed groups like trade unions, on the other hand, achieve their objectives by restricting their membership on the basis of some agreed set of rules.

Thus, in totality, social exclusion denotes the following characteristics of a society at large or individuals at least. i) Inability to participate effectively in economic, social, political and cultural life. ii) Distance and alienation from a so-called mainstream society. iii) Isolation from major societal mechanisms which produce or distribute social resources. Social exclusion is a broader concept. It is a related concept with unemployment and poverty, but not an identical one with them. Social exclusion is a relative term particular to a place or country on certain circumstances. It is always related to a social agent or agents. Exclusion is also dynamic term depending upon people's immediate condition.

IMPACT OF INCLUSION AND EXCLUSION

Though it is generally presumed that exclusion is detrimental and inclusion is for good, in practice this may not be true. Coercive inclusion by market or by dominant social system in any form may cause harm to the social web of the new entity. Coercive inclusion may be in the form of child labour, women in wage labour with differential payments, putting tribal people in unskilled and unprotected labour force and as immigrant workers etc. For similar reason, exclusion is not always bad.

To those who do not accept the value of the market system and do not resemble or depend on a social system outside their traditional domain, any voluntary exclusion from those entities should be perfectly accepted. Both from social and market perspective discourse on inclusion and exclusion of tribal people cater relevance in present situation. Because, it is said that exclusion and poverty are mostly interrelated. Conventional poverty indicators reveal that there is a strong correlation between being indigenous or tribal and being poor or extremely poor. Tribal people are more likely to have lower income, poorer physical living conditions, less access to health care, education, and a range of other services, worse access to labour, land and capital markets and worse returns to work as well as weaker political representation. The poverty and social exclusion experienced by tribal people are largely due to discrimination at social and institutional level during colonial and post independent era. The present chapter tries to highlight the characteristics of inclusion and exclusion of tribal societies in Indian situation.

THE TRIBAL WORLD

Definition of Tribal Societies: On the basis of certain specific characteristic some human societies are defined as tribal societies across the world. These characteristics are not uniform for every society. But there are certain characters universal to all of them; at least they had derived from such a social arrangement at certain point of time.

According to the ILO Convention No. 169 indigenous and tribal peoples are those peoples "whose social, cultural and economic conditions distinguish them from other sections of the national community, and whose status is regulated wholly or partially by their own customs or traditions or by special laws or regulations".

Indian Tribal Groups: In India we come across many social groups or societies who might have some of these characteristics. But all of them are not denoted as tribal groups. The term tribe is more functional in nature in India. There was a purpose to declare or recognize some societies as tribal societies through constitutional Act of the country. Thus, when we talk of tribe, we talk of the Scheduled Tribes, the social groups recognized or listed in the Schedule of the Constitution of India.

Therefore, by definition, the Scheduled tribes are those social groups who are "such tribes or tribal communities or parts of or groups within such tribes or tribal communities as are deemed under Article 342 to be Scheduled Tribes for the purposes of this constitution". This delineation shows that there is no characteristic definition regarding tribal groups.

The recognition is done on purpose or functional aspects only. But it is generally accepted that in selecting the tribal people the following characters are taken some sort of priority: indications of primitive traits, distinctive culture, geographical isolation, shyness of contact with the community at large, and backwardness. The criteria are not spelt out in the Constitution but have become well established. It subsumes the definitions contained in 1931Census, the reports of first Backward Classes Commission 1955, the Advisory Committee (Kalelkar), on Revision of SC/ST lists (Lokur Committee), 1965 and the Joint Committee of Parliament on the Scheduled Castes and Scheduled Tribes orders (Amendment) Bill 1967 (Chanda Committee), 1969.

Tribes are at Different Levels of Transition: Culture and society are dynamic. Culture and society change over time due to several factors -exposure, invention, experimentation and change in surrounding environment. The tribal societies are also no exception. When we observe the social status and cultural components of tribal societies, we find that in our country the tribal societies are in different stages of transition. They are in different stages of picking up or imbibing Components of modern world like education, economic activities, dresses and recreation, food habit, health seeking behavior and world view etc.

There is lack of uniformity in these domains among the different tribes in different regions of the country. These specific characteristic of the tribal groups attach the importance in that while making policies for social and economic development, one has to be aware of such levels of transition. For example, we have come across highly educated tribal groups in north eastern states like Mizoram whereas, areas like Orissa and Bihar the tribal people are very less educated. The situation is same for many other social indicators of development among tribal groups across the country. Thus, tribal policies must be group specific or region specific. Flatly generalized uniform policies may not serve the purpose.

Tribes as a Unique Self-Excluded Group of People: By traditional definition, tribal societies are self-sufficient (though not strictly in economic front). Self-sufficiency means they need not to interact with non-tribal societies for their social, cultural and physical existence. This very nature of tribal people kept themselves away from the rest of the other societies. The tribal people had crude form of trade relations with non-tribal world, but that was not sufficient to penetrate their social core. Thus, it is quite clear that exclusion of tribal societies was a self-imposed criterion. Contrary to this fact, the caste societies were the integral part of Hindu caste system. The Scheduled Castes, generally the lowest in the social rank, have socio-cultural and economic dependency on other caste groups. Thus, exclusion of such societies is due to its social customs, work attachment and legendry mandated by social authorities present among the greater Hindu society.

The perceived and manifested exclusions are mostly due to the fact that the other part of the society think them not suitable to be in the same line of interaction. From these two explanations one can draw the difference of exclusion: Tribal groups are excluded groups because they are not a part of the greater traditional Hindu society. At best they may be termed as the parallel segments in a different domain. Scheduled Castes, on the contrary, a part and parcel of the greater Hindu society, are excluded as neglected parts thereof. Therefore, it is opined that in the nation building process, while the Scheduled Castes need uplifting in social status, the tribal societies need a meaningful integration and positive inclusion.

CONSEQUENCE OF TRIBAL ASSIMILATION

In Socio-Cultural Sphere: Indian tribes and issue of social inclusion and exclusion In both the cases, a lot of tribal traditional entities and identities were either merged or lost to universal religious domain. Along with religion, social and economic front has witnessed a drastic change afterwards.

Thus, we come across a term called detribalization, giving rise to the problems of identity crisis. Identity crisis arises when a group of people does not left with anything unique of their own from others, except the undesirable differential treatment they receive from the others. Needless to say that there is a difference between the Hinduised tribal the Christian tribal groups' assertion. In case of the later, though most of traditional religious norms are lost, it hardly altered the traditional identities and cultural components of the converted tribal groups. Christianity could not evolve as a universal dominant culture among the tribal people and the ethnic and regional variations remained in the core. Thus, being itself in a minority status in the country it could not absorb the tribal into the greater Christian society in the real sense. Moreover, Christianity itself offers as a shield towards loss of identity being a separate entity from Hinduism and so-called greater Indian culture. For the Christian tribes, the ethnic assertion, therefore, seems to be political in nature.

In Economic Sphere: Inclusion of tribal world into the non-tribal domain was mainly aimed at or focused on economic exploitation of tribal people and their resources. Intentional or not, the tribal people lost their traditional authority over their economic resources - land, forest and other resources. Several land reform policies, land acquisition act and land distribution policies deprived tribal people of their livelihood. The colonial laws did not recognize the community or clan ownership over forest and land resources. In the absence of clear ownership title land and forest went to the State. Inclusion also had great impact on tribal social and economic front. This was because the open up of tribal belts became the heavens of fortune runners who were basically non-tribal. During colonial administration numerous nontribal people entered tribal areas as traders, service providers, contractors and money lenders etc. They exploited tribal people in various ways.

The tribal people, ignorant of monetary economy could not cope with the changing situation and reduced to land less wage labourers in most of the cases. Large scale migration and maladjustment occurred in tribal zones. The post independent inclusion of tribal territories into development map of the state has displaced millions of Tribal people of their home, making them dependent on others' mercy. The excluded area concept was mostly used for political gain in terms of security and smooth administration in and around tribal areas in contrast to the general view that it was meant for the betterment of the tribal people. Since the exploitation of resources and the breakdown of tribal tradition were in vogue in those areas, the political exclusion had some definite impact on tribal societies. The economic development, education and infrastructure etc. were suffered in those excluded areas, barring the areas where Christian missionaries were in operation.

Caste Sphere: It has been stated that tribal people, at present, have experienced detribalization and identity crisis. In spite of being self-sufficient groups of people in the past, what have made them bound to come forward to get assimilated with non-tribal domain? To answer this question we have to look into several circumstances the tribal people once went through in their ethnic history. It has already been stated that except a few tribal groups in the north east region, most of the tribal domains were either surrounded by the non-tribal domain or they were aggressively near to non-tribal entities. The political intrusion of non-tribal into the tribal authorities made the tribal people vulnerable to socio-economic exploitation. Thus, the tribal people were bound to come out of their traditional domain in search of better quality of life by accepting jobs, education and non-traditional way of life.

The already penetrated parochial religious identities and resemblances made the tour easier in the initial stage. But there were certain constraints. These constraints were in terms of social recognition. In a caste based ranked society, as it was prevalent during colonial era and at the dawn of Indian independence, the tribal people were unable to identify themselves and place themselves in social strata. They had to identify, at best, as caste people for meaningful social interaction.

Thus, the only way left open for the tribal people was to imbibe several caste components leaving behind their own traditional rites and rituals, customs and food habits and ways of life. There are numerous instances that show that by abandoning the tribal gods and goddesses, by leaving tribal customs, the tribal people could attain the status of lower caste groups in greater Indian society. In this rush for identity formation the tribal people lost a lot - language, customs and even their traditional names and surnames etc.

The legendry stories flourished everywhere linking tribal people with the caste groups and caste literature (mythological) and greater Hindu traditions. We have come across several caste and tribal groups having similar customs and traditions in the lower strata of society. Definitely, such similarities are due to the process described above. Social scientists have forwarded a term very similar to this situation as Tribe-caste continuum.

A very general observation also can make it clear that the parochial legends found at regional level do not find their place in the domain of universal or all Indian level. There are different places known to people for those legends. The Hindu religion never penetrated in the land from where the forefather of the Ahom came to Assam. It might have been due to necessity of the Ahom kings to accept a broader religious ideology to administer the conquered country in later period. The story of the Koch Rajbonshis certainly was coined by the royal priests who were the Hindu Sages. It is to be noted that a lot of legends and stories were adapted and translated to local language using local elements and examples so that the people at local level can accept them as their own. The Koch themselves now-a-days do not accept their kshatriya status and deny the link with lord Siva or so on. The story of Gatotkach is also not above controversy. For logical reason it is very hard to believe that the Pandavas would come to Dimapur from Hastinapur crossing Ganga and the Brahmaputra.

The famous Hadimba temple in Himachal Pradesh reveals the improbability of north-east links. The instances from Assam clearly show that a lot of ethnic groups imbibed Hindu ideology at different degrees. Some of them accepted it in totality and abandoned their traditional rites and rituals and observances. Some followed a dual form of religious belief blending both traditional as well as Hinduism. Following the advent of the colonial rule, the social and political scenario changed a lot in the state. This was a time of formation of greater Assamese society. Modern Assamese language was flourishing under the print media provided by the Christian Missionaries.

To be able to speak and write Assamese language was a matter of pride and was attached to status in society for the non-mainstream Assamese (tribal) groups in the state. In this way, many ethnic and tribal groups left their traditional dialects and accepted Assamese as their mother tongue. Acceptance of Vaishnavism was also a means to raise one's status in the newly emerged society.

The advent of the British rule, open up of market and monetary economy, large influx of outsiders and break down of traditional system and domain among the tribal group made it appealing to catch a new identity and status in the emerging society. By imbibing Vaishnavism they were able to forward their identity to the non-traditional world. Thus a trend of massive detribalization occurred during this period. These were some of the instruments through which tribal people wanted to raise their status or in some of the cases the priest and preacher tried to find their followers so as to build up religious society where they can be benefited financially, physically and others. The contemporary ethnic history of tribal India clearly reveals that this process of identity formation and detribalization was not at all a prudent move from the part of the tribal people. The newly created identity did not serve the purpose to the tribal people. Except a few, most of the tribal groups could not assimilate completely with caste traditions. The converted tribal were, too, placed in the lowest strata of the society and ultimately experienced more severe exploitation and negligence from the greater Hindu society and elite groups.

The same way they also lost their age old dignity as a self-sufficient society. The tribal people who had their own gods and goddesses, had own priest and norms of religion, society and way of living, who were independent lot, now had to obey alien dictatorship of higher castes and elites. Frustrated at the deteriorated condition the tribal groups in many regions of the country have started rejuvenate their age-old tradition to regroup and re-assert their unique or separate tribal identity.

A process of retribalization and revivalism has sprung-up in the country at different times. Thus, an excluded identity began to appear in tribal world again. Tribal societies are now seemed to be smarter than before. The exclusion, now, is selective in nature. They are very much concerned about preservation of their remaining traditional culture and entity, while in economic front and skill formation they are inclusive in nature quite voluntarily. Thus, exclusion is now, again, self-imposed and it is basically meant for group identity preservation aiming at political, social and economic assertion. Thus, we see a different kind of inclusion -exclusion dynamic in case of tribal groups in India. One has to be careful while talking about contemporary trends or dogmas of inclusion-exclusion because the tribals have a complex web of socio-political history to accept or deny them.

THE PROBLEM OF TRIBAL EDUCATION

The vulnerability of tribal populations to exploitation by minor government officials, as well as moneylenders, landlords, and other agents of vested interests, can largely be traced to their illiteracy and general ignorance of the world outside the narrow confines of their traditional environment. Their inability to cope with the many novel forces impinging nowadays on tribal villages and on an economy which had remained virtually unchanged for centuries is by no means due to any innate lack of intelligence.

As long as they operate within their familiar atmosphere, tribals evince as much perspicacity, skill, and even true wisdom as any other population, but as soon as they are faced by social attitudes rooted in a different system they become insecure and often behave in a manner detrimental to their own interests. Brought up in a system in which all communications are by word of mouth, and hence used to trusting verbal statements, they get confused by constant reference to documents and written rules, which increasingly determine all aspects of rural life. Unable to read even the receipt given by an official and obliged to put their thumb impressions on documents which they cannot understand, they are easy victims of any fraud or misrepresentation which more educated exploiters are likely to devise.

It is obvious, therefore, that a modicum of literacy is indispensable as a first step towards enabling tribals to operate within the orbit of the advanced communities dominating the economic and political scene. The disadvantages under which illiterate tribals labour are multiplied in the case of those who do not even speak and understand the language of the dominant population, and hence cannot communicate with officials except through better-educated fellow tribesmen acting as interpreters.

Many of the tribal groups of Andhra Pradesh long ago lost their own language and speak Telugu as their mother tongue. In their case there is no language barrier, and hence no need for any special type of schooling. Other tribes, however, speak languages unintelligible to most outsiders, and it is imperative for them to learn Telugu if they want to communicate with members of the majority community. This is the case of the Gonds and Kolams of Adilabad, of some groups of Koyas of Khammam, and of several of the tribes of Vishakapatnam and Srikakulam.

Among the Gonds there are still many who speak no other language than Gondi, a Dravidian tongue closer to Kanara than to Telugu, and many Kolams speak Kolami and Gondi, but neither Telugu nor any other language understood by officials and members of the advanced ethnic groups. Hence they are handicapped at every step as soon as they move out of the small circle of their fellow tribesmen.

Education for tribals who normally speak their own tongues is beset with difficulties, because the acquisition of literacy has to be combined with the learning of a language other than the mother tongue. Yet the average teacher available for tribal schools has had no training whatsoever in the technique of imparting to children what is to them a foreign language.

The first major educational experiment launched among any tribal community of Andhra Pradesh was the Gond Education Scheme in Adilabad District, initiated by the Nizam's government in 1943. At the time, when there was a determined drive to improve the position of the Gonds, Pardhans, and Kolams, it was realized that no advance could be maintained unless it was accompanied by the emergence of at least a small number of literate tribals. But what was to be the medium of instruction? The vast majority of Gond children did not speak or understand any language other than Gondi, but there were no teachers who knew Gondi and could communicate with Gond children. Hence there was no other solution to the problem than to produce Gondi-speaking teachers before any schools for Gond children could be established. There existed at that time a few young Gonds who had privately learned the rudiments of reading and writing Marathi, the language spoken by many of the Hindus of the western part of the district. A small band of such semi-literate Gonds were assembled at Marlavai, a village in the hills of Utnur Taluk, and initially given systematic training in the reading and writing of

Marathi and in arithmetic. It was hoped that this training centre established in Marlavai would produce enough Gondi-speaking teachers to make it possible to start within a few years a network of primary Gond schools extending over the greater part of the district. The medium of instruction in the first two classes of these schools was to be Gondi, and to provide teaching materials the headmaster of the Marlavai Training Centre and I composed Gondi primers and readers printed in Devanagari script. The idea was that once the children had learned to read and write Gondi in this script, they could more easily be taught Marathi, the script being the same. From the fourth standard onwards Urdu, then the official language of Hyderabad State, was to be added, and in order to make this possible the teacher trainees were also taught Urdu.

By 1946 thirty primary Gond schools were functioning, and by 1949 their number had more than trebled. In order to improve gradually the standard of the Gond teachers, all of them were annually assembled at Marlavai for a course of instruction lasting one month. In this way the level of their competence was raised, and they were familiarized with new developments in the sphere of tribal welfare. In addition to the training of teachers, the Marlavai centre was used for the instruction of literate Gonds in the basic knowledge of revenue matters required for village officers, and some of those trained were subsequently appointed as *patwari*.

By 1951 the Marlavai Training Centre, which in 1943 had begun with the training of five semi-literate Gonds, had produced ninety-five teachers, five village officers, one revenue inspector, five clerks, and seven forest guards. One of the trainees of Marlavai, Atram Lingu, subsequently became *patwari, sarpanch* of the Sirpur *panchayat*, and finally in 1967 president of the Panchayat Samithi of the Utnur Tribal Development Block.

The success of this centre encouraged the Social Service Department to establish a second centre at Ginnedhari, a Gond village in Asifabad Taluk. There Telugu was the language of the non-tribal population, and hence Telugu was taught instead of Marathi.

The high hopes which had been placed in this experiment of imparting education to Gond children in the mother tongue and at the same time familiarizing them with the regional languages were subsequently disappointed. The incorporation of the Telengana districts of Hyderabad State into Andhra Pradesh was accompanied by fundamental changes in the educational system. The government decided to abandon the use of Gondi, and no further schoolbooks in Gondi were supplied to the schools. Instruction in Telugu, now the state language, replaced teaching in both Marathi and Urdu, with the result that many of the Gond teachers became redundant because they could not teach in Telugu.

Yet the young Gonds who had attended the two training centres formed for years a class of moderately educated tribals. Apart from those who worked as teachers, there were some who found employment in minor government posts.

In 1972 the character of tribal schools was changed. Many single-teacher schools were closed and staff and children grouped together in so-called ashram schools. These provide boarding facilities for children from other villages, while children from the same locality can attend as day scholars. The expense of these boarding schools is considerable, for to maintain and educate a child in one of them costs the government approximately ₹ 1,000 per year. There is no coordinated control over the tribal schools, as some are supported by the Tribal Welfare Department and others by the relevant Panchayat Samithi. In 1975 there were 269 primary schools, 46 ashram schools, and 10 Tribal Welfare hostels for children attending upper primary schools and high schools outside the area covered by the Integrated Tribal Development Project. The government also provided scholarships, books, slates, and clothes to tribal pupils. Despite all these facilities only 31.2 percent of the tribal children of school age were enrolled in educational institutions, and the literacy rate of the tribals of Adilabad District, which had been 2.52 percent in 1961, had risen to no more than 3.28 percent. According to the 1971 census there were then many villages the entire population of which was illiterate, and I learned by personal observation that even in 1979 there were still entirely illiterate village communities.

The numbers of the various types of educational institutions in all the tribal areas of Andhra Pradesh in 1979 were as follows:

Ashram schools399 with 26,746 studentsPrimary schools1,740 with 37,729 studentsUpper primary schools115 with 4,052 studentsHigh schools75 with 3,630 studentsJunior colleges6 with 305 students. The number of teachers in ashram schools was 1,171 and that of teachers in other schools 1,821. Despite the existence of all these schools, the percentage of tribal children who pass the tenth standard, i.e. matriculation, and are thus qualified to proceed to intermediate courses in colleges is very low, and in thirty-six years of tribal education only five Gonds and two Pardhans have been awarded university degrees.

What is the reason for this disappointing lack of educational progress, which contrasts so dramatically with the rapid advances achieved by most tribal communities in Northeast India ?

One of the causes is undoubtedly the very low standard of teaching and facilities in tribal schools.

About 75 percent of all schools are housed in thatched huts, many of which leak during the rains, a defect making their proper functioning extremely difficult. There are, moreover, no quarters for the teaching staff, and rented accommodation is unavailable in most tribal villages.

The lack of basic comforts discourages non-tribal teachers from taking on jobs involving residence in remote villages, and among those posted in such villages there is a high rate of absenteeism. While non-tribal teachers are reluctant to work in tribal villages, few Gonds are nowadays available for such posts. The reason is that the Education Department has raised the required standard, so that only persons who have attained intermediate standard are eligible for teaching posts. Gonds who have reached that standard are few; those who have done so can continue their education with the help of scholarships, and if they are successful they have a good chance of obtaining more attractive posts owing to the system of reservation of posts for members of scheduled tribes. Hence, qualified tribals are not very interested in appointments as teachers, and those tribal matriculates who would be glad to take up such posts are not acceptable to the education authorities.

Among the teachers working in tribal schools at present, those of non-tribal origin generally have higher educational qualifications than their tribal colleagues. Nevertheless, their efficiency as teachers is not necessarily higher than that of tribal teachers. Their appointment to schools in a tribal area is usually purely accidental. Few of them have expressed any preference for such a posting, and they are given no orientation or training for work among tribal children. Their difficulties begin with their inability to speak and understand Gondi, the only language most of the younger children know. Moreover, they are total strangers to tribal culture and the values of the society within which they have to operate. Those who persevere in tribal schools usually pick up a working knowledge of Gondi, but their own cultural background stands in the way of an understanding and appreciation of tribal culture and traditions. As quarters are not provided by government and rented accommodation is usually unobtainable, most non-tribal teachers are separated from their wives and children, with the inevitable result that they take every opportunity of leaving their posts and visiting their families. The majority of these teachers try to obtain posts outside the tribal area as soon as possible.

As a result of the shortage of efficient teachers, as well as of the inadequate facilities in most schools, few tribal boys and girls pass the tenth standard, and the majority of those enrolled drop out long before.

The reasons for this wastage are many. At the age of ten to twelve, boys and girls are useful for work on their parents' farms, and many Gonds are unwilling to spare their children, particularly if they see that the schools are not well run and the teachers' frequent absences condemn the children on many days to virtual idleness. Perhaps more important is the realization among parents, as well as the older pupils, that school education is of limited usefulness. While those who have passed the tenth standard are eligible for minor jobs in government service, by no means all have obtained such jobs, and there is, moreover, the large category popularly described as "tenth failed."

Boys who have read up to the tenth standard but failed to pass the final examination have few chances of employment in government service, and as nearly all commercial activities down to small village shops are in the hands of non-tribals who employ on principle only members of their own caste or community, there are no other openings for such youths. Yet ten or more years at school have given them the ambition to find an occupation other than the ordinary farm work for which they are no better qualified than their illiterate contemporaries.

In the tribal societies of Northeast India, superior educational institutions allow many young people to obtain good academic qualifications which enable them to compete even outside their own sphere on equal terms with men and women of other communities. There many tribals have been appointed to gazetted government posts, and others have proved successful in the professions and in commerce.

Hence education has so high a prestige that a few failures do not marr its image. But the Gonds see hardly any of their fellow tribesmen elevated to respected and lucrative positions, and numerous school-leavers are without any jobs. Their disillusionment with school education is therefore understandable. The advantage of having some literate persons in the village does not weigh heavily with the individual family which for years has forgone a son's help on the farm without enjoying any financial reward for the time he spent at school.

A certain disenchantment with the results of school education prevailing among many of the illiterate tribals accounts for the fact that in villages where tribals and non-tribals live side by side the latter are much keener on making use of educational facilities. In an investigation conducted in 1977 by Y. B. Abbasayulu in nine villages of Utnur Taluk, it was found that 62.28 percent of the non-tribals, but only 33.72 percent of the tribals, sent their children to school. Of the tribals interviewed, 22.15 percent gave poverty as their reason for not sending their children to school, 12.5 percent claimed the children's involvement in agricultural activities, and 3.75 percent gave as an excuse their general inferiority complex vis-à-vis non-tribals.

Some of the non-tribals also claimed poverty as an excuse, but none invoked the need for children to do farm work, and reference to a feeling of inferiority did not figure in their replies. Interestingly, more tribals than non-tribals replied positively to the question of whether they thought of education as good and valuable; 98.46 percent approved of school education, whereas only 76.3 percent of the non-tribals professed so positive an appreciation.

Abbasayulu interprets this surprising result of his enquiry by pointing out that non-tribals, engaged mainly in making money, were confident of their ability to be economically successful even without formal education, whereas tribals realized that their depressed status could be bettered only by education, despite the disappointing results of the schooling of so many of their children.

As an illustration of the impact of education on individual villages, we may consider the situation in Marlavai and Kanchanpalli. The former was the first centre of Gond education and is still the site of an ashram school, and the latter also has some tradition of literacy as the seat of a raja family literate for at least three generations. At Kanchanpalli, too, there is at present an ashram school.

Among the fifty households of Marlavai, there were in 1977 eleven literate adults and fourteen children attending the local school. Apart from one retired school-teacher, no one in the village had ever held a paid post.

Among the sixty-four households of Kanchanpalli, there were in 1977 twenty-two literate adults and twenty-four children were attending the local school.

In both villages there were among the literate adults men who had attended school for only three or four years, and had only a very limited knowledge of reading and writing.

By the beginning of 1980, the educational scene in both villages had considerably improved, probably because of the Gonds' general increased awareness of the need for education. Forty children of Marlavai were attending various schools. Twenty-one of these went as day pupils to the local ashram school, 15 were boarders in other ashram schools, and 4 attended schools in two taluk headquarters and stayed there in hostels for scheduled tribes where they got free food and lodging.

In the Marlavai ashram school there were then 139 pupils, including 21 girls. Attendance in the Kanchanpalli ashram school had also increased: there were altogether 89 pupils, including 50 boarders and 39 day pupils.

There can be no doubt, however, that part of the money and effort devoted to the teaching of tribal children is wasted because many children leave school after the third or fourth year and soon relapse into virtual illiteracy. This is borne out by the relatively small number of literates in Marlavai.

This village has had a primary school since 1945, and in 1943–44 it was the focal point of an adult literacy project for which special charts in Gondi had been printed. Yet thirty-four years later there were only eleven literate adults among the villagers. In a study of tribal education in Adilabad District, E. V. Rathnaiah investigated the attitude of Gonds to school education. In the course of this investigation he found that in the opinion of the teachers interviewed 13.7 percent of parents were positively cooperative, 56.3 percent were favourable to education but not active, 23.7 percent were indifferent, 1.3 percent were unfavourable, and 5 percent were antagonistic.

The reasons given by parents for not sending their children to school were as follows:

Need for help in household work	35.7 percent
Occupation with herding cattle	30.0 percent
Children's lack of interest in education	25.3 percent
Ill health	6.6 percent
Don't know	2.4 percent

In the opinion of the teachers questioned, the reasons for the poor enrollment of tribals in schools were:

Lack of interest in education among parents	64.5 percent
Poverty	31.5 percent
Lack of interest in education among children	4.0 percent

Even more important factors impeding the spread of education among tribal children are the distance of many villages from the nearest school and the limited places in ashram schools. There are many villages whose children would have to walk five or six kilometers to attend a school, and there are not enough boarding schools to accommodate more than a fraction of the children from villages without primary schools in a vicinity.

For tribal children who are eligible for admission to upper primary and high schools, most of which are situated at some distance from tribal villages, there are hostels in which pupils are provided with free board and lodging, and in some cases also with extra tuition. Without such facilities few tribal children could attend high schools, because for most parents it is economically impossible to maintain a child in a taluk or district headquarters. Notwithstanding all the material facilities provided by government for tribal students, few progress beyond the fifth from. The following figures relating to 1976 make this clear.

Of 5,599 tribal children enrolled in the schools of Adilabad District, 4,555 were boys and 1,044 were girls. Distribution in forms I to X was as follows: I, 3,302; II, 832; III, 363; IV, 298; V, 345; VI, 194; VII, 119; VIII, 58; IX, 43; X, 40.

Table. Higher Education Scholarships, 1974–75

Institution	**Number of Scholars**	**Amount of Scholarships**
Government College, Adilabad	4	Rs 3,400
Degree College, Nirmal	2	1,648
Junior College, Sirpur-Kaghaznagar	3	2,863
Government College, Chennur	1	364
Government College, Mancherial	14	10,371
TOTAL	24	Rs 18,647

The rapid drop in attendance was particularly noticeable in the blocks of Wankdi and Utnur.

There the relevant figures were as follows:

Form	I	II	III	IV	V	VI	VII	VIII	IX	X
Wankdi	284	24	9	3	4	1	2	0	0	0
Utnur	912	192	60	28	34	28	23	6	15	7

For the years after 1976, statistics for the indigenous aboriginals are not available because in 1977 the immigrant Banjaras were notified as a scheduled tribe, and henceforth counted among the tribals.

But my personal enquiries in primary, upper primary, and high schools confirmed the trend apparent in the above statistics. After the first form, in which many children are enrolled, there is a dramatic drop, and between forms II and III, and III and IV, the figures are each year more than halved.

Only a very small percentage of pupils reaches forms VIII, IX, and X. Of those reading in form X, many fail the Secondary School Certificate examination, and the number of Gond children attaining eligibility for college education is thus infinitesimal; this explains the disconcertingly small number of graduates. In the school year 1976–77, 797 boys and 109 girls were attending high schools in Adilabad District, but only one boy attended a junior college.

There is no shortage of scholarships for those eligible for higher education.

In the Government Degree College, Adilabad, the enrollment in the first-year intermediate course from 1969–70 to 1975–76 was twenty-five, out of which only six students completed their courses.

The high degree of wastage was probably due to the students' inadequate previous education, which did not enable them to compete with non-tribal students in a course demanding not only learning by rote but also independent judgement.

Table. Educational Performance of Tribals in Government Service, to 1977

Tribe	Designation and Office	Qualification	Home Village or Taluk
Gond	*Subinspector of Police, Sultanabad, Karimnagar District*	*Pre-University Course*	*Madaguda, Both Taluk*
Pardhan	*Radio Licence Inspector*	*Higher Secondary Certificate*	*Adilabad*
Gond	*Inspector of Vaccinations*	*VIII standard*	*Kapardevi, Adilabad Taluk*
Pardhan	*Agricultural Assistant, Parbhani (Maharashtra)*	*B.Sc. Agriculture*	*Kapardevi, Adilabad Taluk*
Pardhan	*Lower Divisional Clerk, Revenue Department*	*B.Sc. failed*	*Deepaiguda, Adilabad Taluk*
Pardhan	*Lower Divisional Clerk, Social Welfare Department*	*Higher Secondary Certificate*	*Adilabad*
Pardhan	*Lower Divisional Clerk, Revenue Department*	*Secondary School Certificate*	*Lakshetipet Taluk*
Gond	*Lower Divisional Clerk, Public Works Department*	*Secondary School Certificate*	*Madaguda, Adilabad Taluk*
Gond	*Lower Divisional Clerk, Forest Department*	*B.A.*	*Korstkal Taluk*
Gond	*Lower Divisional Clerk, Forest Department*	*Intermediate failed*	*Kapardevi, Adilabad Taluk*
Gond	*Lower Divisional Clerk, Forest Department*	*Intermediate failed*	*Bhutai, Both Taluk*
Pardhan	*Lower Divisional Clerk, Local Funds*	*Secondary School Certificate*	*Akrula, Adilabad Taluk*
Gond	*Lower Divisional Clerk, Post Office*	*Secondary School Certificate*	*Both*
Pardhan	*Lower Divisional Clerk, Girijan Corporation*	*Secondary School Certificate*	*Thendoguda, Asifabad Taluk*
Pardhan	*Telephone Operator*	*B.A. discontinued*	*Asifabad*

Tribe	Designation and Office	Qualification	Home Village or Taluk
Pardhan	*Telephone Operator*	*Secondary School Certificate*	*Ginnedhari, Asifabad Taluk*
Gond	*Lower Divisional Clerk, Police Department*	*Intermediate failed*	*Bhimpur, Adilabad Taluk*
Pardhan	*Lower Divisional Clerk, Registration Office*	*Secondary School Certificate*	*Jaturla, Adilabad Taluk*
Gond	*District Revenue Officer*	*B.A.*	*Utnur Taluk*
Gond	*Police Constable*	*Intermediate failed*	*Dhanora, Utnur Taluk*
Pardhan	*Reserve Police Constable*	*Higher Secondary Certificate failed*	*Adilabad*
Pardhan	*Lower Divisional Clerk, Cooperative Office*	*Intermediate failed*	*Adilabad*
Naikpod	*Lower Divisional Clerk, Post Office*	*Intermediate*	*Thami, Adilabad Taluk*
Naikpod	*Lower Divisional Clerk, Public Works Deptartment*	*B.A. failed*	*Nirmal*
Naikpod	*Lower Divisional Clerk, Forest Department*	*B.A. failed*	*Manoor, Adilabad Taluk*
Naikpod	*Lower Divisional Clerk, Forest Department*	*Higher Secondary Certificate*	*Mancherial*
Pardhan	*Market Inspector*	*Pre-University Course*	*Asifabad*
Pardhan	*Market Inspector*	*Higher Secondary Certificate*	*Thari, Adilabad Taluk*
Gond	*Market Inspector*	*Secondary School Certificate failed*	*Dharampuri, Adilabad Taluk*
Gond	*Market Inspector*	*Secondary School Certificate failed*	*Dharampuri, Adilabad Taluk*
Pardhan	*Salesman, Daily Requirement Depot*	*Higher Secondary Certificate failed*	*Dehgaon, Adilabad Taluk*

The standard of educational performance by tribals, i.e. Gonds, Pardhans, and Naikpods, is reflected in the qualifications of those who succeeded in obtaining employment in government service up to 1977. The fact that no Kolam figures in this list indicates the exceptionally low educational level of that tribe. From which individual names are deliberately omitted, contain information on the tribe, the type of employment, the educational qualification, and the home village of the tribal employees in 1977.

This list of tribal government employees illustrates both the successes and failures of tribal education in Adilabad District. Among the successes must be considered the fact that thirty-seven tribals received an education which enabled them to enter the ranks of government service at all. Seventeen of them acquired sufficient skills to enable them to attain and hold positions as lower division clerks in a variety of offices.

Tribe	Designation and Office	Qualification	Home Village or Taluk
Pardhan	*Salesman, Daily Requirement Depot*	*Secondary School Certificate failed*	*Jaturla, Adilabad Taluk*
Gond	*Salesman, Daily Requirement Depot*	*Higher Secondary Certificate failed*	*Godumalle, Adilabad Taluk*
Gond	*Excise Constable*	*Secondary School Certificate failed*	*Jatuarla*
Pardhan	*Vaccinator, Health Department*	*Higher Secondary Certificate failed*	*Indravelli, Utnur Taluk*
Gond	*Vaccinator, Health Department*	*Secondary School Certificate failed*	*Bhutai, Both Taluk*
Pardhan	*Vaccinator, Health Department*	*Secondary School Certificate failed*	*Tantoli, Adilabad Taluk*

Their qualifications range from secondary school certificate to B.A., but a number of them failed either in the intermediate or in the degree examinations and had to content themselves with minor clerical positions though success in their examinations might have made them eligible for gazetted posts. Thus one Gond graduate has recently attained the elevated position of district revenue officer. The number of those who failed in the examinations for which they had studied is relatively large, but even they managed to obtain such minor government posts as market inspector, salesman, or vaccinator. But there must be many more who failed to attain the secondary school certificate and who did not manage to secure even the humblest of government posts.

A further fact emerging from this list is the disproportionately large representation of Pardhans among government employees. They outnumber Gonds, even though the total Pardhan population is less than 10 percent of the number of Gonds. As traditional bards and chroniclers they were always the "intellectuals" among the local tribesmen, and it is hardly surprising that they could overtake the Gonds in the competition for jobs which require some intellectual gifts.

The list further reveals the advantages enjoyed by tribals in the more progressive areas, such as Adilabad Taluk, and the more backward status of the tribal population of Utnur Taluk. Proximity to district headquarters seems to have had a positive influence both on education and on the people's awareness of the opportunities for entering government service.

A study of tribal manpower resources in Adilabad District undertaken in 1977 by the Tribal Cultural Research and Training Institute, Hyderabad, has diagnosed some of the factors which impede the recruitment of young tribals to government service and private industry. Both in government enterprises and in industry there are numerous vacancies for posts requiring technical skills, but the number of tribal candidates with such qualifications are few.

There is an Industrial Training Institute in Mancherial, entry into which is open to candidates with a pass in the eight standard. In the year 1973-74 one tribal joined one of the courses but dropped out, and in the years 1971–72, 1972–73, and 1974–75 there were no tribal students. In the year 1975–76 six tribal candidates joined this institute; three in the course for fitter's trade and three for tractor mechanic's trade. In 1976–77 three candidates joined the course in mechanic's trade, and in 1977 altogether six tribal students were enrolled in the institute.

This is a very small number considering the fact that the Singareni Collieries Company Limited alone has an annual requirement of three thousand candidates to fill vacancies in all grades and has to import labour from other districts because of the lack of sufficient qualified local persons. In 1977 there were seventeen vacancies for holders of certificates of the Industrial Training Institute on the register of the employment exchange, but there were only two tribal candidates.

As early as 1946 I advocated in my pamphlet *Progress and Problems of Aboriginal Rehabilitation in Adilabad District*the systematic training of Gonds and other tribals in mechanical skills. I wrote:

I believe that Gonds could be trained as skilled workmen, and I would suggest that the training of young literate Gonds as carpenters, mechanics, fitters etc. should not be deferred until the industries of the new towns have come into being, but should be taken up at once. If we can build up a small stock of trained Gond workmen of fairly high qualifications... these young men can become the nucleus and leaders of an industrial Gond colony and serve as an example that for the aboriginal industrial employment does not necessarily mean casual labour at low wages and life in an uncongenial, squalid environment, but that an industrial worker can enjoy as high or higher a standard of living and as good housing as an independent cultivator.

Had this proposal been taken up, the involvement of tribals in the industries of Bellampalli and Mancherial might have begun when these industries were still in an early stage of gradual development and hence capable of integrating small groups of tribal workers. Today Gonds can enter industry only as individuals and only at the cost of total alienation from the traditional life-style of tribal society.

In the course of the study of manpower resources quoted above, tribals in various boys' hostels were questioned about their career preferences.

The results of the interviews showed that 40.9 percent wanted to become teachers in arts subjects; 22.7 percent wanted to become science teachers; 18.2 percent wanted to study medicine and become doctors; and 18.2 percent wanted to enroll in technical courses and become engineers. Of those interviewed, 82.8 percent hoped for employment in Adilabad District, preferably near to their home villages. An interesting feature of this enquiry is the preference for such familiar professions as teaching, medicine, and engineering, while none of those asked mentioned careers as veterinary surgeons or agricultural extension officers.

More surprisingly none of the boys stated that he wanted to become a *tahsildar* or superior revenue officer, an interesting contrast to the aspirations of tribal students in Arunachal Pradesh, many of whom told me that they hoped to join the administrative service and to attain ultimately the position of deputy commissioner or another post involving responsibility and authority. The tribals of Adilabad have for so long been ruled by outsiders that they cannot envisage the possibility of occupying positions of authority and power, although one of them was recently appointed to the prestigious position of district revenue officer.

The situation in other tribal areas is similar to that prevailing among the Gonds of Adilabad. In the 1940s teacher training centres identical to those at Marlavai and Ginnedhari were established in Koya villages of Warangal District, and in 1979 some Koya teachers trained in those institutions were still in service. Most of the Koyas have the advantage of speaking Telugu as their mother tongue, and Koya children therefore face fewer difficulties than the Gondi-speaking children of Adilabad. The absence of a language barrier accounts perhaps for the fact that among the tribals of Khammam district the literacy rate was 5 percent, compared with 3.28 percent in Adilabad District, both figures relating to the 1971 census. Another explanation may be the inclusion in Khammam District of some areas which in the days of British rule belonged to the Agency Tracts of Madras Presidency, where educational standards were more advanced than in Hyderabad State. In the area of Sudimalla, one of the Koya training centres established in 1946, several Koyas have had fairly successful careers. In 1978 there were two Koya subinspectors of police, and one Koya who had entered the central police service held the appointment of district superintendent of police at Imphal in Manipur State, a highly responsible position in a sensitive frontier region.

In recent years special efforts have been made to develop educational facilities in Srikakulam District, where the administration is anxious to regain the confidence of the many tribesmen who were involved in the Naxalite uprising. Saoras, Jatapus, and various minor tribal groups number a total of 213,928 and thus constitute 8.2 percent of the population. Most of them are economically backward and, dwelling in remote hill villages, had until recently no access to any kind of schools.

A further obstacle to the spread of education was the fact that such tribes as Saoras and Gadabas speak Munda languages, whereas teaching was available only in Telugu, even where schools had been opened in the vicinity of tribal settlements. By 1978 there were 227 primary schools, 5 upper primary schools, and 4 high schools, in which nearly 12,000 children were enrolled. In addition, there were 61 ashram schools, 25 of which had been opened in 1977, and altogether 6,000 tribal children were maintained as boarders in ashram schools and hostels. The annual expenditure on education was then ₹ 5,000,000. Some of the results seem to have been rather better than those from Adilabad quoted above. Thus, between 1974 and 1979, 35 tribal pupils of the high school at Bhadragiri succeeded in passing the matriculation examination. Even in some Saora and Jatapu villages situated on high hills and accessible only by footpaths, ashram schools have recently been opened and seem to be well attended.

The overall literacy rate for all the tribal areas of Andhra Pradesh was 5.34 percent in 1971, and had risen to 8.62 percent by 1978. The system of ashram schools providing boarding facilities for tribal children extends to all the districts containing tribal populations, including Mahbubnagar and Kurnool, where school education is provided even to the children of the semi-nomadic Chenchus.

It appears that the low economic level of the foodgathering Chenchus has no adverse effect on the children's ability to absorb the instruction provided in schools, and in the ashram school at Mananur some Chenchu girls are studying in the tenth standard.

In Kurnool District, where education for Chenchus was started in the British period, there are a few families of educated Chenchus who have obtained positions in government service, but in Mahbubnagar District there are as yet no adult Chenchus who have gone through the school system. It remains to be seen whether those Chenchus who have spent several years in boarding schools will be able to readjust to the forest life of their parents. If they have lost the skill of gathering marketable forest produce or have developed wants which cannot be met from the income Chenchus derive from the sale of such produce, education may be a mixed blessing except for those young people who obtain jobs outside their traditional habitat.

The educational backwardness of most of the tribal populations of Andhra Pradesh is a correlate of the generally adverse economic conditions under which the tribesmen labour, and cannot be attributed to a lack of funds available for educational institutions. In the financial year 1978–79, a total of ₹ 56,340,000 was allocated for tribal education, and of this total budget ₹ 52,245,000 was provided by the Tribal Welfare Department.

The number of educational institutions in 1978, together with the number of pupils within the area covered by the plans for tribal development. The boarders accommodated in hostels were also given special coaching. The number of teachers in ashram schools was 1,171, and the number of teachers employed in primary, upper primary, and high schools was 1,821. The number of students in receipt of post-matric scholarships was 1,950, 468 tribal students were admitted to reputable private schools and public schools, and 90 students were enrolled in the special residential Kinnarsani school for tribals.

Table. *Pupils Covered by Tribal Development Plan, 1978*

Number of Educational Institutions		Pupils within the Area	
Ashram schools	399	*Boarders enrolled*	26,746
Hostels	343	*Boarders enrolled*	24,383
Primary schools	1,740	*Students enrolled*	37,729
Upper primary schools	115	*Students enrolled*	4,052
High schools	75	*Students enrolled*	3,630
Junior colleges	6	*Students enrolled*	305
Aided schools	375	*Students enrolled*	24,970

In Andhra Pradesh the funds spent on educational institutions accessible to tribal populations have not yet brought about a fundamental change in the tribals' unfavourable position, largely because the social, political, and economic forces arraigned against them have so far prevented all real progress. However, that in Northeast India educational progress among tribals has played an important role in securing for them a position of political equality and growing economic prosperity.

Chapter 8

Development and Poverty among Tribal People in India

Tribal people are often considered as a 'blockage' towards development and progress. Development, like growth, corresponds to different meanings. However, the ideology of 'development' is generally used and rightly understood as 'dominant development paradigm' that brings only negative effect on the tribals. Although it is considered as an essential part of enhancing economic growth through which social justice can be brought in, its experience of today is of anti-poor and pro-rich. According to a noted Indian economist C.T. Kurien, poverty does not continue to exist in spite of "development" but because of it. The state has consistently using development concept to solve poverty problem in India especially in the tribal areas. Because of development there has millions of tribals are displaced. Development which boasts of as 'progress' and 'modernity', on the one hand deprives the tribal people of the right and access to resources and the same time destroys the non-renewable natural resource base rapidly.

In India many development projects such as construction of roads, airport extension, uranium mining for industries, dam construction etc., have forcefully dislocated/displaced millions of people. The World Commission on Dams, estimates that 40 million to 80 million people have been physically displaced by dams worldwide, a disproportionate number of them being indigenous peoples. Indeed, this 'development cleansing' may be well constitute ethnic cleansing in disguise, as the people dislocated so often were from minority ethnic communities. In India, 40 per cent to 50 per cent of those displaced by development projects – a total estimated at more than 33 million since 1947- are tribal people.

In the case of Sardar Sarovar project- the number of displaced tribal stood at 57.6 per cent. North East India which has large concentration of tribal population is facing the heat of development today. Arunachal Pradesh government has signed hundreds of MOUs for dam constructions with companies. Such dams would have destructive effect on the people, its livelihoods and ecological balance. Timothy Z Zote wrote about the Tipaimukh dam in Manipur thus: "The Government's final decision for the construction of the Timaimukh Dam is really a knell to the affected people of Tipaimukh Sub Division. Economically or politically, the Hmars, inhabitants of Tipaimukh Sub-Division will certainly be exploited by the outsiders who are more advanced. Half of the population will leave the place for some economic and political reasons, almost half of the land, orchards, gardens and public jhum land will either be submerged by water or will be acquired for township, colonies or other types of construction."

The Barak River on which the Tipaimukh dam is contructed is the life line and their mother who gives them all domestic needs in season and out of season. For the Hmars and Nagas tribes living on the bank, the river has been the carrier of uncountable source of income and wealth to the people, and in return this river carries away poverty. The people sell their agricultural products in Silchar and carry their domestic needs through this river; their economic activity entirely depends on this river. Therefore, the construction of Tipaimukh Dam means the destruction of the economy of its inhabitants.

Another example of a development project that affect the tribal people in Manipur is Khuga Dam (multi-purpose project). In the construction of the Dam, many villages and households had been affected and displaced. The people especially the meiteis, who had been allotted land under the provision of the MLR and LR Act 1960, are made genuine land owners. Such people only got land compensation. The tribals who had been living there even before the framing of the land laws and owned the land on the basis of the traditional and customary laws are made encroachers in their own land. The extension of the Act had deprived the people of ownership of land based on traditional and customary practices. Government of North eastern states have allowed Special Economic Zones (SEZ) to be set up in their states as part of economic development. The Indian government in collaboration World Bank is constructing new roads almost every part in NE India. With its Look East Policy (LEP), the Indian government is planning for transnational highways which would cross through Arunachal Pradesh to China, Nagaland to Myanmar and Manipur to Thailand and Malaysia.

The poor tribal will be wipe out from their own land as is happening in many parts of mainland India (as in Narmada valley and Chhattisgarh, Orissa etc). An intensive research needs to be done about these projects to educate the rather ignorant tribal people about the benefits and ill-effects of such development in the region. Certain quarters and concerned individuals have already started to raise voice about the dangers of such development works in the region. Many villages will be wiped out by developmental projects. Traditional livelihoods will be destroyed. Social system will be broken.

Such development will intensify commercialization of natural resources that has been already threatened by money-oriented economy in the region. Only few will people (both local elites and outsiders) will become richer at the expense of poor masses. India state has been ruthlessly efficient in the way it has appropriated its resources –its land, its water, its forests, its air – and redistributed it to a favoured few (in return, no doubt, for a few favours). While the government is keen to alleviate mass poverty through development, tribals fear that this could lead to gain control over their lands.

Today, India's poorest people are subsidising the lifestyle of her richest. Most tribal people have no formal title to their land and therefore cannot claim compensation anyway. They were forced to migrate to cities and end up in slums. The price of the mega development projects has been paid by the rural poor, particularly the tribal, the Scheduled Castes and the other landless category of people. They have paid the price in terms of their dislocation and consequent dispossession in the event of meagre compensation by the State for their losses.

Arundhati Roy said that contrary to what we were often told in public speech that India lives in her villages, in fact, India doesn't live in her villages. India dies in her villages. India gets kicked around in her villages. India lives in her cities. India's villages live only to serve her cities. Her villagers are her citizens' vassals, and for that reason must be controlled and kept alive, but only just. If India wanted to remove mass poverty among the tribal people, reviving, protecting and enhancing village economy is a must. Without this, various welfare schemes of the state (mostly given through cash) alone will not be able to solve the problem.

Under the patronage of government, the corporates are taking over everything –water, electricity, minerals, agriculture, land, telecommunications, education, health –no matter what the consequences. Almost everywhere in India, the tribal people are struggling with one problem or the other as their very survival is threatened. The Dongria Kondh tribe in Niyamgiri region was fighting against the giant company Vedanta from mining bauxite. The government allows "market forces" to mine resources "quickly and efficiently" in most of the mineral rich regions of tribals. The tribal lands are forcefully acquired and turn it over to private mining corporations which is illegal and under unconstitutional under the Panchayat (Extension to Scheduled Areas) Act or PESA. Passed in 1996, PESA is an amendment that attempts to right some of the wrongs done to tribal people by the Indian Constitution when it was adopted by Parliament in 1950. It is a law that acknowledges the deepening marginalization of tribal communities and is meant to radically recast the balance of power.

As a piece of legislation, it endowed the community -the collective- a legal entity and it confers on tribal societies who live in scheduled areas the right to self-governance. Certain powers were conferred to gram sabha such as management of community resources, resolution of disputes, approval of plans and programmes and mandatory consultation before the acquisition of the land. The gram sabha is also entitled to ownership of minor forest produce, enforcement of prohibition, restoration of unlawfully alienated lands, control over money lending and marketing., etc under PESA. Under PESA, "compulsory acquisition" of tribal land whether it is for reserved forests, mining, or for any other developmental projects cannot be justified on any count.

In spite of this provision, tribal people continue to suffer in the name of development. The adivasis and the tribals' lands are being grabbed and distributed to the rich for Special Economic Zones (SEZs). In places like Lalgarh, the tribals held a stiff opposition to land grabbing by the rich companies who works in connivance with the state government. People who dreamt of equality and justice and who demanded land to the tiller are often branded as 'Maoist' or 'insurgents" and are booked under criminal laws.

The armed forces, the state controlled media, the state and the companies all work together to grab the resources of the poor tribal and at the same justify this act in the name of development. Economic growth based on heavy industry, mega dams, steel industry, transnational highways, etc, has ecological concern on which the lives and livelihoods of the tribals depend. Destroying ecological health is tantamount to destroying tribals' lives and livelihoods as they have symbiotic relationship with forests, land and rivers. So often our government interprets poverty as lack of cash to buy food. This belief has destroyed forests, rivers and land for growing cash crops. By growing cash crop, it is believed that more money will be earned, income will increase, and living standard will be raised. But it turn out to be opposite for the majority poor. Seeing poverty simply as a lack of cash is dangerous. This is abolishing food security. Cash incentive is given to the people and they were told to buy food. Land resources and other productive are privatized and commoditized to make more money. People have to search job in order to earn. This is unreasonable. If public investment in agriculture sector is neglected, agricultural land and forest diverted for other commercial purposes, poverty and high rate of unemployment will be the fate of poor masses.

The deficiency of understanding poverty in terms of cash poverty is that it directed all economic policies and activities are turn towards earning money. Growth in that condition will not be able solves mass poverty. It will benefit few at the expense of the majority poor. Cash crops have been intensively encouraged to earn money and buy more from the market. This will uproot them from their subsistence economy. Giving money directly to tribal people is likely to destroy their food security rather than solving poverty problem.

The plan of government to give cash in lieu of subsidised food and kerosene directly to the poor is not going to help the poor tribal. Even the money that comes through NREGA has been used unmindfully like buying mobile phones, eating and drinking and gambling and so on. This makes them lazy too. In spite of its defects, such welfares schemes are necessary, but it should not be taken as a sure way to solve poverty problem in the country. Proper education and awareness about various schemes and its importance towards enhancing their living standard needs to be given to the tribal people. This calls for the involvement of civil societies, NGOs and leaders from the grass-root level.

Lack of money to buy minimum needs cannot be the only yardstick to measure poverty in the tribal area. It is imperative to look poverty from food security perspective especially when it relates to tribal people. This calls for investment in agriculture and its allied activities which will be of great help towards solving mass poverty if such is taken up in accordance with the tribal knowledge and ecological viability.

The government negligent attitude towards agriculture and its allied activities is a cause of great concern. This will leave millions of workers unemployed and hungry. Protection of the commons (land or forests or rivers) from privatization and restriction of mega developmental projects is a must in protecting and promotion of tribal people. In many parts of North East India, where forests and other resources are completely at the control of local people, deforestation takes place partly due to poverty on one hand and commercial interest on the other hand. There is a need to makes them realize about the importance of conservation of forests as they have been doing since long. Proper education will lead them to preserve and nurture forests. This would lead to sustainable living.

Perhaps it is time to revisit Gandhi's vision of Gram Swaraj which has ecological relevance, empowerment of local masses through decentralisation of planning according to local needs. But one must not neglect the problem of internal class, caste and patriarchal divisions of traditional society on an organisational level. Decentralised local initiatives, flexibly determined by local needs, resources and opportunities may be better way of dealing with poverty.

To alleviate poverty therefore is not an individual enterprise. We all need to put our heads together and fight against global capitalist force from grass root level.

Arundhati Roy, a writer activist, aptly put it this way: "Most important of all, India has a surviving adivasis [Tribals] population of almost 100 million. They are the ones who still know the secrets of sustainable living. If they disappear, they will take those secrets with them....If there is any hope for the world at all, it does not live in climate change conference rooms or in cities with tall buildings, it lives low down on the ground, with its arms around the people who go to battle everyday to protect forests, their mountains and their rivers because they know that the forests, the mountains and the rivers protect them."

ALIENATION OF TRIBAL LAND: TENURIAL INSECURITY

The provisions regarding tenurial insecurity recognise that this is the 'single most important cause' of poverty amongst tribals. However, all the current provisions relating to protection of tribal land apply only to 5th Schedule areas. Tamilnadu does not have a law preventing alienation of tribal lands. Only a government order in the case of lands assigned by government to tribals states that these lands cannot be alienated to anyone outside the class to which the assignee belongs. If such land is alienated there is no provision to return the land to the adivasi – in fact it is reclassified as government land and so thus forever loses its tribal characteristic. Therefore it is strongly recommended that Adivasis living in non-scheduled areas must be brought within the ambit of the provisions under this chapter.

Recommendations:

- A Tribal Committee at the district level, as well as Panchayat Tribal Welfare Committee must undertake the assessing and classification of alienated lands, as well as ensuring their restoration and distribution of pattas and forest lands. The Committee must decide whether pattas will be distributed to individuals, families or village-wise – in general it will be best to issue family or village pattas.
- Traditional sacred groves, burial grounds and pathways must be identified, listed and demarcated village-wise. Villages must be given possession of encroached or alienated lands, or suitable alternatives found, depending on the traditions and cultural practices of the tribe.

- There are cases where land has been set aside for tribals for subsequent use and distribution. For example in Nilgiris district there are two instances: a) is a particular classification of land called RHT or Reserved for Hill Tribes – where pieces of land had been identified during the 70's for subsequent distribution to adivasis. These lands have never been distributed and have either been encroached upon by outsiders and the forest department. Many have been reclassified as government assessed waste lands. These lands must be identified and repossessed and handed over to landless adivasis. And b) a large portion of land - The Kollapally division of TAN TEA – The Tamilnadu Tea Plantation Corporation was earmarked for tribals. In fact this land was not administered by the Corporation but by the Forest Department who it was felt had better contact with the tribals. However since none of them were aware of this they were not able to take advantage of this provision and in the late 80's the land was handed over to the Corporation without a single tribal benefiting.
- Due to certain complications arising out of the Gudalur Janmam Abolition Act – many lands have in Gudalur and Pandalur have been classififed under Section 17 of the said Act. The matter has been in court for several years and it has proved to be a huge stumbling block for adivasis who have traditionally been in possession of lands long before the passing of the Act. All lands such as these under possession of adivasis must be immediately reclassified as "tribal land".
- In fact all tribal land must come under a special classification with special survey numbers and all registrars must be supplied with a list of these survey numbers stating that sale or other documents relating to these lands cannot be registered. Laws notwithstanding, it is common practice to register sale deeds of tribal lands. This must be stopped immediately.

TRIBAL FOREST INTERFACE

The consultation appreciated the recognition that tribals have been in the "forefront of the conservation regime". This section, in keeping with the Schedule Tribes (Recognition of Forest Rights) Bill 2005, ensures the right of adivasis to their forest homelands.

It is the most vital element of adivasi development. Adivasi without forests and forests without adivasis is an unthinkable proposition.

Recommendations:

- Forest produce has been a vital nutritional source for adivasi communities and food security must be viewed broadly to include these traditional foods as well as carbohydrates provided by PDS
- Right to propagate certain medicinal plants and fruits, such as jackfruit, Indian gooseberry (amla) etc in forests must be recognised
- The usage of chemical pesticides and insecticides inside and around forests must be discontinued
- Building of infrastructure in forests, like roads, electricity lines, check dams etc, must be done after consultations with adivasis in the area and built with their involvement
- Adivasi staff must be taken into administrative and advisory roles in the Forest Department enabling them to become more sensitive to the interactions of adivasi communities within forests
- Adivasi communities must be involved in dealing with and preventing poaching of wildlife in forests and Controlled ritualistic hunting of certain species may be introduced during identified seasons

DISPLACEMENT, REHABILITATION AND RESETTLEMENT

Clarifications are sought on the nature and scope of 'development' projects as referred to in these sections.

Project affected persons must include those adivasis displaced in the creation of national parks, wildlife sanctuaries and biosphere reserves.

Recommendations:

- Displacement of adivasis from their traditional homes in forests must be minimised, even while creating wildlife sanctuaries and reserves

ENHANCEMENT OF HUMAN DEVELOPMENT INDEX

Education, Vocational Training and Sports

The functioning of Ashram Schools or Government Tribal Residential Schools as they are called in Tamilnadu leave a lot to be desired. These schools neither provide basic education nor do they provide adequate care as hostels.

Recommendations:

- Adivasis must be free to choose the institution to which they want to send their children.
- Rather than fund schools government should provide an outright amount per child which will be paid to parents as long as the child goes to school. Though the amount may vary from state to state or district to district it must be over and above the school fees. This will both act as an incentive to ensure retention and also minimise the loss of family income when a child goes to school. This will also give the parents freedom to choose the school and will give their children the right to be seen as "fee paying" students rather than as charity cases. It will further give the parents a right to intervene in the school which is sorely lacking now.
- Establishment of a Panchayat Tribal Welfare Committee which will work with the Parents Committee to supervise the education and vocational training of children and young people. School curriculum and administration must be developed and managed by this committee
- Government Tribal Residential School (GTR) to be replaced by Government Tribal Residential Hostels for school and college going students. GTR Hostels will have facilities to take the children to school, and provide uniforms, and other support.
- Traditional knowledge must be recognised and seen to be part of the school curriculum. Apart from mainstream subjects like maths, science etc, a subject in tribal knowledge must form part of the syllabus. Childrens traditional knowledge gained from their parents must be formally recognised as education.

- Schools must grant leave of absence to children during tribal festivals and rituals and allow flexible rules to re-admit drop-outs, especially during cropping or harvest seasons.
- Village escorts will be paid to take children safely to school and bring them back home after classes especially where children have to trek long distances to school.
- Girl students must receive academic and psychological counselling. Regular follow-up of drop-out girl students must be conducted.
- Training and other inputs must be provided, by adivasi trainers, to teachers who work in adivasi areas. They must be tested and pass a basic exam on local Adivasi culture and tradition
- Study centres, libraries or tuition centres to be started and cultural camps to be conducted in each village. These will be built and run by the village rather than outside contractors.
- In areas removed from forests, arrangements must be made for children to go into the forest and learn about them, as part of school curriculum
- When there is a minimum number of adivasi children in a school, a 'gram sahayak', volunteer or staff, may be appointed and act as a link between students and teachers, the village and the school

Health

Recommendations:

- To address the problem of vacancies in tribal areas, appropriate qualification criteria must be used while selecting health care personnel. Positive discrimination may be exercised to ensure that people from these areas are employed to cater to the needs of their people.
- Tribal Health Staff must be trained to ensure that health care needs are adequately met. Village level workers must be trained so that each village will have access to basic health care. Further, Tribal health promoters must be trained to act as a link between the village and the tertiary health care centre in the town, and guarantee that health

services reach the people. Health Education programmes, like street theatre, posters, banners etc must be taken up at the village level, since tribal people are hardly exposed to these programmes which are currently limited to larger towns

- The number of balwadis and Anganwadis in Tribal areas must be increased to create greater accessibility, and improve child health and nutrition. The Balwadis must also be linked to geriatric health care for elderly persons in the village, who are especially vulnerable due to malnutrition etc. Cirteria for anganwadis must be based not on minimum numbers but on villages.

CREATION OF CRITICAL INFRASTRUCTURE

Recommendations:

- Land and other tenurial issues must be sorted out prior to the implementation of infrastructure development schemes
- Plans for infrastructure development, such as housing plans, must be custom-made with the involvement of stakeholder families, rather than being mass produced. Funds for housing infrastructure must be given to the village committee which can develop plans tailor-made for each village. Habitat planning focusing on water facilities, sanitation and drainage, roads etc will encompass more than just a narrowly focused housing plan.
- Release of funds for infrastructure development must be made by and to village level committees and contracts given by them. Budgets, schemes, their implementation and follow-up must be shared with Panchayat level Tribal Welfare committees on a yearly basis.

CONSERVATION AND DEVELOPMENT OF PARTICULARLY VULNERABLE TRIBAL GROUPS (PTGS)

It is appreciated that the Policy proposes to reclassify Primitive Tribal Groups as Particularly Vulnerable Tribal Groups. Since all the tribes of the Gudalur and Pandalur areas fall within this category there are some specific recommendations.

Recommendations:

- There should be village level micro planning for the development of the members of these groups.
- These plans should be family specific
- These plans must be drawn up by the community themselves drawing on expertise and support from the government as well as NGO's.
- These plans must be time bound and drawn against very strict measurable indicators.
- Local NGO's must be drawn into this process.

ENLISTING SUPPORT OF NGOS

While the impact of NGOs in the development sector has been significant, the role of adivasi organisations in the process of their development must be emphasised. Many of those who have been working with adivasis for many years and have been attempting to protect the very rights as envisaged in the Draft Policy are often seen as "trouble makers' and will therefore be bypassed when deciding "good" ngo's. Ngo's must be selected on the basis of their track record and on the basis of acceptance by the community.

Further, the policy does not recognise tribal organisations – who may not strictly fall into the category of NGO or development organisations. These membership based organisations can play a vital role in the development of the tribals.

TRIBAL CULTURE AND TRADITIONAL KNOWLEDGE

As Nehru's Panchsheel suggests, *People should develop along the line of their own genius.* Traditional knowledge must be protected and learning gained at village festivals and seasonal practices must be recognised as important part of education. This may be introduced into school curriculum as a paper on Adivasi Culture and Traditions.

DEORI PEOPLE

Deori or Deuri is one of the major ethnic tribes in Assam, India. The Deori community has its own culture and traditions which is a hidden treasure for the sociologists. The Deoris were originally priests and worshipers and depended mostly on agriculture for their livelihood.

RELIGION

In North East India the Deoris are known as well civilized people. They have their own language to converse amongst themselves. History says that the Deori language was the original language in the Chutian kingdom before the reign of the Ahoms in Assam. They worship Kundi-Mama (Shiv-Parvati) and hence fall under Hinduism by default. The Deoris are God fearing people. Since ancient days Deori people worshiped God by singing hymns and holy songs. Later on the experienced priests known as Boderi and Bharali started sacrificing animals in their temples; they not only worshiped God, but also administered the kingdom. They also built some important "Kundi Ku" (Temple) in their ancient city or nagar called "Khundi Nagar". Now the ruins of these temples are in the District of Lower Dibang Valley, Lohit and Changlang of Arunachal Pradesh.

HISTORY

However, history says that the homeland of the Deoris is in the North Eastern states of India or in the east of undivided Assam. According to the book *Mataks and their kingdom*, the Deoris had their abode on the bank of the Kundil river which flows through the Sadiya (Chapakhowa) area and for this reason their Kingdom was known as Chutam in the North Eastern region of the Brahmaputra Valley.

In the book "Siva Purana", the late Ahom king Rudra Singha narrates that the Deoris were living at Chaug-Chu-Kul, Chakati-Chaliya, Laibari, Lataubari, Kundil, Joidaam, Arem-Kerem and Mamaru-Pichala (Now in Arunachal Pradesh). According to the book "Boroni Jaiminaw Swamasarnai" the Dimichiya Gonarajita whose capital was Kundil Nagar was ruled by the Deori tribe. They had an honorable and prestigious king called Patgauan or Tanugiria. The first king of Dimichiya Ganarajya was late Bisusing Borkoyo in 1500BC and the last king was Bismoksing Borkoyo who was most famous and well known for his brilliance. These days the capital Kundil Nagar of Dimichiya Ganarajya is known as Bismok Nagar due to the strong Endeavour and enterprise of the late king Bismok

Sing. It is said that in 1602AD the three main sub cast of Deoris namely Jimochayan or Dibang-Diyongial, Midoyan or Tengapania and Luitugan or Borgoya took different temples like Midiya (Bolia Baba), Luituwasi (Tamreswari), Midi Gira-Girasi (Burha-Burhi) and Daramji (Parsuram Kundha). They had been serving the 4th sub cast called Patgayan or Tanugirian. These areas are now in the Lower Dibang Valley, western Lohit and Northern Changlang and North East Tinsukia Dist. of Assam.

The Deoris proudly introduce themselves as 'Jimo-Chhayan', meaning 'the children of the sun and the moon'. In fact, the Deoris were respected among the tribal communities as priests or worshipers.

FINDINGS

As there is lack of scientific study about the indigenous tribes of the State, one cannot find a general acceptable term on the Deoris. Again, history books mention that the Deoris faced a serious crisis from 1794 AD for which the Moamoria rebellion widely spread up to Sadiya and the Ahom monarchy gradually declined. Then the Khamtis, who were Buddhists, occupied Sadiya from the Ahoms and as a consequence, the Deoris were stopped from making human sacrifice in the Tamreswari temple. They lost their support from the Ahom kings and felt insecure due to the Khamtis who killed chief priest Kendukolai Bor Deori in the temple. Without royal patronage, they had no resources to repair the Tamreswari and other temples of the region that were damaged in natural calamities like earthquakes. So, in 1800 AD, when the Ahoms re-occupied Sadiya, the Deoris had already left Sadiya for the Choikhowa area.

Bishnu Rabha says 'Kundil' is a two-phase word Kundi meaning God and la denoting place, according to the Sutiyas. So, Kundil ignifies the place where God is omnipotent. Archeologists believe the relics of Malini Than in the border area of Assam and Arunachal Pradesh are of the ancient Bidarbha Kingdom.

One English scholar discovered a fort, some broken bricks and a tank there, some 25 miles from Sadiya.

But it has created confusion among the historians, because no reliable ancient document exists on the original place of the community. Obviously, without proper investigation and systematic study they have done some work.

In this connection, WB Brown says: "In the upper ward of Sadiya, Deoris lived here originally and before first century they came there to inhabit the area. The people are generally called Deoris simply; the language is more properly known as Sutiya. The Sutiya language indeed, may fairly claim to be the original language of upper Assam." Gait says, "the traditional rulers of Assam do not profess to be at all exhaustive. Religious books and other old writings contain lists of many other kings, but it is impossible to say if they are genuine, and if so', who the kings were and where they reigned; and to refer to them at length would be a waste of time and space.

The dynasties mentioned above are those that are best known and although a great part of the stories told of them may be fictitious, it is probable that there is nevertheless a basis of actual fact."

The Deoris are believed to have come to Sadiya before the 1st century. Up to the 4th cen-tury AD was the 'pre-history period' of Assam history and our sources for that period are the relics like caves, pots, megaliths and legends and traditions as found in the ancient literature like the epics and the Puranas. We find mention of some rulers of ancient Assam like Mohiranga Danava, Ghatakasur, Narakasur. Bhagadutta, Bana, Bhismak, etc. Bhagavat mentions the legends of a king named Bhismak who ruled over a kingdom called Vidarbha with its capital at Kundima.

This kingdom was in the northeast corner of Assam, *i.e.* near Sadiya. The Deoris were royal priests of the kingdom. The legends also provide us other important information, that Lord Krishna appeared in Bidarbha and forcibly married Rukmini Devi, daughter of Bhismak, after defeating Sisu-pal, a prince of a neighbouring kingdom, to whom Rukmini was betrothed. Gait writes in his book: "Bhismak had five sons and a daughter named Rukmini. Krishna, having heard of her beauty, was anxious to marry her, but the father had arranged to give her to another prince named Sisupal, whose fort may still be seen a few miles to the east of the one attributed to Bhismak. Rukmini secretly sent news to Krishna and on the day fixed for her marriage, the latter suddenly appeared and carried her off in his chariot. He was pursued by the crowd of princes, who had come to assist at the wedding, but he defeated them."

Some folk songs and unwritten form of literature provide us information about the origin of the Deoris. They had moved from one place to another before Christ and at last reached Joydham (presently Arunachal Pradesh) from Arema Kerema.

THEY SING IN A HUSARI GEET

"Aremat arilo Keramat dharilo Joydhamat patilo than, Joydham Parbatar Para sai pathiyalo Sadiyar batate sura, Tarepasate sai pathiyalo Sadiyar putala ghunra."

Historians say about the legends that most probably they heard the story from the locality as a fact and gave a shape to it without any systematic study and proper evidence. The episode is known as Rukmini Harana and in the 10th chapter (skandha) of Bhagavat it is also described that Rukmini had offered puja in order to get Krishna as her husband and visited a few temples.

Except for these legends, the Sutiyas first came to the limelight of history in the 13th century. Under Brahmin influence they wrote their traditional history which shows that the founder of the Sutiya kingdom Birpal, who claimed descent from the mythical Bhismak, ruled over sixty families on a hill called Sonagiri. After defeating the king of the Pala dynasty in a battle, the Sutiyas ruled over the upper part of Assam and the kingdom was known as the Sutiya Kingdom.

When the Ahoms established their kingdom in the southeastern corner of Assam or south bank of the Brahmaputra between the rivers Burhi Dihing and Disang in the 13th century, one of their immediate neighbours were the Sutiyas, who ruled the land east of the rivers Subansiri and Disang. During that time both were independent powers and faced uo problems from each other. Both came into contact in the middle of the 14th century AD.

Nowadays, Deori people are living in various places of Assam, Especially, Sivsagar, Jorhat, Dibrugarh, Lakhimpur, Sonitpur, Dhemaji, Tinsukia district and Lohit and Changlang Districts of Arunachal Pradesh are the major habitation of them. According to the Census Report of 1951, the total populations of Deori people were 12,503.

But it is quite strange that only 6715 of them can speak their own language. There were four classes of Deoris one of them are mysteriously missing when they migrated from Sadia trough River Brahmaputra.

(a) Dibongia (b) Tengaponiya, (c) Bogeenya. and (d) Patorganya

Only the people of Dibongiya class can speak their own mother tongue, and almost all the other classes mysteriously lost their language.

THE TERM "DEORI"

The real explanation of the term 'Deori' is not given convincingly by the Sociologists.

The word 'Deori' comes from the word Deu meaning great and wise. O and R denotes male and female respectively. Deori thus refers to a great or wise male/female. According to UN Goswami's Deori-Chutia, the term Deori refers to a person who is well-versed in worshiping God. Hemkosh (1900) refers to Deoris as one of the disobedient tribes who live on the plains of Assam. Chandrakanta Abhidhan (1933) says they were originally hills people, now living in Assam plains as a priestly class of the Sutiyas. Sir Edward Gait says the Deoris are the priestly section of the Sutiya kings of Sadiya who worshipped the Goddess Kundi-Mama or Gira-Girachhi, Tamreswari or Kechaikhati and Baliababa.

Dr. Banikanta Kakoti opines that the word Deori is originated from a Sanskrit word "Debagrihik". "They (Deoris) are a new Indo-Aryan for-mation connected with devagrhika."

According to that point the ancestors of Deori came to Assam from the mountain "Himgiri"and lived in the North of Assam.

Himgiri may probably be the Himalayas. It has already mentioned above that Deoris are classified into four groups. Each group is known as according to their habitation.

(a) Dibongia –Who live in the bank of the river Dibong (River Dibang). (b) Tenaponya – The inhabitants of the riverside of Tengapani. (c) Bogeenya – Who live in the bank of the river Bornoi. (d) Patorganya – officially not traced yet.

The Deoris were leading a prosperous and peaceful life in Sodiya when some hilly tribal people invaded them. They left Sodiya for good within a night making their way to an uncertain destination sailing through the river the Brahamaputra. Proceeding downward through the river the Brahmaputra. Ultimately they reached Sivsagar and Lakhimpur Districts and established themselves there. They tried to keep relationships with Assamese people to promote mutual cooperation and give their mother tongue. Only Dibongia Deoris use their own language and now keep it well.

House Type

Deori people build their traditional house by using bamboos, woods, canes, reeds etc. They believe in typical "Chang Ghar" (Stilt house). The lower part of the house is used as an enclosure for the animals. The floor has certain holes in it and they pass the unnecessary victuals to the animals. A corridor is enclosed to the mid of the house or in a side by which they can differ various rooms for certain purposes. The fireplace is attached with the 'Chang' and they call it as "Dudepati".

They cooked various meals in it and eat them sitting around the fireplace. A platform remains enclosed to the house for cleaning various things. Such a platform is also built (by somebody) at the entrance of the house. It is to be noted the Deori people keeps faith in God and hence they build a place (in the home) containing an altar for praying.

DRESS AND ORNAMENT: Every society be it Assamese, Mishing or Bodo – has a particular dress habit. Every man tends to form society and in society they create their own peculiarities among themselves in various fields according to their religion, belief and century long experiences support it. As a matter of fact, the Deori community has their own century long adornment and now in the 21st century they are nourishing it, using it with heartfelt devotion. They use particular adornments in particular occasions. Deori Couple A Deori male uses a loin cloth called "Ikhoon" while they stay at home and the "Ikhoon" usually combines with a shirt or sporting. While going out of their home or village they generally use trousers and shirt. They adorns white cloth and use a necklace (called 'Konthamoni') while they take part in traditional social function.

The Deori women wrap up a kind of skirt (called 'Ujaduba Igoon', which hangs loosely down wrapping tightly the breast) along with a sheet called "Jokachhiba" which is enclosed in the waist. However they sometimes wear 'Riha' (a traditional outfit, sheet) and it is called "Tegihra". Particular to Deori women, they use a towel (Gamucha) to cover their head which is known as "Gathiki". It's a peculiar dress code of Deori woman. Deori woman often find their happiness in wrapping various ranges of traditional ornament. They wear a ring called "Gema" and use bangles called "Uchoon" in their wrist. They also wear necklace which they called as "Igawa". Lee, Kotu, Madoli, Joonbiri, Dugdugi etc. are some of the ornaments they use while performing 'Bihu'. The Deori young girl wrap up a kind of skirt (Called "Igoon") same like women but there has some differences; they wrap it up within stomach along with Blouse and Gamocha (for helping to hide Breast). In the Ritual performed (*e.g.* Puja, Marriag Ceremony, Bihu) place they are wrap up the breast with a sheet (Called Baika Mariba) along with Igoon and Blouse and cover their head with "Gathiki" also wear various ornament like "Gema, Lee, Junbiri, Madoli, Dugdugi" etc.

MARRIAGE CEREMONY

Marriage is one of the major social traditions of a society. The customs that involve in marriage ceremony of Deori community is quite interesting. The wooer or his parents visit bride's family first and seeks her for the groom. The first side has to give various commodities to the other in that day and both side cheerfully enjoy. A holy day is fixed for the marriage ceremony by conversation.

Bridegroom sends various ornaments, clothing and significant others to the bride before the marriage ceremony. This is known as "Chhubi- huta- duba". Later on, the marriage ceremony is performed with great religious attitude by them and people are received with various recipes. Hence the ceremony ends and bride is brought to the house of the groom.

MAJOR FESTIVAL

Assamese culture is by no means poor. Their different fairs and festivals have enriched our culture. The Deoris observe two major festivals during a year. One of them is "Bohagiyo Bisu", *i.e.* Bohag Bihu, while the other is "Magiyo Bisu" *i.e.*, Magh Bihu. They have some special rules for the Bihu Festivals. The Bohagiyo Bisu is the most important one and the Deoris observe this festival for a period of seven days with unlimited joy and merry makings. Generally they start it from Wednesday when the "Sangkranti" of "Chot" falls on that day. On the first day of the festival the Deoris offer a Puja in a "Than". It must be mentioned here that both the Bihu festivals of the

Deoris are connected with the agricultural activities and so they are observed rightly before starting the agricultural operations in the fields. The Deoris must sacrifice a goat in the Bihu Puja. The ceremonial bathing of the animals take place in the morning of the day of the Bihu Puja. It is on this day, the "Suwasani Puja" is duly observed by each and every household. Thus the household deity is prayed in the "Suwasani" room by the headman of each household for the welfare of the members of the family.

In the midday all the villagers irrespective of age and sex go to the "Than" and gather there for getting sacred water and "Prasads". First they are purified by the sacred water prepared in the "Than" and then the Bor Deori and Deori Bhorali of the Than distributes "Prasads" among them after his due prayers inside the same. The sacrifices of birds and beasts as goats, ducks and fowls are performed duly and after the puja only the male people of the village take part in the feast.

During the Bihu the elderly people of the village do visit all the households of the village and shower blessings on the members of the households. In return the members of each household greet them well and entertain them with "Suzen" and "Kajii".

Meanwhile the young, both male and female do not remain idle. The young male and female performed dance and song at "Chhaje Khula" (A place which are situated either Isolated from the Village or Middle of the Village) at night, this course had begun from Pohila Chot (Middle of March) and end with "Bisu Uruwaba".

Deori People are could not performed Husari Party without declaration by Deori Bharali's on first Day at Than. Husari are not performed in every year. Declaration of Husari had depended on Village Economy. But probably Husari must be performed after 2 or 3 years gap; if there is no any natural disaster in these year. After declaration of the Husari on the second day of the Bihu the dancing starts from the "Than" and then the parties go on visiting each and every household. They first visit the house of the Bor Deori who is the best respected person of the village. However, the Husari party wishes the members of the household a prosperous year and then the party comes back to the than with different Bihu greetings. The musical instruments used by the Husari party are mainly dance is followed by melodious songs which make the situation filled up with un-restricted joy and merry-makings. The Bihu dances are performed in each household of the village. If the singing of the Husari songs cannot be completed on Thursday, then it is kept for the next Thursday. In big Deori villages the Bohag Bihu seems to last for a period of two weeks. On the day of Bisu Uruwaba (Ending Ceremony of Bohag Bihu) Midi Girachi of Dibongiya Clan, Boliya Baba of Tengaponia Clan and Khesai Khaity of Bogyaan Clan are blessed to all the villagers for whole year and people are seems to be very glad to dance with him/her. The Deodhani Dance is a very important and essential part of the Bohag Bihu. Dr. Moheswar Neog opines that Deodhani is a holy female dance or a god's woman. However, during the Bohag Bihu no man is allowed to go into the Than wearing colourful clothes.

LAND ALIENATION AND TRIBAL PEOPLE'S RIGHTS

Tribal people's rights being a part of the broad human rights phenomena has acquired significance in recent times. As human beings the people who live in tribal lands acquire a similar set of rights like others. Being citizens of the country they are entitled to a number of privileges as well.

From time immemorial there have been violations of their fundamental rights. In contemporary society the state comes to their rescue to some extent. The increasing awareness of the concept of human rights under the aegis of the UNO, world media, NGOs etc. proves beneficial to the victims.

Human rights are those conditions which are inherent to nature and without which one can not live as a human being. These rights and fundamental freedoms allow one to develop fully and use one's human qualities, intelligence, talents and conscience to satisfy one's spiritual, physical, social and other needs. They are based on human kind's increasing demand for life in which the inherent dignity and worth of each human being will receive respect and protection.

Human rights constitute a variable category as is adequately demonstrated by the history of the last few centuries. The list of human rights has been modified and continues to be modified in changing historical circumstances. Thus rights may not be fundamental by nature. That which appears to be fundamental in a given historical era or civilization is not fundamental in other era or civilization. Since the time of Hobbes and Locke, liberal political theorists have made it their primary purpose to explore relationships between the individual and the State.

It is not enough to think in terms of two level relationship, the individual at one level and the State at another nor is it enough if the nation is added. Considering the heterogeneity of mankind and of the population of virtually every existing State it is also necessary to think of ethnic communities and certain other kinds of groups, and to include them among the kinds of rights and duties bearing units whose inter relationships are to be explored.

Rights that belong to individuals may go the them either as human beings or as members of a group. The Universal Declaration of Human Rights enumerates rights of the first sort; they go to, "everyone.... without distinction of any kind, such as race, colour, sex, language, religion, political or other opinion, national or social origin, property, birth or other status".

With regard to the legal rights of groups, ethnic communities are sometimes treated as political units within countries, both through territorial delimitations and through the use of separate electoral rolls. Ethnic communities in many countries are differently treated with respect to rights of property and residence; it is not only a question of territorial reservation for the indigenous but also a question of special measures designed to make it possible for the communities to preserve their distinctive identify.

In case of less advanced groups that have suffered discrimination, it is now not uncommon to give them a right to expect special measures (affirmative action) designed to promote their quality, *e.g.* in the educational and economic realms.

Human rights are often held to be inter-related and mutually complementary. According to this view the 'first generation,' civil and political rights form the bedrock of 'second generation' economic, social and cultural rights, while collective and solidarity rights, such as the evolving indigenous rights constitute a 'third generation' of human rights. Further human rights are often said to be compatible with the rule of law and representative democracy. As per Stig Toft. Madsen's (State, society and Human rights in South Asia) hypothesis, "some instances of human rights do not form an integrated whole but are rights in intergenerational conflicts." The conflict according to Madsen is between the presently dominant 'first generation', civil and political rights professed and guaranteed by a liberal State accepting the ideals of democracy and rule of law and the rights of legal and political, cultural and economic autonomy enjoyed by tribal groups. The outcomes of the conflict between the two incongrous orders of rights has been a working understanding or compromise. While this compromise has guaranteed the survival of tribal cultures, it has also meant that the tribal in question have been denied many of the rights enjoyed by others. So the question is how the tribal autonomy or collective right to autonomy including legal autonomy have circumscribed first generation rights, democracy and the rule of law.

The recent international thinking on indigenous rights is exemplified by the draft of Universal Declaration on the rights of indigenous peoples. According to this draft, "indigenous people have the right to participate fully in the political, economic, social and cultural life of the state while maintaining their distinct political,. economic social and cultural characteristics".

The Rio de Janerio Declaration on Environment and Development, adopted on 14th June, 1992 by the United Nations conference proclaims that states should recognize and duly support indigenous peoples' identity, culture and interest and enable their participation in the achievement of sustainable development.

Indigenous people and their communities have an historical relationship with their lands and are generally descendants of the original inhabitants of such lands. They have developed over many generations a holistic traditional knowledge of their lands, natural resources and environment. According to the Rio Declaration, they shall enjoy the full measures of human rights and fundamental freedoms without hindrance or discrimination. Their ability to participate fully in sustainable development practices on their lands have tended to be limited as a result of factors of an economic, social and historical nature.

The International Labour Organisation also in its convention No. 169, year 1989, on "Indigenous and Tribal Peoples", suggested that governments must consult with indigenous and tribal peoples within their countries on development projects and other activities effecting them. It provided for respect for their land rights. This right include protection of their lands and right to refuse displacement form their lands except in exceptional circumstances and against compensation.

TRIBAL RIGHTS IN INDIA

At the time of independence the Indian Government inherited a large tribal population. The Govt. of India has made a number of plans to protect the rights of the tribals and to integrate them into national developmental planning. The Minority Commission, the National Human Rights Commission etc., are there to prevent atrocities against them and to bring their plight to national lime light. In the Constitution of India the rights of the tribals were explicitly recognized and clauses were included to permit positive discrimination in their favour.

But the evaluation reports have pointed out that these special provisions have so far failed to bring about any positive gains to the tribal population. As per the Planning Commission Document 1973, "Reviewing the policies and programmes of the proceeding Five Year Plans we are of the opinion that the efforts so far made for social and economic development of the scheduled tribes have not brought an appreciable change in their condition."

There can be a number of explanations for the failure of the governmental programmes for tribal development. However, the oppression and appropriation of the tribal people by the economically and politically more powerful groups have led to tribal movements or tribal unrest.

For instance, the Santal rebellion, the revolt by Birsa Bhagwan, the Praja Mandal Movement, the Tana Bhagat Movement, the Naxalbari Movement, the Jharkhand Movement etc., are all attempts by the tribal people to shake off the yoke of exploitation.

In recent times the traditional territories of the tribal people have been subjected to incursions. Their lands are taken away in the name of economic advancement of the country. But in return they receive landlessness, impoverishment and long term degradation of the environment on which they totally depend. For almost two centuries now, tribal communities, like many other non-tribal peasants and forest dwellers, have been witness to the collapse of their multiple relationship with the land, the forest and among themselves. The basis of their cultural ethos, their systems of meaning have faced the collective unslaught of outsider exploiters, the disruptive impact of proselytizing Christianity, and of foreign models of economic betterment which have been conceived without their participation and implemented without their consent. Laws like Land Acquisition Act and the Indian Forest Act legitimise the continuing decline in access and control over forest resources that are the basis of their subsistence economy.

Initiatives from the Bharat-Jan-Andolan, Shosit Jan Andolan, the Indian Council of Indigenous and Tribal Peoples, Adivasi Sangamams in South India, PUCL, PUDR etc., are indicative of these modest attempts to raise - fundamental issues and define an alternative political agenda that frontally challenges the institutions and structures of our bourgeois democracy.

STATE POLICY AND THE TRIBALS

The edifice of colonial forestry was inherited by the Government of Independent India and immediately put to work in the service of the State's primary goals of repaid industrialization.

The National Forest Policy 1952 underlies continuity of the colonial policy. It reinforced the claim of the State to exclusive control over forest protection and production. Significantly this policy identifies shifting cultivation as one of the main threats to State forestry.

But in turn this affects the basic rights of the tribals to be dependent on forest resources. Hence, many tribal groups mounted a sustained challenge to the continuing denial of their rights. The Khanwar tribes of Madhya Pradesh protested in 1957 against revenue collection and called upon the people to defy forest laws which violated their customary rights.

Their slogan, "Jangal Zamin Azad Hai", (forest and land are free gifts of nature) succinctly expressed the opposition to external control and commercial use. Another concept of conflict is the 'Contractor System' which is the modus operandi of forest working in India. The State's unwillingness to replace the contractor system has given rise to militant movements. Naxalite movement is one of the results of this type of exploitation.

PROCESS OF DEPEASANTIZATION AND LAND ALIENATION

An overwhelming majority of the tribals are agriculturists. They owned the land in their own rights. Their entire life process was centered and built upon two major means of production *i.e.*, the forest and the land. To understand the dynamics of land problem in the totality, one needs an understanding of the logic of the underlying forces that govern its ownership pattern. The specific economic form in which unpaid surplus labour is pumped out of the direct producers, determines the relation of the rulers and the ruled. Hence land problem of a particular area has to be understood from its historical perspective. Historical evidences are ample which proves the conception of depeasantization as a net result of the uneven structural changes that have taken place from time to time due to the commoditization of the tribal economy in which land plays a critical and predominant role.

LAND ALIENATION AS A CONCEPT

As per Marx, in a Capitalist society an alienated man lives in an alienated nature and he performs estranged labour and the product of his labour becomes alien to him. Alienation as a concept is used by many social scientists in India, merely as a sociological phenomenon. Since land alienation is the crux of the depeasantization of the tribals, the concept assumes utmost importance in the analysis of tribal rights as a part of human rights discourse. The problem of land alienation is a much deeply connected phenomenon with full of contradictions related to the existing socio-economic order. The separation of land from the tribal communities can be understood in a more scientific way with the assistance of the theoretical formulations of the concept of alienation.

Alienation was defined by Hegel and was used by Marx to describe and criticise a social condition in which man far from being the active initiation of the social world seemed more a passive object of determinate external processes. Marx says, alienation is fundamentally a particular relation of property, involving involuntary surrender to autagonistic 'other'. Alienation is inherent in exploitative relations of production and its nature varies with that of exploitation. Hence alienation's manifestations also differs among societies based on slavery, serfdom and capitalism etc. Thus the concept of alienation may be interpreted to understand a specific problem of the tribals where land becomes the primordial source of exploitation and results in the creation of a society where exploitative production relations exit.

VIOLATION OF LAND RIGHTS

The question of land is not just result of the existing situation but its origin may be traced to the periods of deprivation of tribal lands or to periods of the withdrawal of their rights to exploit forest. Gradually, due to various structural changes within and outside the tribal systems, the more advanced groups forced the tribals either to retreat to the nearest jungles or to become landless labourers. Though land is the only source of their livelihood, as their other assets being extremely meagre, tribals were severally deprived. Basically, moneylenders, traders, the feudal lords, or the rich peasants exploit the tribals most. It is an established fact that there is a large scale alienation of lands which belong to the tribes and grabbers invariably in all cases are the non-tribes. This phenomenon has further been ruined by the emergence of new forces of production. Commenting on this, the National Commission on Backward-Areas Development (1980) says, “In a number of areas new industrial and mining complexes, many major irrigation projects were located in the tribal areas resulting in the submergence of extensive lands belonging to the tribals”.

Also in the operations of denudation of forest on a massive scale tribal labour had been used to a great extent to clear off the forest area which was a method of the land lords to alienate the tribals from the forests. This further widened the gap between the tribal landless and landed gentry of the non-tribal communities.

Commenting on the problem of land alienation in tribal areas, the Committee on Plan Projects, Planning Commission, presented a report on the Tribal Development Programmes in 1969. The committee noticed that tribal lands in many areas passed into the hands of non-tribals, the legal prohibitions against such transfers notwithstanding. Sample studies in Andhra Pradesh, Orissa and some other States have shown that transfers have taken place on large scale without the permission of the collector or other competent authorities as required by law. The loopholes were exploited by the money lenders and others and they continue to circumvent the legal provisions by entering into 'benami' or other clandestine transactions with the native tribals. The impotency of legislation to arrest this growing menace to the economic advancement of the tribal in such a situation is thus obvious.

FORMS OF LAND ALIENATION

The first and foremost is the manipulation of land records. The unsatisfactory state of land records contributed a lot to the problem of land alienation. The tribals were never legally recognized as owners of the lands which they cultivated.

The second form of land alienation is reported to have taken place due to 'benami' transfers. The report of the study team of the Union Home Ministry (May 1975) pointed out that large scale transfers of ownership of the Adivasis' lands are being allowed to go out of hands through illegal and benami transactions, collusive civil proceedings etc., in which land remains to be in the names of the original owners who are reduced to the level of share croppers.

Another form of land alienation is related to the leasing or mortgaging of the land. To raise loans for various needs the tribals have to give their land as mortgage to the local moneylenders or to the rich farmers.

Encroachment is another form of dispossessing the tribals of their lands and this is done by the new entrants in all the places where there were no proper land records. Bribing the local Patwari for manipulating the date of settlement of land disputes, ante-dating etc., are resorted to claim the tribal lands.

Concubinage or marital alliance is another form to circumvent the law and grab tribal lands at no cost at all.

Fictitious adoption of the non-tribals by the tribal families is also another method to snatch the lands of the tribals.

Also the slackness in the implementation of the restrictive provisions encourages the non-tribals to occupy the tribal lands. Lands alienation which takes place in various ways has assumed alarming proportion threatening the right to life of the tribal population. Though the problem lies elsewhere, it is being unfortunately always interpreted as the handiwork of certain individuals like the moneylender, traders, land lords, etc, without understanding the class connection of these individuals. The unsystematic land records of the pre-colonial and colonial periods was followed by the present State. There was collection of taxes, (a strange phenomenon for the natives and it was the beginning process of alienation) in the tribal areas.

In the name of protecting the interest of the tribals stringent laws were enacted by the government but the non-tribals found the loopholes to their advantage. This double edged nature of State policy in one of the facets of the existing contradictions in the Indian Tribal Society. The process of land alienation is not an accidental one, but it has arisen because of the concerted efforts of the antagonistic class interest that are operating in the tribal areas. This is not just migration of the non-tribals into tribal areas rather there is a history behind this migration and the State has supported the migrant non-tribals to the settle down in the tribal lands.

However, being the natural owners of forests and its adjoining lands the tribals are being deprived of their rights to own them. They have been relegated from their earlier 'self-reliant' status to a 'dependent' one. Coupled with the exploitation by the non-tribals, the State legislations also proved detrimental to their interests. Therefore to understand the root causes of the land alienation process of the tribal communities its relationship with the changes in the socio-economic structures have to be understood properly.

Case Study of Mayurbhanj District in Orissa

Orissa occupies a special position in the tribal map of India. In the State the Scheduled Tribes Constitute 22.21 per cent. There are 62 different types of tribes in the State. Mayurbhanj is one of the most tribally dominated districts, lying at the Northern border of Orissa. This district was formed in 1949 out of the ex-State of Mayurbhanj.

The percentage of Scheduled Tribes in the district in nearly 58.56 per cent. The district is extremely important from anthropological point of view. It is inhabited by almost all the important tribes found in the eastern region of India through it is a fact that only a few of them have a concentrated settlement here *e.g.* the Santals, Hos, Bhunyas, Bhumijas, Bathuris and Gonds etc. The basic tribal population of the district is therefore formed by these six principal tribes.

As it has happened in other tribal parts of this country, the tribals of Mayurbhanj are also not spared off. Land alienation is rampart here. Due to poor economic conditions and illiteracy the tribes have not been able to understand the vicious circle thrown by their non-tribal exploiters. The Tribal Research Bureau conducted surveys and studies to analyze the relationship between the tribals and non-tribals who settled down in tribal areas *e.g.* an untouchable caste, Dom and Pano, the first non-tribals to settle down on the hills, live in intimate relationship with the Kandhas and Saoras of South Orissa. Similarly milkmen oilman and others live with the Juangs and Paudi Bhunyas of North Orissa. Many researchers put this relationship of the tribals with the non-tribals as parasitism but sometimes a symbiotic relationship is also found between them. Indebtedness among the tribals is a chronic malady. Schemes by the State Government have been bogged down in bureaucratic red-tapism. According to the Tribal Research Bureau the original purpose of these schemes is lost sight of. The two major steps by the Govt. of Orissa to prevent land alienation of the tribals are,

(i) Orissa Scheduled Areas Transfer of Immovable Property (by STs) Regulation, 1956, provides for the control and check of the transfers made by the scheduled tribes to the non-scheduled tribes in the Scheduled Areas.

(ii) Also outside the Scheduled Areas, alienation of land of the scheduled tribes has been restricted under Orissa Land Reformed Act, 1960.

Though Mayurbhanj possesses enormous forest wealth, the tribal people have no freedom to enjoy its benefits. Even for making agricultural implements they have to seek permission of the authorities. Permission to cut fire wood is available on payment of a stipulated amount. Sardari system of collection of land revenue gave enough scope for the feudal practices to survive. In the Colonial revenue administration Sardars, Tehsildars and Lakrajdars were the intermediaries. Notwithstanding various welfare measures introduced by the Colonial Government, there seemed to be a deep-seated unrest among the peasants of Mayurbhanj which provided congenial atmosphere for the growth of Prajamandal Movement during 1930s and 40s. The tribal composition of Mayurbhanj is another important aspect of its history. The tension between the tribals and non-tribals often resulted in violent outburst leading to direct intervention by the Govt. The Kol insurrection and the Bamanghaty disturbances were instances which speak of tribal's refusal to accept a alien system.

However, in order to understand the present tribal problem of land alienation in Mayurbhanj a general background of the land structure of the district is to be analyzed starting from the pre-colonial phase. Also an analysis is to be made to understand the changing pattern of the land structure in Orissa's plains and its effect over the neighouring forest regions that lead to the fast depeasantisation of. the tribal communities. As this depeasantisation has emerged as a criteria of the class antagonisms, its effects are to be examined in the district. The failures of State Govt.'s policy and the result of such failures are to be found out.

However, there is an imperative to project the land alienation of the tribals as human rights violation and to bring to attention of the government as well as non-government agencies. Nowadays the awareness of human rights brings about a certain awakening and often generates courage of tribals to stand up for their own rights. As far as the concept of tribal rights are concerned the challenges are to make the tribals aware of judicial systems, prepare them for political participation, create opportunity for equality, prepare them for self-governance to guarantee rights to traditional natural resources, provide them land rights etc.

Also the Tribal - Sab-Plan, the Bhuria Committee Recommendations, the Constritution's 73rd and 74th Amendments etc., are the recent endeavours by the State to remove socio-economic backwardness of the tribal population and to integrate them into the national mainstream of development and progress.

LIVELIHOOD RATIONALE OF TRIBAL PEOPLE

The traditional livelihood system of tribal people (also known as adivasis) has been based on shifting cultivation and collection of edible forest produce. Such a system was rendered sustainable by a level and pattern of utilisation of land and forest resources, which ensured their self-generating capacity. Sustainability was also ensured through adoption of a highly diversified pattern of production and shifting cultivation. When shifting cultivation began to decline from about the second decade of the 20th century, and tribal people took to settled agriculture mainly on the uplands, they actively adapted to upland conditions by growing a large variety of crops. While the physical yield of these crops was quite low in comparison with that of modern mono-crop agricultural practices, it minimised the risk of complete crop failure. Such a livelihood system also provided for a nutritionally balanced food consumption basket. All in all, one may say that tribal people were perhaps the earliest 'social ecologists': tribal people's economic conditions of existence were rooted in both subsistence and conservation ethics.

In social terms, the traditional livelihood system was based on customary, usufructuary rights of tribal communities over land and forests. It was also an 'extensive' system of production. The 'common pool' nature of resources supported customary rights and prevented the intensification of production, in the interest of conserving and sustaining the long-term productivity of livelihood resources. The sustainability of tribal people's livelihoods was thus firmly rooted in a system of 'property' rights over land and forests. As a consequence, the livelihood system's 'carrying capacity' was relatively low and it typically supported sparse populations relative to the size of the 'territory'.

The customary rights of tribal people over livelihood resources and their territorial sovereignty (insofar as land was territory, not property) increasingly came in to conflict with the forces of 'modernisation', which was defined by the developmental state and by 'outsiders' (whom we may call the plains people). In this discourse, it was thought that tribal people's traditional livelihood system was characterised by underutilised, wasteful and 'inefficient' use of productive resources. Thus, the developmental state, mainly using the logic of the market, created a policy and legal framework for gaining control over resources from the 'tribal territory'.

The territories of tribal people were thus broken open. There was widespread resentment and organised protests by tribal communities when this process of territorial intrusion was initiated by the colonial state through its land tenure policies in the uplands of Orissa in the mid-19th century and through forest conservation policies introduced at the end of that century. This indirectly facilitated the entry of caste Hindus into tribal territory for the commercial exploitation of productive resources. Thus, the space for the penetration of varied forms of commercial capital into the tribal hinterland was created. All this threatened to undermine the viability and sustainability of tribal people's livelihood base as their access to productive resources started to narrow. It is against the above background that we can understand the role and effectiveness of developmental interventions by the Indian nation-state and international development agencies for the protection and promotion of tribal livelihoods, and how tribal people have played a role in this.

BROAD OBJECTIVES

The following are the main objectives this chapter seeks to cover:

- A critical review of tribal policies and programmes of the state within the broad framework of planned development efforts;
- The impact of state interventions on the livelihood base and structure of tribal people;
- How and why the rationale and approach of the state's development interventions have changed;
- The manner in which the tribal people have articulated their collective concerns from the point of view of the prospects of their livelihood promotion and protection;
- The major limitations of state tribal policies; and
- Recommendations on how the livelihood question for tribal people needs to be addressed in order to mainstream tribal development processes in an era of rapid macro-economic changes.

MAJOR FOCUS OF THE PAPER

We give a brief account of the physiographic conditions and historical factors, which together carved out a niche for the tribal people of Orissa and gave them a pre-eminent position in the state. The critical natural resource base, and customary access to it, of tribal people's livelihood structure is presented. How this has changed over time is described to provide a backdrop. The extent and causes of development-induced displacement and the poor record of rehabilitation and indebtedness as conditions of livelihood insecurity. The nature of and approach to planned interventions by the state and central government. The examines certain major government initiatives specifically aimed at improving the livelihood base of tribal people, as well as some from bilateral funding agency and non-governmental organisation (NGO) bodies. The changing nature of state interventions through adoption of a participatory mode and autonomous institutional support. An account of the different forms and contexts of the open articulation of tribal rights in the recent past.

ORISSA, ITS PHYSIOGRAPHY AND TRIBAL PEOPLE

Physiography of Orissa

The administrative division of the state comprised 13 districts and was restructured into 30 districts in 1992, which are sub-divided into 59 sub-divisions, consisting of 314 Community Development Blocks (CD Blocks) and comprising of 56,887 villages. Around 3.74 percent of India's population is in Orissa. Since 1921 the state has experienced a progressive decline in the female-male sex ratio. Despite immense diversity in its agro-climatic conditions, it can be classified into four distinct agro-climatic zones.

They are the coastal plains, the central table land, the northern Plateau and the Eastern Ghats. The major rivers of this region are the Mahanadi, Brahmani, Baitarani, Budhabalang, Rushikulya and their many tributaries. Orissa has 480 km of coastline. It has an essentially undulating topography, with highlands constituting 64.2 and 50.6 percent of the cultivated area in the northern plateau and Eastern Ghat regions, respectively. The tribal people, who constitute about 22 percent of the total population of the state, are concentrated in this highland region.

Formation of Orissa State

The history of Orissa dates back to antiquity. The territorial boundaries of the state were never fixed in the past and in ancient times this land was known variously as Udra, Kosala, Tosali, Kalinga and Utkal, representing the different territorial, political and cultural contexts of the Rajas and Maharajas. Cultural links between the regions bear testimony in the field of art and artefacts, music and dance and in the processes of amalgamation of different cult groups by the dominant religion of Hinduism, with the Jagannath Cult and the Oriya as a numerically powerful linguistic group. The important dynasties that ruled over Orissa at different periods had their capital in the coastal region. Orissa lost its independence to Afghan invasion (1568- 78), Moghul domination (1578-1751), Maratha control (1751-1803), and British rule (1803-1947).Towards the end of the 19th century more than half the land area of present-day Orissa was under the control of 24 feudal chiefs; this area contains most of the ethnic minorities and major land area of the present state. In 1936 Orissa became the first state (after Sindh) to be formed on the basis of language. Its inland regions are by and large inaccessible thanks to ecological conditions.

The heavily forested Eastern Ghat hill range runs across the state in a north-south direction, which has made the tract inaccessible. Tribal people are the original settlers of this region. These inland regions, which were divided into *Garjats* were more-or less-independent of the kings of coastal Orissa until the Maratha and Moghul rule. During British rule most of these *Garjats* were raised to the status of princely states and maintained their identities until India achieved independence.

Tribal Communities of Orissa

Orissa has always taken an important, distinct and colourful position on the national map by harbouring various culturally unique ethnic groups from time immemorial. In 1956 the President of India declared 62 different tribal communities in Orissa to be 'Scheduled Tribes' (STs), of whom 13 communities are considered Primitive Tribal Groups (PTGs), and were assigned special treatment. Almost 44.25 percent of the total land area in Orissa has been declared as Scheduled Area.The major tribes of Orissa, in terms of their numerical strength, are the Kondh, Gond, Santhal, Saora, Bhuiyan, Paraja, Koya, Oraon, Gadaba, Juanga and Munda.

There are also several smaller tribal communities living in the state. They are the Chenchus, Mankiridia Kharia, Baiga, Birhor and Ghara. Tribal communities such as the Santhal, Gond, Munda, Ho, Birhor, Koya, Lodha, Kondha, Bhumija, Kharia and Oraons cut across state boundaries and are found in the neighbouring states of Jharkhand, Chhatishgarh, Andhra Pradesh and West Bengal, while tribal communities like the Juanga, Bonda and Didaye are found in the region of their origin in the districts of Keonjhar and Malkangiri, respectively. These tribal communities can be classified on the basis of geophysical zones, geographical regions, ethno-language, and crude techno-economic development.

They have rich social institutions, dwellings, natural habitats, folk dance, folk music, musical instruments, festivals and festive occasions, folk art and artefacts, a nature-based economy and life skills. In spite of the impact of outside forces on the socio-cultural processes, many tribal communities are trying to maintain their ethnic boundaries, reflected in various fronts of their life. These communities by and large possess certain common characteristics, like animism, use of crude technology, concentrated habitations, use of dialects, subsistence economy, etc. and other characteristics that distinguish them from complex and hierarchical societies.

TRIBAL LIVELIHOOD RESOURCES

Customary Land Tenure and Land use Systems of Tribal Societies

The survival of tribal communities critically depends on land and forest resources. For historical and ecological reasons, most tribal people inhabit the forest and highly inaccessible regions of the state. These communities practise various customary land tenure systems, which have often been modified by state policies and legislation. The clan-based land tenure system was based on customary rights over land, trees and forest. For example, the Kondhs clans were called muttas, who may be further sub-divided into their linkage-based territories, as observed in the case of Dongaria Kondhs and Kutia Kondhs The land use and tenure systems vary from tribe to tribe, as reflected in the practice of swidden and terraced cultivation. In general, tribal communities cultivate valley bottoms as paddy lands and kitchen gardens, while in the uplands they pracitise swidden or shifting cultivation as observed among the Kondhs, Saoras, Parojas, Gadabas, Bondas, Juangs and Bhuiyans. Juangs, Bhuiyans and Kondha enjoy community ownership over certain valleys and hillsides. It may be noted that the tribal-dominated regions of Orissa inherited land and forest administration systems from the Madras presidency (south Orissa), central provinces (parts of western Orissa), Bengal Province (coastal Orissa) and many princely states like Mayurbhanj, Keonjhar, Bamara, Bonai, Boudh, Kalahandi and Rairakhol. During the pre-British period most of the tribal areas were autonomous. During the British period the inclusion of tribal areas in the state and state administration was often violently contested. Much of this resistance was brutally put down.

This often led to the dispossession of tribal people as zamindars (village headmen) and tribal cultivators with usufructuary rights within the customary land tenure system. This was perhaps the beginning of the forced displacement and forced migration of the tribals to the plains. In the subsequent period, both the British and Princely States increased their administrative control over tribal areas and settled lands with non-tribals who carried out settled cultivation. In Gangpur Princely State most Gountias (intermediary tenure holders responsible for rent collection) were tribals in the early 1800s; but by the1890s there was a great preference for non-tribal Gountias from the Agharia and Teli castes. The major motivation for encouraging the settlement of upper caste cultivators in lands customarily held by tribals was to increase land revenue.

In 1882 the policy of the Kalahandi king to settle Kultas, an agricultural caste, in tribal areas led to a Kondh rebellion, which was suppressed with great brutality with the support of the British (District Gazetteer, Kalahandi, 1980). The policy of encouraging Oriya cultivators in tribal areas had led to a rebellion by 20,000 Juang in Dhenkanal and Keonjhar Princely State in 1868, and was again boldly suppressed with the help of the British.

Thus, the entry of non-tribal peasantry, encouraged by the ruler to open up settled agriculture and wet rice cultivation, led to the transfer of land from tribals to non-tribals and, in the plains areas, converted tribals into landless labourers or pushed them into marginal lands. Since the non-tribals were given virtually free passage into the cultivable plains lands, large-scale alienation of such lands occurred. In terms of future access, it should be noted that the power of assigning wastelands to cultivation was vested in the village headman - a colonial policy.

Immediately after independence the land administration in the state moved from an intermediary land system to a rayatwari system following the principle of tillers as owners, accompanied by laws to regulate the concentration of land holding through a process of fixing a land ceiling. The process of land reforms in Orissa was piecemeal and full of loopholes, and it failed in its goal to ensure equity and efficiency in agriculture.

The Orissa Estate Abolition Act, 1952 provided for abolition of all intermediary tenure holders and vested all the rights in the state and intermediary tenure holders. The Orissa Land Reforms (OLR) Act, 1960 provided for permanent heritable and alienable land under the principles of land to tillers and the Act was amended in 1965 and 1972.

The corporate and joint rights of tribal people over land did not allow it to be a saleable commodity. Uncritical adoption of the colonial concept of land ownership in the post-Independence era thus made it difficult to determine how much land, over which they had customary usufructuary rights, tribal people have lost in practice. How much land owned by tribal people has been alienated into the hands of non-tribal landed elite and upper caste cultivators through illegal transfers? It is a fact that the loss of land affects tribal people's social and sacred relationship with the land, which is reflected during ploughing, collection of non-timber forest products (NTFPs), utilisation of stream water, maintaining sacred groves, etc. One can say that among the tribal communities loss of land seems to be equal to the loss of social identity, not only for the present generation, but also for future generations. Whatever quantity of land tribal people cultivate, only a negligible percentage of it is recorded against their name. Land above a 9^0 slope from sea level is normally declared government land. The land patches used for shifting cultivation and terracing are normally above 9^0 elevations.

The Government of Orissa (2000) recently realised that the non-conferment of entitlement rights to tribal people for cultivation of land in the hill slopes within 30° represents a major non-performance of the state in the matter of land reforms and a reason for unrest among tribal communities.

Now the government has made a conscious policy to carry out a special survey of unsurveyed hill slopes within 30° in Scheduled

Areas (except Kasipur Tehsil), with the purpose of transferring ownership of such lands to tribal cultivators who in many cases have been practising terraced cultivation and adopting indigenous techniques of cultivation.

Shifting Cultivation

Shifting cultivation is a primitive farming technique known by different names in different tribal communities of Orissa. Increased population pressure has not discouraged the shifting cultivators much, mainly because of the non-suitability of 'better' farming and multi-cropping (mixed cropping of ten to 20 varieties) which have proved to be more productive and agriculturally viable for tribal people. Different estimates of shifting cultivation in Orissa carried out by different agencies and experts suggest that around 11 tribal communities follow this practice, constituting around 30 percent of the total tribal population of the state. However, estimates of the extent of shifting cultivation in terms of area contain wide variations and thus it is difficult to assess with any degree of certainty their relative reliability.

The crop cycle, crop quality and quantity depends on the cultivation cycle and distance of podu patches. This type of crop diversity ensures conservation of minerals of the soils, checks damage from pests and diseases, ensures food grains for couple of months, conserves soil nutrients and acts as an insurance against total crop failure, unlike under mono-culture systems. There is no doubt that over the decades the growth of population, restricted government forest policies, commercial plantation, deforestation, land alienation, non-availability of suitable hill slopes and availability of viable livelihood alternatives have reduced the cycle of shifting cultivation and its production substantially.

Many scholars interpret shifting cultivation as a form of subsistence economy. While looking at the strengths and opportunities of tribal societies in general and the non-availability of infrastructure facilities in tribal areas in particular, it is very difficult to say that shifting cultivation is a subsistence economy. Pathy (1987) points out that cash crops are more or less of equal importance to staple crops because in many cases in tribal societies crops are found mortgaged even before they are harvested. It has been observed that the shifting land is community land, where the individual households are given usufructuary rights over a patch of land. However, over time, as a result of increasing pressure on land, a tendency towards heritable rights in shifting land has emerged. As a result, tribal people have moved from cultivating shifting patches to cultivating permanent patches. Although they have been cultivating the same patches for years, together with back up social support, the Revenue Department of the State Government still considers them to be encroachers on forest land, even in areas where there has been no forest for the past couple of decades. In this regard Fernades et al. (1984) write:, 'in this marginalized stage a large section of tribal cultivators instead of living from forest as earlier, now live on forest'. As podu cultivation did not supplement their subsistence, and forest encroachment prevented them from engaging in collecting forest products they have been forced to look for other sources of income from outside the region as migrant wage labour in irrigated areas inside and outside the state.

Denial of rights over shifting lands and considering this practice as an encroachment on government land has always been the principal guideline for the state. Most shifting cultivation has been on 'objectionable' land, *i.e.* categories of revenue land not eligible for the issuance of entitlement rights as per law, and such lands are not settled under the provisions either of the OLR or of land encroachment laws.

Alternative measures to win tribals away from shifting land cultivation were adopted during the 1960s and 1970s through large-scale plantations of cashew and sisal, etc. The Economic Rehabilitation of the Rural Poor (ERRP) provided the rural poor with usufructuary rights on plantation programmes on shifting lands. Such rights were handed over to eligible beneficiaries when these plantations bear fruit; however, absolute rights over the land were to remain with the state. The right of usufruct was heritable and transferable in favour of similar beneficiaries with the approval of the Tehsildar. The allotment of podu affected government land for plantation by podu cultivation in accordance with circular no GE (GL) S 69/79-3755/ Revenue Department, Government of Orissa alt.18 January 1980, which envisaged the planting of commercial fruit trees like mango, tamarind, jack fruit, guava and orange by the podu cultivators. Notwithstanding the debate on the desirability or otherwise of shifting cultivation, one can say that many among the tribal population still practise it and from it generate their livelihood, which helps ensure the flow of food. It is a fact that, in the wake of capitalist approaches to land and land-based resources, planners, development workers and the state at large have started viewing shifting cultivation negatively. But none of the welfare services provided by the government during the past five decades to discourage tribal people from practising shifting cultivation seems to have been effective.

Forest Resources

The relationship of tribal people and forest resources has been symbiotic in nature. The life-way processes of Orissa's tribal people are reflected in their economy, religion, polity and social institutions, which cannot be understood without understanding various aspects of the forest surrounding them.

Until the intervention of the British, tribal people believed that they were the owners of the forest and forest resources that surround them. Their attitude towards forest resources as a source of food did not change much until Independence. They were more forest-friendly and were not exploiting forest resources randomly. Almost all the tribal communities in Orissa observe various forms of social sanctions related to undertaking or not undertaking certain forest-related activities: eating or not eating certain products, when and how to eat forest produce, and performance of rituals on a community basis before the first intake of forest food items. The customary laws of various tribal communities have become the guiding force for binding them closely with the forest. This can be seen when one examines the folk taxonomies given by tribal communities to flora and fauna, and from their classification of plants as more and less useful, edible and non-edible, hygienic and poisonous, ritualistic and non-ritualistic, medicinal and non-medicinal.

A large extent of land in tribal areas is categorised as forest, hence the laws related to forests also have a major impact on access to land for tribals. The Orissa Forest Act 1972, the Forest Conservation Act 1980 and the Orissa Forest (Grazing of Cattle) Rules 1980, all have an immense impact on the livelihood resources of the tribals. The state's forest, can be classified as reserve forests, demarcated protected forests, undemarcated protected forests, unclassified forests and other forests. Prima facie the forest laws provide protection for settlement of the rights of local people and communities before land is declared forest land, but this does not always hold because some reserve and protected forests are so deemed without any settlement taking place, and there is often non-recognition of rights on land used for shifting cultivation, and a lack of settlement of rights and family settlements.

This implies that once an area has been classified as forest of any sort, it can not be used for cultivation or any other purpose without the permission of the Ministry of Environment and Forest (MOEF) and ownership rights cannot be given without the Supreme Court's permission. In this process the regional variations of customary practices are not taken into consideration. In most cases the rights of the tribal people, which were prescribed in the/FA/927 audits amendment in 1954, were not followed and forests were created in ad hoc survey and settlement processes. The reservation of forests has often been made with little consideration of the interests of cultivation. The areas declared as forest very often carry tribal villages where no settlement has in fact taken place.

In this context Saxena (1995) points out that 'Protected forest (demarcated or un-demarcated) is invariably classified as non-forest area in the Record of Rights (ROR) prepared and maintained under the Orissa Survey and Settlement Act and in function issued by Revenue Department for reservation of Government land for specific purposes in rural areas.

There is dual control of both the departments over such land/ forests and virtually no management exists. Most of the Protected Forests are either declared as such under subsections 4 of section 33 of the Orissa Forest Act 1972 or deemed to be Protected Forests under sub-section 4 at section 81. The realities on the ground regarding the issue of the status of forest villages in Orissa.

The identification of such villages could not be completed until 1980, when the Forest Conservation Act 1980 was passed. This ultimately neutralised the process of regularisation of the cultivation of forest land which was later treated as encroachment. In this way the tribal people are unable to access their age-old livelihood sources.

Since they are deprived of entitlements over land, they are not eligible for certain state programmes and welfare measures intended for them. Despite the various attempts made by the state government, the MOEF, Government of India and the Tribes Advisory Council of Orissa to expedite the process of land settlement as per the Orissa Forest Act, little progress has been made. In 2000, the Government of Orissa (GoO) submitted a proposal to the MOEF to regularise 4,429 ha of forest area for cultivation. While this is an underestimation of the actual figure, the GoO has, through an affidavit, submitted to the Supreme Court of India a proposal for regularisation of 42,605 ha of such land in the whole of Orissa.

Recognition of rights of the Forest Dwellers over the Encroached land will Strengthen their Livelihood basket

In the Sunabeda sanctuary area, there are 30 revenue villages and 34 unsurveyed settlements, mostly inhabited by Chuktia Bhunjias, a PTG who are considered by the Forest Department as encroached villagers in the forest, although these people have been living there for generations together. Similarly, such villages in reserve forests are also observed in the Kutia Kondh-dominated region of Belghar in Kandhamal district, whose rights have not been settled. Such situations are observed in many sanctuary areas of the state. Likewise, Nabarangapur, Umarkote and Koraput district have a number of such villages. Since these tribal people do not have legal rights over their habitations, they are unable to access many state livelihood-related programmes.

The restrictions on them entering into the forest have multiplied their poverty to a situation that is chronic in nature. Again the data show that in 11 districts, a total of 0.276 million acres of forest land was under cultivation, while 0.316 million acres of government waste lands were fit to be reserved as forests. The Campaign for Survival and Dignity is a coalition of tribal organisations and NGOs lobbying for recognising the rights of such forest dwellers who have encroached to the extent of 20,000 hectares. The Nabarangapur division of the Working Plan enumerates 23,039.45 hectares as per 1980 encroachment.

There has been controversy over the Scheduled Tribes (Recognition of Forest rights) Bill, 2005, which specifies 13 rights for the adivasis, including access to and ownership of minor forest products, grazing rights, habitat and habitations for primitive tribes, settlement for old habitations and unsurveyed villages, and community rights to intellectual and traditional knowledge relating to forests and cultural diversity. Entitlement over land will be given to those adivasis who have been cultivating forest land since 1980, up to 2.5 hectares per nuclear family. The bill aims to look at the rights of adivasis along with their responsibilities for conserving the forests and protecting wildlife, while seeking to end the inefficient and monopolistic exploitative hold of the Forest Department over the adivasis by nominating the Gram Sabha (village council) as the authority to recognise and verify their claims. But the fact remains that the rights of the Gram Sabha seem vague. The bill has not properly reflected the principles of the Panchayat Establishment of Scheduled Areas (PESA) Act. It seems that the bill has made tribal people dependent appendages of the state, instead of making them free citizens, on a secured livelihood basis. In addition, misconceptions with regard to land distribution, old rights vs new rights, rights of non-tribal forest dwellers, etc. have multiplied the confusions over the new bill.

In the post-Independence era in Orissa, serious damage to forest resources, 'the food basket' of the tribal people, has been caused by the establishment of development projects. These projects can be categorised as multi-purpose irrigation dams, mines, roads, railways, new townships, refugee settlements and major industries. A few of the development projects so far established in Orissa's tribal-inhabited forest areas, which have had a tremendous impact on the forest resources and tribal life, are hydroelectric-cum-irrigation projects like Hirakud, Balimela, Machakund, Sileru, Upper Kolab, Upper Indrabati, Mandira and Rengali; mineral-based industries like the Rourkela Steel Plant, National Aluminium Company and Hindustan Aeronautics Ltd; and mining projects for cement, iron, dolomite and limestone.

A detailed estimate of the deforestation carried out for various purposes, like irrigation, mines, roads and housing, railways, defence and industry shows that there were 190 projects established in Orissa by1999, and 24,124 hectares of land have been deforested. The massive social cost of modern development projects - which are mostly borne by the local tribal people - have not been taken into account in the project pre-appraisal and impact assessment documents, either in the private or public projects. The distribution of forest areas released for non-forest use under the Forest (Conservation) Act 1980 (up to June 2001).

Table. Diversion of forest areas released for non-forest use under Forest (Conservation) Act 1980 (up to 1 June 2001)

Sl No Name of the sector	Proposals finally approved by government	
	Numbers	Forest area diverted (ha)
1 Irrigation	51 (23.50)	5739 (22.64)
2 Industries	4 (1.84)	2403 (9.48)
3 Mining	74 (34.10)	8228 (32.46)
4 Transmission on line	37 (17.05)	2488 (9.82)
5 Roads and bridges	21 (9.67)	221 (0.87)
6 Railway line	4 (1.84)	1909 (7.53)
7 Defence	4 (1.84)	3865 (15.29)
8 Miscellaneous	19 (8.75)	163 (0.64)
9 Human habitations	3(1.38)	322 (1.27)
Total	217 (100)	25,343 (100)

The impact of massive deforestation has been observed in the life-way processes of tribal people, and can be categorised as environmental effects, social effects and economic effects. The social effects of deforestation restrict tribal people's access to the forest and affect their religious activities, lifecycle rituals, customs, practices and habits. Similarly, the economic effects of deforestation have drastically influenced the traditional livelihood resources of tribal people, which were providing them with food and economic security.

In the Orissan context, studies have shown that tribal people have followed best practice in managing their land-based resources. Tribal people have protected 150,000 to 200,000 hectares of forestland in 3000 villages. At a certain level this reflects the functioning of various formal and informal village-level organizations in protecting their forest resources. In addition to the protection of village forests, such local level organisations have also been playing constructive roles in maintaining common resources, organising the community and establishing social harmony by resolving community conflicts. The Forest Department of the GoO tapped these resources only much later and formed Village Forest Protection Committees (VFPCs), which by and large maintain the traditional authority structure of tribal villages. In this regard the role of a few regional people's organisations, like 'Brukshya O' Jeevara Bandhu Parishad' (BOJBP) in Kesharpur, Nayagarh district, 'Budhikhamari Joint Protection Party' (BJPP) in Baripada, Mayurbhanja district and Budatika Anchalik Committee, in Negipalli, Balangir district, is remarkable.

Orissa shown the path to start Joint Forest Management of forest resources

In 1988 Orissa was the first state to introduce Joint Forest Management (JFM), which was later adopted as a policy by the Government of India. In 1990 the GoO passed another resolution to include all the reserved forests under protection by tribal villagers and to recognise the role of VFPCs in the management of both reserved and protected forests.

Again during 1993 the GoO provided a 50 percent share over any major harvest of produce, in addition to meeting all intermediate requirements of the protecting communities. The distribution of (VFPCs in different Forest Divisions of Orissa reflects the fact that there are certain Forest Divisions like Koraput, Sundargarh, Kalahandi and Rayagada, which have suffered from encouraging community participation in forest protection when compared with other Forest Divisions in Orissa.

MINOR FOREST PRODUCTS AND TRIBAL LIVELIHOODS

Because of the uncertainty of agricultural yields, tribal people largely depend on minor forest products (MFPs) as a source of food security, as well as for household medicines. As a result, in the recent past policy makers, environmentalists, researchers and government have been highlighting the significance of MFPs in the life and livelihood of tribal people.

Although MFPs are the sustainable sources of livelihood for poor tribal people, middlemen, traders and forest contractors have affected the prices received by primary producers through unfair trade practices. This has no doubt adversely affected the livelihood sustenance and food basket of a large number of poor tribal households. Tribal people are denied a fair price and most often receive a price lower than the prevailing market price. The collection and sale of NTFPs by the tribal population of Orissa have been drastically and systematically curtailed as a part of state strategy. In addition, the growth of the tribal population, which increased its dependency through adoption of commercial ways, conversion of tribal rights into concessions through the National Forest Policy, 1952, unscrupulous use of forest resources by middlemen and traders, and lack of interest on the part of the government in regenerating forest resources through plantations have affected the natural and only livelihood base of the forest dwellers. This is the reason why the Dhebar Commission suggested that the Forest Department should not function via an exclusive obligation to trees and vegetation but should also accept an obligation to utilise the forest as much as possible from the angle of the economic development of the tribal population. This chapter will end by discussing what the GoO has done in respect of giving tribal people a greater flow of income from MFPs.

The Government of Orissa has from time to time formulated and implemented a host of policies and enacted laws with regard to the collection, processing and marketing of NTFPs. Trade in kendu leaf, sal seed and bamboo was nationalised in 1973, 1983 and 1988, respectively. The objectives behind the nationalisation were partly to enable the primary collectors to obtain a remunerative price for their produce. Despite various policies formulated by the state at different times regarding the optimal collection, fixing of fair prices and processing of NTFPs, there still exist rampant corrupt practices, exploitation of tribals, state monopoly over forest resources, lack of management skills and non-responsive attitudes of the government agencies working for the procurement, processing and marketing of NTFPs.

Index